Gluten-Free
Baking

with The Culinary Institute of America

Chef Richard J. Coppedge Jr., CMB
with Cathy Charles

Photographs by Keith Ferris

Avon, Massachusetts

Published by
Adams Media, a division of F+W Media, Inc.
57 Littlefield Street, Avon, MA 02322. U.S.A.
www.adamsmedia.com

ISBN 10: 1-59869-613-0
ISBN 13: 978-1-59869-613-4

Printed in the United States of America.

10 9 8

Library of Congress Cataloging-in-Publication Data
is available from the publisher.

This publication is designed to provide accurate and authoritative information with regard to the subject matter covered. It is sold with the understanding that the publisher is not engaged in rendering legal, accounting, or other professional advice. If legal advice or other expert assistance is required, the services of a competent professional person should be sought.
—From a Declaration of Principles jointly adopted by a Committee of the American Bar Association and a Committee of Publishers and Associations

Many of the designations used by manufacturers and sellers to distinguish their product are claimed as trademarks. Where those designations appear in this book and Adams Media was aware of a trademark claim, the designations have been printed with initial capital letters.

Photographs by Keith Ferris.

This book is available at quantity discounts for bulk purchases.
For information, please call 1-800-289-0963.

Dedication

We all eat food as part of our daily sustenance, but food can also satisfy a need or make bad feelings pass quickly. Food should not be something that makes us feel bad by promoting harm or discomfort to our bodies, inside or out.

These gluten-free recipes are bound and printed for all of you, including your loved ones and friends. This way, you can "break bread" with them, without digestive pain or any other reactions to mar the pleasure of eating together. Enjoy!

Regards,
Chef Richard J. Coppedge Jr., CMB

. . . .

For Max
—Cathy Charles

Contents

Acknowledgments

To President Tim Ryan and the administration, faculty, and staff at The Culinary Institute of America: In 1992, you all welcomed me with open arms. Your encouragement and commentary were helpful in my formulations for this book.

Adams Media: When other publishers balked, Adams believed in the concept.

My deepest thanks go out to the publishing department here at the Institute. Lisa Lahey, Shannon Eagan. Patrick Decker and Keith Ferris: Your eyes for arrangement, lighting, and of course 'focus' make the photos more delectable than the recipes themselves.

Cathy Charles, the hired text writer: You accepted the challenge of listening to all of my lectures and demonstrations on this subject.

Students and recipe typists Polly Conway, Nicole Bonafante, Kaitlin Barthmaier, Jessica Briggs, and Andrea Roshore.

My gratitude also extends to Bob and Ruth Levy's gluten-free dining-travel club; to Suzanne Bowland who heard about my teachings and has invited me to her conferences each year. Special thanks go to George and Ceil Chookazian, owners of Foods By George—thanks for all of the advice and technical support.

Dr. Peter Green and the Columbia University Celiac Disease Center.

Robert Cray and his band: Your music has always been present, which helps motivate my work.

To all of my current, past, and future students: This book is for all of you.

To fellow Certified Master Bakers, teachers, and authors Jeffrey Hamelman, and Peter Greweling: Robert La France and Kim Koeller, developers of the gluten-free and allergy-free passport booklets.

To my most devout friends, Indy, Cody, Max, Emmylou, Kiah, Lucy, and Mom-Mom: You always acknowledge my arrival home from work, and always in a happy manner.

To my friends and family: This book displays some of my talents—talents that you have all supported in many ways.

Finally, to my wife of twenty-two years, Julie Keef: Because of your unfailing help, your tolerance of my ways, and your understanding, this book is yours as much as mine.

—Chef Richard J. Coppedge Jr., CMB

· · · · · · · · · ·

First of all, I would like to thank Lisa Lahey and Chef Coppedge for hiring me. Chef, this project has been an enriching and enjoyable experience. Thank you for your generosity as a teacher, mentor, collaborator, and friend.

Thanks also to the many people I met at and through the CIA who shared their stories with me.

I am indebted to my husband, Steve Kaye, for supporting me in so many ways throughout this project, and to my children, who never complained (instead endlessly requesting more visits with Chef Coppedge).

I would like to thank my parents, Bill Charles and Carolyn Cavallone, for giving me a strong work ethic; my stepparents, Colette Matsui and Joe Cavallone, who are important role models in my life; my parents-in-law, Bernard and Evelyn Kaye, for their nurturing and encouraging phone calls; and my godparents, Roger and Marilyn Ray, for planting the idea in my head (years ago) that I could do this kind of project.

Thanks, too, to Adele Cohen, Ann Brenesal, and all my siblings, siblings-in-law, and their families: the Dokurnos, the Bonitos, the Charles/Killian family, the Charles family, the Uhers, and the Kayes. The examples you set, as well as your support, encouragement, and understanding, mean so much to me.

—Cathy Charles

Foreword

George Chookazian, founder, Foods By George

Imagine for a moment being in the scenic Hudson Valley of New York, with the beautiful river in clear view. You have arrived at a renowned school, as mighty as the river itself, with state-of-the-art kitchens and world class chef/instructors. . . . The Culinary Institute of America.

That was my life in the early 1990s. During a thirty-week baking and pastry program, when I was immersed in techniques, processes, and craftsmanship, I met Chef Rick Coppedge. Although Rick was not one of my instructors, he took an interest in the gluten-free business I had started a few years earlier. We shared an enthusiasm for the science and chemistry of baking—things like yeast's dependence on time and temperature, and the principles of how ingredients interact—always with the goal of creating a superb finished product. Rick shared his time and talent, and from these conversations, I learned how to think like a professional baker.

Rick's skills as a professor of baking and pastry arts shine through in his well-thought-out, diverse, creative, and delicious recipes. Someone once told me "Find something you do better than most others; then do it." That is what Rick has done. He has put his signature on the gluten-free world as the first Certified Master Baker to fully embrace this important field.

Thank you, Rick, for your dedication to this discipline.

Preface

Cathy Charles

Picture a steaming loaf of perfectly browned French bread, straight from the oven. Break off a piece and hear it snap, see the beautiful latticework of cells inside. Now bring it to your lips and inhale the yeasty aroma as you take your first bite. Crusty and delicious! This is how real bread is supposed to be. Or at least that's how you remember it, before you had to give it up.

Wait a minute—this is gluten free? No. Impossible.

It sounds too good to be true, but it really is true. Welcome to Bakeshop 2 at The Culinary Institute of America in Hyde Park, New York, where Chef Richard Coppedge Jr. is turning out delectable baked goods without using wheat flour or gluten.

Chef Coppedge developed the innovative gluten-free baking program at the CIA in 2001. He is a pioneer in food industry education, the first Certified Master Baker to focus on adapting classic, wheat-based baking recipes into flavorful gluten-free versions that are hard to distinguish from their conventional counterparts.

After 15 years of teaching traditional baking, Chef Coppedge was asked to enter into a new realm: nutritional baking. The now-titled Advanced Baking Principles class at the CIA began with Chef Coppedge's acceptance to teach outside the box. His many trials and errors led to the writing of this book.

Chapter 1

Living Gluten Free

A growing number of people are being diagnosed with celiac disease, wheat allergy, and wheat intolerance. It means they cannot eat wheat, and in the case of celiac disease, cannot eat rye or barley either, because the proteins in those grains, commonly referred to as gluten, are toxic to their bodies. If you are one of those people, you probably thought you would never enjoy another moist cake, tender muffin, or chewy brownie again, or at least thought you might never learn how to bake safe versions of these things for yourself. In the pages that follow, you will learn about techniques for baking without gluten, including the special ingredients used, specific approaches, and the equipment preferred, given with both the home baker and the professional in mind.

CELIAC DISEASE

Most people who avoid eating gluten have celiac disease (CD), an autoimmune disease that affects any organ of the body. It affects about one percent of people in the United States. Although the classical baking definition of gluten refers to the proteins gliadin and glutenin that are formed, for example, when making bread, the term "gluten" is used in the medical community to describe the proteins found in wheat, barley, rye, and anything derived from these grains that are dangerous for people with celiac disease. It is the gliadin portion of the wheat protein that causes the problem. Some people avoid oats as well, since in the United States oats are often grown or processed near wheat. An easy way

---

PREVALENCE OF CELIAC DISEASE (CD) IN THE UNITED STATES

- About one percent of Americans have CD, but most of them don't know it because they appear healthy. That translates to 3 million people, 97 percent of whom are undiagnosed.
- 1 in 22 people is estimated to have CD if he or she has a parent, child, or sibling with the disease.
- It takes an average of 11 years to be diagnosed with celiac disease in the United States.
- 60 percent of children and 41 percent of adults diagnosed with celiac disease showed no symptoms during the five years they were tracked for a multicenter study of celiac disease.

Sources: Celiac Disease Centers at Columbia University; University of Chicago Celiac Disease Program; University of Maryland Celiac Disease Center.

Profiles in Gluten-Free Living:

DARIA ASTORINO, CONYNGHAM, PA

Adapting to the gluten-free diet is hard, especially the first year, but then there are transition times in life that also challenge people—such as when young people leave home and start lives on their own. Daria Astorino was on a gluten-free diet, along with her mother, for three years before heading off to attend The Culinary Institute of America at Hyde Park, NY. Neither one of them has been formally diagnosed with celiac disease, but they were both very sick for many years and only started feeling better after a vegan friend advised them to cut gluten out of their diets.

"I have Italian heritage and we always ate a lot of bread and pasta," Daria says. Early on in high school her stomach hurt all the time and she would double over from pain when she got nervous before a test. She also suffered from asthma and heartburn, and slept for years with her bed propped up. Once she changed her diet, she felt better. She says the fact that her mother was going through the same thing helped her, especially when she'd see other people eating some of her old favorites, like pizza. "There were so many times I cried and told my mom, 'I want to eat it,' but she got me through it."

Daria says her first year at college was hard. "I was shy about telling people. I skipped a lot of meals because I was afraid of getting sick," she says. She doesn't have any weight to spare now, but she looks healthy and energetic. She says she spends about $80 a week on food above and beyond what she has to pay for the school meal plan, and it's hard to fit the gluten-free foods she buys into the tiny freezer in her dorm room refrigerator.

"I'm afraid to get tested four years into it," she says, because she'd have to eat gluten for a few months to get an accurate test result. When she does accidentally eat gluten, the results are debilitating, and she doesn't know how she could function. This is a trap that a lot of people fall into. Doctors say it's important not to self-diagnose because there's too much at stake. If you're not completely certain you have celiac disease, you're more tempted to cheat on the diet. If it turns out you really do have celiac disease, consuming gluten causes internal damage even if you don't notice anything. And your chances of developing additional autoimmune diseases or cancer are increased if you don't stick to a strict gluten-free diet.

Daria, meanwhile, has her sights set on working as a pastry chef, and sees herself ten years down the road with her own wedding cake business. "I'll never know how regular puff pastry is supposed to taste," she says, but she doesn't question her career choice. She thinks it is worth doing whatever she has to do to follow her dream.

A SHORT HISTORY OF CELIAC DISEASE

Celiac is a Greek word referring to the abdomen. What we've come to know as celiac disease was first referenced by the Greek physician Aretaeus of Cappadocia, writing during the first or second century A.D. He described a chronic disorder in which "pepsis," thought to mean digestion, was incomplete, leading to a "starvation of the body." In 1888, British physician Samuel Gee wrote of celiac disease, "if the patient can be cured at all it must be by means of diet." But it wasn't until after the Dutch famine of World War II, when wheat flour was scarce, that the connection between celiac disease and the ingestion of wheat was made. A Dutch pediatrician named Willem Karel Dicke put it together in 1950, and within a decade gluten was isolated as the cause, atrophy of the villi was discovered, and the idea of small bowel biopsy was born.

Sources: Dowd, B. and J. Walker-Smith. "Samuel Gee, Aretaeus, and the coeliac affection." *Abstract, British Medical Journal* 1974, April 6; 2(5909): 45–47.

to remember which grains are off-limits to people with CD is to think of BROW (barley, rye, oats, wheat).

For people with celiac disease, ingesting even a small amount of gluten causes the immune system to damage the villi, the tiny fingerlike projections that line the small intestine and absorb nutrients. This leads to malnutrition, vitamin deficiencies, and a host of other serious health problems if left untreated. It is a genetic disease that can be present from birth, or switched on at any time in life by trauma, illness, or stress. Avoiding gluten can be difficult, since it appears in many food additives and can easily be transferred through contact with kitchen tools. Once gluten is out of the diet, the small intestine can start to heal, a process that can take anywhere from a few months to several years.

How Do You Know if It's Celiac Disease?

Symptoms of celiac disease vary. Some people have classic abdominal symptoms including diarrhea or constipation, bloating, vomiting, stomach pain, and unexplained weight loss; others have symptoms that are less obvious including fatigue, joint pain, tooth discoloration, or infertility. Irritability is a common symptom in children. Celiac disease can be hard to diagnose because it presents similarly to other disorders and sometimes there are no symptoms at all. If celiac disease is suspected, a doctor will advise the patient to continue consuming foods with gluten, and then test the blood for the presence of these antibodies:

- The anti-gliadin antibodies:
  - Immunoglobulin A (IgA) and/or
  - Immunoglobulin G (IgG)
- The antibodies that indicate the body is attacking itself:
  - Anti-tissue transglutaminase (tTGA)
  - IgA anti-endomysium antibodies (AEA)

If a positive blood test is found, the next step in the diagnostic process is to perform an intestinal biopsy. The patient must continue to eat a regular diet or the results may come back as a false negative. To perform the biopsy, a doctor runs a small tube called an endoscope through the mouth and stomach to the small intestine, then takes a small sample of tissue. If the villi in the tissue sample appear blunted or flattened, the doctor will consider it "consistent" with celiac disease. The next step is to send the patient to a registered dietician to learn about the gluten-free diet, and to see whether the patient improves while on it. Only then, after improvement is shown, is celiac disease considered confirmed.

Some people also suffer from a skin condition linked to celiac disease called dermatitis herpetiformis (DH). DH usually appears as an itchy, blistery rash on the elbows, knees and buttocks. People who develop this rash may or may not have the intestinal symptoms of celiac disease, but must adopt a gluten-free diet to control it.

TO BIOPSY OR NOT TO BIOPSY

Some people who have a positive blood test for celiac disease choose not to have the biopsy because they are concerned about being uncomfortable during the procedure, which is usually done with a local anesthetic. But when you consider the commitment required for people with celiac disease, enduring an endoscopy is a small tradeoff. The commitment is to a lifelong gluten-free diet that is expensive and socially inconvenient. It should not be taken lightly, especially in children. If you are going to the trouble of adhering to a strict gluten-free diet for life, why not know for certain that you must do so? On the other hand, if celiac disease runs in the family, one can argue that the outcome of the biopsy is a foregone conclusion. Most doctors say the biopsy is the gold standard for diagnosis of celiac disease and warn against diagnosing yourself. It's not unheard of for the blood test to come back with a false positive. In other cases, celiac disease does not show up on the blood test, but is found through a biopsy when the doctor was checking for something else.

Profiles in Gluten-Free Living:

GEORGE CHOOKAZIAN OF FOODS BY GEORGE, MAHWAH, NJ

*L*ove can sometimes lead to business opportunities, as in the case of George Chookazian, founder of the gluten-free Foods By George line.

George's entrepreneurial journey started in 1989, when he and his future wife Ceil began dating. They shared a love of fine food and got to know each other over traditional restaurant meals, including many crusty loaves of bread. As George tells it, "The more we saw of each other, the sicker Ceil got!" She wound up in the hospital, dropping 25 percent of her body weight over a few short weeks, which is hard to believe but is true. The cause: celiac disease (CD). Ceil had been diagnosed as a child but was allowed to introduce gluten into her daily meals when she became asymptomatic in her mid-teens. Symptoms returned in adulthood, even before she started dating George, but doctors repeatedly missed the diagnosis, as they commonly believed children outgrew the disease in adolescence.

Meanwhile, George, a stockbroker at the time, felt inspired to restore Ceil's health through the gluten-free diet. They both remember him standing by Ceil's hospital bed, telling her, "I think I know a way to make you a pizza." Early attempts failed, but after much experimenting with a gluten-free flour formula he personally developed, George got it right. That gluten-free pizza he promised to deliver went on to become an award-winner in 2005, besting seventy-one other food items to take the Best New Food Product title at that year's Natural Products Expo East. That's the Holy Grail for individuals with CD—finding safe foods that are enjoyable in and of themselves and not just "okay" when judged by typical gluten-free standards.

George says he got there by taking "a grass-roots approach, paying attention to each step in the process, with the best possible product being the goal." When he formed Foods By George in 1991, he began offering gluten-free baking mixes, handling most of his business by phone. He built a clientele by catering gluten-free "Pasta and Dessert" dinners at celiac support group meetings, which led to orders for his mixes. To perfect his baking skills, George completed an eight-month baking and pastry certificate program at The Culinary Institute of America in 1993. That is where he met Chef Coppedge, who became a friend and mentor, critiquing George's efforts at baking wheat-based breads. While at the CIA, George would return to his apartment after class and apply his newly acquired baking skills to making gluten-free versions using his own formulas.

By 1994, George had to stop making gluten-free pasta: although his pasta machine was equipped with a motorized crank, the intense kneading that was necessary beforehand had nearly given him carpal tunnel syndrome. Now the core of the business is breakfast muffins, English muffins, brownies, pound cake, crumb cake, and, of course, the pizza.

George believes that gluten-free products share a "trailing similarity" to organic foods in that major supermarkets will probably start offering their own branded gluten-free items in the near future. The market has started to explode, and major supermarkets are already stocking Foods By George products and several other gluten-free brands.

Celiac Disease, Wheat Allergy, and
Wheat Intolerance: What's the Difference?

As previously mentioned, celiac disease is a lifelong, inherited condition in which the ingestion of gluten causes the body to attack the lining of the small intestine. There is no cure for it, but the disease can be held in remission by removing all gluten from the diet. If left untreated, celiac disease can lead to malabsorption, anemia, osteoporosis, short stature, cancer, and other autoimmune diseases including lupus.

In the case of wheat allergy, the immune system responds to the protein in wheat as if it were a toxin, producing antibodies to attack it. The response can be immediate or can occur a few hours after eating the food. The presence of the antibodies leads to the release of the chemical histamine, which in turn causes allergic symptoms ranging from a mild stuffy nose and tingling lips to life-threatening anaphylactic shock. A wheat allergy may occur in anyone at any time in life. Children with allergies often outgrow them, but adult-onset allergies tend to remain for life.

As noted by the American Celiac Disease Alliance, food intolerance does not involve the body's immune system and is thought to be a chemical response that causes no long-term damage. Symptoms can develop over several hours or several days after a person eats a particular food. In the case of wheat intolerance, the symptoms are often gastrointestinal and will pass once the wheat is out of a person's system.

The Autism Connection

Some parents of children with autism spectrum disorders find that removing both gluten and milk protein from the child's diet helps. The theory is that children with autism do not process gluten and casein correctly, and that these proteins act like narcotics. In other words, the more wheat and dairy a child with autism eats, the more he or she craves it, which contributes to a fogged state of mind. Once free of these substances, it is believed, the child can think more clearly and function better, as found by GFCF Diet Support Group and Autism Network for Dietary Intervention. (See "Baking Without Casein or Gluten" in Chapter 2.)

GLUTEN-FREE BAKING STRATEGIES

Earlier, you were introduced to the grains that must be avoided in a gluten-free diet (remember BROW?). Here is a closer look at the ingredients and safeguards that are necessary in gluten-free baking.

The Five Cs of Gluten-Free Baking:

1. Content
2. & 3. Contact & Contamination
4. Communication
5. Common Sense

Content

Make sure that there is no gluten, the protein portion of wheat that is dangerous to people with celiac disease, in the ingredients of food you buy or consume. As mentioned before, you can think of the prohibited grains as BROW: barley, rye, oats, and of course, wheat (though inclusion of oats remains controversial).

Durum, graham, kamut, semolina, einkorn, and spelt are types of wheat that must be avoided. Triticale is a cross between wheat and rye and is also off-limits. It sounds fairly straightforward, but it's not: gluten can also be hidden in many common food ingredients. Couscous and most breading are made from wheat. Malt is usually made from barley, and brown rice syrup often contains barley malt. Regular beer and malt vinegar, which are brewed, contain gluten. Distilled (as opposed to most brewed) vinegars and alcoholic beverages are okay because the gluten peptide and all proteins do not pass through the distillation process. Modified food starch and hydrolyzed vegetable protein can be made from wheat. Soy sauce most often contains wheat. The words "natural flavors" can mean anything. And "wheat-free" does not necessarily mean "gluten-free," since the item could

THE FOOD ALLERGEN LABELING AND CONSUMER PROTECTION ACT

As of this writing, the federal government is considering labeling laws that will define the term "gluten" and make it easier for people avoiding gluten to know whether a product contains it. Currently, eight common food allergens must be listed on all packaging: wheat, eggs, milk, soy, seafood, peanuts, tree nuts, and shellfish. Barley, rye, and oats are not included yet, but this is likely to change when the new gluten-free labeling laws take effect in 2008. How to classify oats is especially complicated. Oats can be tolerated by most people with celiac disease. However, oats are frequently contaminated with other grains by crop rotation, processing, and shipping. The FDA considers a gluten level not exceeding 20 parts per million safe for most people with celiac disease.

Profiles in Gluten-Free Living:

Mary Mueller has been cooking gluten-free meals for her family for fifteen years. Her husband Chuck was diagnosed with dermatitis herpetiformis in 1985 during a high-stress period when he was applying for dental school. Chuck managed to keep his skin cleared up for seven years by using the drug dapsone. "Then," Mary says, "another doctor told him he had to get off of that stuff and go gluten free." Mary, who stays at home with their three sons, plunged into the gluten-free lifestyle by adapting recipes from her own cookbooks and started an informal coffee klatch out of her home that grew into the official Celiac Sprue Association's Green Bay, Wisconsin support group. "I hate that term, 'support group,'" she says, because it makes her think of people sitting around complaining. "It's really just us chit-chatting." Interestingly, even though Chuck backs Mary's efforts, he is not part of the group. "He's very supportive of me," she says "But he'd rather be with [the boys] at night," coaching their sports teams.

The Muellers are careful about watching their sons' health, and Mary has come to rely on free annual screening offered by the University of Chicago's Celiac Disease Program. All of her sons had a negative test result four years ago. But two years later Michael got sick and she knew it had to be celiac disease: "One day, it hit him. I took him right in." He was 12 at the time and it has changed her perspective. Mary says she never worried about her husband feeling upset if there was little for him to eat at a restaurant or a party—he could always have a salad or go without and not care about it. But Michael's diagnosis concerns her more as a

mother. Even though she wouldn't describe him as a "food person," and says he often tells her "It's not a big deal," she worries that he feels left out at school pizza parties and thinks he is too secretive about his condition. "I worry about my son going off to college. I think about that all the time. He's going to have to pick a small private school that can work with him." She says Michael is extremely sensitive to gluten and once missed school because he ate fast-food ice cream that had been cross-contaminated with cookie crumbs. "One-eighth of a teaspoon can make him really sick," she says.

The Muellers are Catholic and the boys go to parochial school, where Michael brings his own lunch. When they attend Mass they sit in the front row, and during the communion part of the service, when bread and wine are offered, they go up first and receive low-gluten hosts. The hosts contain .01 percent gluten, which Mary says is low enough to cause no problems for Chuck or Michael.

The family members take responsibility for each other. The Muellers' other two sons—David, the eldest, and Matthew, the youngest—know what to look for on labels and, in a pinch, can shop for foods that are safe for everyone.

Mary says that they enjoy eating out, too, and that she does not check ahead. "I don't walk in panicking. We are very careful. We don't go to chain restaurants. In better restaurants I just walk in with my dining card ... and talk to the chef." She says if you are going to limit yourself to a dry baked potato and a dry piece of chicken, you might as well stay home.

contain rye and/or barley. A basic rule: don't use any ingredient unless you are sure it's safe. The Celiac Sprue Association (*www.csaceliacs.org*) annually publishes *The CSA Gluten-Free Product Listing*, which includes food industry contact information. If it is not clear from a food's label that it is gluten free, then you must either go without it or check with the manufacturer. (See page 8 for more information on food labeling.)

Safe grains include rice, corn, sorghum, buckwheat, quinoa, millet, amaranth, and teff. Flours made from tapioca, arrowroot, soy, potatoes, beans, and nuts are also gluten free. Unprocessed fruits and vegetables, meats, poultry, fish, legumes, and dairy products are naturally gluten free.

Contact and Contamination

Even a trace of gluten can cause damage to a person with celiac disease. Make sure you are using clean tools, that food preparation surfaces and grills are free of gluten, and that the kitchen itself where you are working is clean. Flour dust can linger in the air for a long time, so if gluten-containing flour is used where you are baking, either wait for the dust to settle or work in another room. It is a good idea to keep a separate set of tools for gluten-free cooking and baking. Sifters, colanders, and pasta forks have lots of crannies where gluten can adhere, so it's best to have GF-dedicated versions of those. A separate toaster is a necessity. If you have to share a toaster oven, put foil under the gluten-free item and toast one side of it at a time. Another potential area for contamination is frying oil. Do not fry regular and gluten-free foods in the same oil. Designate a separate fryer or drain the oil and clean the fryer with baking soda before adding fresh oil for frying gluten-free items. Also, do not reuse cooking water if the ingredients you were boiling contained gluten.

Contamination can easily occur through absent-mindedness, especially if your kitchen is not entirely gluten free. One way to avoid this problem while baking is to focus on one thing at a time. Set aside a specific time for gluten-free baking and make sure gluten-containing ingredients are out of reach. Also, see to it that any ingredients you plan to use have not been contaminated. Example: Let's say you are at home preparing a gluten-free tart that contains jam, a condiment that is often spread on toast at breakfast time. Earlier that morning, someone put a spreading knife right back into the jar after spreading some jam on toast—a natural thing to do. But if that toast contained wheat, some crumbs could have adhered to the knife and ended up in the jar, making the rest of the jam unsafe for a person avoiding gluten. Lesson: Train yourself and others to use a spoon to drop condiments onto bread without touching it and then use a separate knife to spread. You could also use squeezable containers, or keep separate containers of condiments that are specifically for gluten-free use.

Contamination can also occur when bread is sliced and crumbs are left on the counter or a cutting board. Use cutting boards that can be submerged in hot water or put in the dishwasher, or try placing waxed paper under the item to be cut and then discard the paper when you are finished. Make sure everyone who uses the kitchen cleans up carefully after him- or herself—and don't forget about contaminated sponges and cleaning tools. Wash those well or place them in the dishwasher after you are done.

If a gluten-containing item has come into contact with a food that should be gluten free, you must start over. You cannot, for example, remove wheat croutons from a salad and then serve it to someone with celiac disease. It will make the person sick. Make a new salad.

Communication

If you are on a gluten-free diet and dine out at a restaurant, or someone else is preparing food for you in a home kitchen, be specific about your needs. If you are preparing gluten-free food for someone else, make sure you identify those needs and then pay attention to details. Keep an open dialogue with each other and double-check everything. It helps to have a "gluten-free dining card" that explains what is necessary. These cards can be obtained through celiac support groups or allergy magazines (e.g., *www.csaceliacs.org* or *www.livingwithout.com*).

Common Sense

It cannot be said too many times: if you are not sure about something, don't use it. If you don't remember whether you cleaned something that might be contaminated, clean it. If you are shopping for gluten-free ingredients, check the label every time. Food manufacturers are known to change ingredients and suppliers.

KEEPING CURRENT

If you have celiac disease or are raising a child who has it, you owe it to yourself and your family to be as knowledgeable about the condition as possible. After the first couple of years of getting used to the gluten-free lifestyle, you may feel you already know enough and want to spend your time thinking about something else. But advances are being made all the time. Why keep doing something you no longer need to do? There is a mountain of information in bookstores and online, and some of it is dated, partly inaccurate, or conflicting. So what can you do? Here are some tips:

Regularly scan some of the celiac disease advocacy group Web sites. If you choose to join one or more of these groups, annual memberships usually come with newsletter subscriptions, and these publications will keep you updated on developments in science and government legislation. You will read about upcoming conferences, symposia, and trade shows. Attend some of these events if you can, and you will get good information from lecturers, meet leaders in the industry, and learn about gluten-free products. The newsletters also tend to have coverage of these events, so you can read about them after the fact. You could also join a local support group and meet people in your area who are coping with the same circumstances.

- American Celiac Disease Alliance: *www.americanceliac.org*
- Celiac Disease Foundation: *www.celiac.org*
- Celiac Sprue Association: *www.csaceliacs.org*
- Gluten Intolerance Group: *www.gluten.net*

The two major gluten-free diet magazines, *Gluten-Free Living* and *Sully's Living Without*, are published quarterly and contain newsworthy articles, advice on coping with the gluten-free lifestyle, and helpful gluten-free recipes. There is also a subscription-based celiac disease newsletter, and a gluten-free cooking Web site with weekly recipe updates.

- Gluten-Free Living: *www.glutenfreeliving.com*
- Sully's Living Without: *www.livingwithout.com*
- Scott-Free Newsletter: *www.celiac.com*
- Glutenfreeda cooking Web site: *www.glutenfreeda.com*

Look for the latest books on the subject of celiac disease, gluten intolerance, and the gluten-free diet. How do you know if you've found a reliable source? When you consider buying a book or borrowing it from your local library, look at when it was published. If it's been a while since the pub date, keep that in mind while you're reading it, or try to find a book that was published more recently. (See the "Readings and Resources" section, page 247, for suggested books). Reliable information is also available from university celiac disease center web sites such as *www.celiacdiseasecenter.org*.

Attend gluten-free cooking classes, or join a gluten-free travel club. Not only will you have a good time and learn something new, but you will meet other people who know what you are going through. Some sites to keep in mind include The Culinary Institute of America (*http://ciachef.edu/enthusiasts*) and Bob and Ruth's Gluten-Free Dining and Travel Club (*www.bobandruths.com*).

Chapter 2

Ingredients and Equipment
for Gluten-Free Baking

*W*hen you take wheat flour away from a baker, it's like asking him or her to reinvent the wheel. But it can be done, and done well, with the right combination of ingredients, techniques, and equipment.

THE UNIQUE TRAITS OF WHEAT

To understand what is required for gluten-free baking, it is helpful to know about the specific attributes of wheat and the role it plays in ordinary baking.

Take, for example, bread. When liquid is combined with wheat flour and the mixture is kneaded, the proteins glutenin and gliadin in the wheat turn into stretchy strands of gluten. The strands form a web that captures the gas given off by the yeast, allowing the dough to rise. Some wheat flours have more protein than others. Breadmaking requires a "stronger," or higher-protein, flour, typically made from "hard wheat." Cake flour is a "softer" flour made from "soft wheat," which contains less protein. All-purpose flour is a combination of the two.

Wheat flour, when combined with various fats, liquids, and leaveners, can make a flaky pie crust, a tender cake, a chewy cookie, or a crusty, beautifully shaped loaf of bread. When wheat is taken out of the equation, there is no single substance that can make up for it. So in gluten-free baking you must blend together various flours, add binders, and supplement the proteins. You will also probably need more liquid, more leavener, and the right equipment. Even so, you will not get a dough that can be easily stretched and shaped. Gluten-free bread doughs are more like batters and cannot be kneaded. They take on the shape of the pan into which they are poured. But, as you will find in the following chapters, you can make gluten-free doughs for pie crust, cookies, and tarts that can be rolled out, shaped, and fluted like their wheat counterparts, something lacking in many other gluten-free recipes.

ACCEPTABLE GLUTEN-FREE GRAINS, FLOURS, AND STARCHES

- Rice
- Corn
- Soy
- Potato
- Tapioca
- Beans/Legumes
- Flax

- Buckwheat
- Sorghum
- Quinoa
- Arrowroot
- Amaranth
- Millet
- Indian rice grass

- Teff
- Wild rice
- Almond meal and other nut flours

THE GLUTEN-FREE PANTRY

If you are a first-time gluten-free baker, the array of ingredients necessary to make a good product may seem vast, and blending a bunch of flours together may sound like it's not worth the trouble. It is! Don't give up. Once you get the hang of it and see the quality of the end product, you will realize that blending your own gluten-free flours is well worth the effort. Before you get started with the recipes that follow, you will need to do some shopping—but first, take an inventory.

Some of the ingredients you will need to make gluten-free baked goods may already be on your pantry shelf or in your refrigerator, such as salt, sugar, and eggs. Other things you may already have on hand, such as baking powder, require a closer look to see whether they contains ingredients that are off-limits or questionable. Once your homework is done, you will need to shop for alternative flours, starches, and binders that work together to simulate the properties of wheat.

Gluten-Free Staples

Store starches on your pantry shelf and flours in your refrigerator, unless otherwise noted.

Rice flour: white and brown—White rice flour is ground from rice after the bran and germ have been removed. It has a bland taste and sandy consistency, and is lower in nutrients and fiber than brown rice flour. White rice flour is one of the most common ingredients in gluten-free baked goods and recipes because of its subtle flavor, relatively affordable cost, and long shelf life. It is featured in all five of the featured flour blends.

Brown rice, which contains the bran, is higher in fiber, nutrients, and fat and contains more protein than white rice. It adds a slightly nutty flavor to baked goods and can increase the nutrient value, but the oil it contains makes it more perishable, so store it in the refrigerator or freezer. It is an ingredient in Flour Blend #2.

Potato starch (sometimes called potato starch flour)—Potato starch is a finely textured starch made from raw white potatoes, and appears in Flour Blends #1, #2, and #3. Do not substitute potato flour for potato starch: the two are very different substances. The flour, made from cooked potatoes, is much heavier than potato starch.

Tapioca starch (also known as manioc) and tapioca flour—Tapioca starch and tapioca flour are the same thing: ground from the starchy, tuberous root of the cassava plant. Tapioca adds body and a chewy texture to gluten-free baked goods. It is a key ingredient in most of the flour blends.

Albumen (egg whites)—Powdered albumen, or egg white, is added to dry ingredients in a recipe to help leaven the product and to increase a batter's viscosity and protein content. Albumen can be found in the baking section of many supermarkets and has a long shelf life of up to one year. Powdered albumen is featured in Flour Blend #3. Egg white powder tends to have a strong flavor so it is best used in small amounts.

Whey powder—Whey is the watery component of milk left over from cheesemaking. It contains protein and other nutrients. A powdered version can add strength and color to gluten-free flour blends and is featured in Flour Blend #5. Keep this refrigerated.

Gums: guar vs. xanthan—Gums such as guar gum and xanthan gum improve the viscosity of gluten-free batters and determine the "mouth feel." Guar gum, ground from the endosperm of guar seeds, tends to have a lot of fiber and some people have trouble digesting it. Xanthan gum was created in a lab using natural ingredients, and is a widely used food additive. Although guar is the gum listed in these recipes, you can substitute xanthan gum in equal amounts if you prefer. Note: Be sure to add gums to the dry ingredients in a recipe. Once combined with liquid, guar gum and xanthan gum become extremely sticky. If you get this mixture on your hands, it's very hard to get off.

Soy flour—Soy flour is ground from roasted soybeans. The defatted version, which is used in Flour Blends #4 and #5, has had the oils removed during processing and is less prone to rancidity. Soy flour is high in protein and isoflavones. It has a strong yellow color and a distinctive soy taste, and should be stored in the refrigerator or, for longer term use, in the freezer.

Bean flours—Bean flours may be made from any legume. Some of the most widely used in gluten-free baking include navy, pinto, garbanzo, and garbanzo-fava bean blends. Bean flours are made by grinding up whole dry beans into a fine powder. Some of these flours can cause flatulence, so look for a brand that is precooked to avoid or reduce this problem. To keep bean flour fresh, store it in the refrigerator or freezer.

Cornmeal—Cornmeal is coarsely ground from whole dried corn and is available in yellow, white, and blue varieties. It can be combined with gluten-free flour blends to create cornbread and muffins. Corn flour is a more finely ground than cornmeal and has a lighter texture and detectable corn taste. Store these products in the freezer to prevent mold.

Cornstarch—Cornstarch is a highly refined product made from the endosperm, or starchy portion, of the corn. It has a bland flavor and works well as a thickener in pastry cream and in fruit pies.

Baking powder—Baking powder is a powdered chemical leavener typically consisting of baking soda (an alkali), acids, and starch (sometimes made from wheat) to keep it from sticking together. Look closely at the label to make sure the baking powder is gluten free. (See page 38, "Make Your Own Baking Powder.")

Baking soda—Baking soda contains just one ingredient: bicarbonate of soda. It is an alkali that reacts with acids in a recipe (such as buttermilk, lemon, or vinegar) to create carbon dioxide, which makes a baked good rise. Baking soda is commonly used in cookie recipes, to help them spread.

Butter—Butter is the fat of choice in many of the pastry recipes in this book. It can be used cold, cut into small pieces that are then rubbed into a flour blend; softened, in recipes that require the creaming method; or melted, to use as a liquid. Choose unsalted grade AA butter in sticks or blocks.

Yeast—Yeast is a living, single-celled microorganism that has been used for centuries to make alcoholic beverages and to leaven bread. Yeast requires moisture, food, oxygen, and warm temperatures to grow and ferment, which in turn produces carbon dioxide to make bread dough rise. All yeast sold in the United States (except for brewer's yeast) is gluten free, grown on a potato or corn base. The yeast used in these recipes is instant yeast, which is the most widely available type. Store yeast in a cool, dry place.

Eggs, whole—The recipes in this book are made with large eggs. Eggs can add leavening power to recipes, bind the ingredients together, and add protein and richness.

Egg whites—Egg whites can serve as a leavener, or, in the case of meringue and angel food cakes, as the basis for a recipe.

Egg yolks—Egg yolks are often used to add richness to custards and pastry creams, and are a key ingredient in the egg bread recipe.

Buttermilk—Buttermilk was once made from the slightly sour liquid left over after butter is churned. Nowadays buttermilk is made from cultured skim milk. It is naturally acidic, and therefore often combined with baking soda to provide leavening for pancakes and biscuits (one tablespoon of vinegar or lemon juice combined with one cup minus one tablespoon of milk may serve the same purpose).

Cocoa powder—Cocoa powder comes in two varieties: natural unsweetened and Dutch-process. Natural unsweetened cocoa provides a deep chocolate flavor and dark color to baked goods, and can serve as the acid needed for leavening in recipes using baking soda. It is often used in brownies and cookies. Dutch-process cocoa is also unsweetened, but treated with an alkali to remove its natural acids. It is red-brown in color, lighter in flavor than natural cocoa, and it works in recipes with baking powder where no additional acids are needed for leavening. Be sure to use whatever type of cocoa is specified in a recipe.

Chocolate—Chocolate sometimes contains gluten. Look for products that do not contain unspecified modified food starch, barley malt, unspecified natural flavors, or artificial colors.

Carbonated water and soda—These can add leavening power to gluten-free breads because of the carbon dioxide they contain. See the recipe for gluten-free Egg Bread (page 61). Cola Cake is another example (see page 184). Diet sodas do not work the same way, so avoid using these. Although caramel coloring is an ingredient found in most colas, caramel coloring in products sold in the United States is made from corn.

OTHER NOTABLE GLUTEN-FREE INGREDIENTS

Here are some alternative gluten-free flours and other gluten-free ingredients that are not typically used in these recipes. They are worth considering if you want to improvise or experiment. If a flour has a high fat content, you should store it in the refrigerator or freezer. Starches keep well on your pantry shelf. If in doubt, refrigerate or freeze.

Almond meal (sometimes called almond flour)—Almond meal is blanched almonds ground finely into flour. It is a staple for people following grainless diets and sometimes an ingredient in "flourless" cakes. It can also be used for breading. Because it is a nut product, it should be stored in the refrigerator or freezer to avoid rancidity. You can make your own almond meal in a blender or food processor. Take care not to overprocess it, or you will have almond butter.

Arrowroot—Arrowroot is a powdery white starch extracted from the root of a tropical plant. It is a good thickening agent and can be used as a glaze for fruit tarts. Arrowroot may be substituted for cornstarch when corn must be avoided.

Amaranth—Amaranth is a very nutritious flour made from the tiny, ground-up amaranth seed. It was first cultivated thousands of years ago and was a major crop of the Aztecs. Amaranth is often found in commercial cereals—just make sure if you are buying the cereal that the amaranth is not blended with wheat or other gluten-containing grains.

Buckwheat flour—Buckwheat flour is an ingredient often used in commercial gluten-free frozen waffles. Buckwheat itself is gluten free and is not related to wheat—it is in the same botanical family as rhubarb. Buckwheat is not considered a grain even though it is often used like one. Look carefully at the label when shopping for buckwheat flour or mixes: sometimes it is blended with wheat flour. Kasha, also known as groats, is another form of buckwheat that is widely available. It makes a good, starchy side dish.

Chestnut flour—Chestnut flour is far lower in fat and much higher in carbohydrates than most nut flours. It is expensive to produce, and therefore expensive to buy, but it is of high quality. You can buy the flour on its own, or in cake or bread mixes.

Gelatin powder—The unflavored, unsweetened kind of gelatin powder is often used as a binder in gluten-free recipes.

Indian rice grass—Indian rice grass (sold under the registered trade name Montina) is available as a flour on its own or as a blend combined with rice flour and tapioca starch. Indian rice grass originally grew wild in the northwestern part of North America. Its small, nutritious black seeds were ground into flour by Native Americans and used to make flat bread.

Millet—Millet is a variety of grass with a very nutritious, round seed that is high in protein and B vitamins. Some types of millet are used to feed birds and other animals, but there are two widely grown species you can find in the grocery store for yourself: pearl and finger millet. The whole, cooked seeds can be used as a breakfast cereal or a side dish. Millet grits and flour are also available. It has a flavor similar to corn.

Mesquite flour—Mesquite flour is made from ground-up bean pods of the mesquite tree. It is high in fiber and carbohydrates and has a sweet, nutty taste.

Nut flours—See almond meal—Filbert and pecan meal can also be found on store shelves and may be used in the same way as almond meal.

Quinoa—Quinoa is often referred to as a "super grain" because of its high-quality protein. Some gluten-free commercially made pastas use quinoa flour. The flour itself has a strong taste and should be used in small quantities with other gluten-free flours.

Sorghum—Sorghum is often paired with bean flours. Some gluten-free beers on the market are made from this grain. (See the "Readings and Resources" section, page 247.)

Sweet rice flour—Sweet rice flour is frequently used as a thickener. It is ground from short-grain sushi rice, also known as glutinous rice. Despite the name, it is safe for those on a gluten-free diet.

Teff—Teff is a tiny grain that makes a dark, nutritious flour and is best used in savory recipes. It grows well in hot climates, and is therefore a major food crop in Ethiopia and Eritrea.

For more information on gluten-free grain alternatives, see *Gluten-Free Diet: A Comprehensive Resource Guide, Expanded Edition*, by Shelley Case, BSc, RD, Case Nutrition Consulting, Regina, Saskatchewan, Canada.

AVOIDING CASEIN IN GLUTEN-FREE BAKING

As previously mentioned, many families with children diagnosed on the autism spectrum find that a gluten-free/casein-free diet is helpful. Casein is the protein found in bovine milk and milk products, including cow, sheep, or goat. A casein-free diet is more restrictive than a lactose-free one, because people who are lactose intolerant can still consume dairy products, as long as the lactose has been removed or is not present, or if they take an enzyme supplement. Those on a casein-free diet can have no dairy products at all, unless the casein has been removed (ghee, for example).

Obvious sources of casein:
- Milk, cream, half-and-half, buttermilk, yogurt, sour cream, butter, cheese, whey
- Desserts including ice cream, frozen yogurt, sherbet, ice milk, puddings, custards
- Candy, such as milk chocolate, white chocolate, caramel
- Soup bases, cream soup, creamed vegetables

Look closely at these foods:

- Margarine (sometimes contains milk)
- Lactose-free cheese, soy cheese, rice cheese
- Ghee (clarified butter in which the casein is supposed to have been removed—make sure it's guaranteed casein free)
- Hot dogs, lunch meat, sausage, tuna fish
- Casein, caseinate, and lactic acid as ingredients
- Lipstick, medicines

Baking Without Casein or Gluten

The gluten-free recipes in this book can be made casein free as well. To make a casein-free version of Flour Blend #5, substitute navy bean flour for the whey. You could

GLUTEN-FREE DIET GUIDELINES

Avoid in all forms:
- All varieties of wheat, including spelt, einkorn, kamut, emmer, durum, faro, semolina, graham, bulgur, unspecified flour
- Rye
- Barley, barley malt, malt flavoring, malt syrup, malt extract, malt beverages; beer, ales, and similar fermented beverages
- Triticale (a cross between wheat and rye)

Foods to question:
- Oats. Make sure they are from an uncontaminated source.
- Caramel coloring, natural flavors, and, in products sold outside the United States, artificial flavors.

Processed foods that may contain gluten:
- Brown rice syrup
- Breading and coating mixes
- Soy sauce and condiments
- Gravies, marinades, sauces, dressings, soup bases, bouillon, and thickeners
- Lunch meat, hot dogs, sausage
- Imitation fish, imitation bacon
- Self-basting poultry
- Communion wafers
- Matzoh
- Bread and cereal products including stuffing, croutons, and pasta
- Energy bars and snack foods
- Candy
- Flavored beverages and rice milk

Look out for yourself:
- Read labels.
- Call food manufacturers if you're not sure a food is safe, or go without.
- Remember that wheat-free is not the same as gluten-free, since "gluten" also means rye and barley.

Sources: American Dietetic Association; Gluten Intolerance Group; Celiac Disease Foundation; Celiac Sprue Association

Gluten-Free Shopping List

*I*t helps to cross-reference the products you buy with either a list of forbidden ingredients (see page 21) or the latest *CSA Gluten-Free Product Listing*, updated each year in late fall by the Celiac Sprue Association, *www.csaceliacs.org.* Additionally, contact information for food manufacturers is included in the "Readings and Resources" section at the back of this book.

Now, on to the market—and don't forget your list!

To make all five of Chef Coppedge's flour blends, you will need the ingredients that follow. (Note: Buy prepackaged flours and grains, as those sold in open bins risk being contaminated by commonly used scoops.)

- Rice flour, brown and white
- Potato starch
- Tapioca flour (or tapioca starch, same thing)
- Whey powder
- Soy flour, defatted
- Navy bean flour, precooked
- Guar gum, or xanthan gum if you prefer (see page 16)
- Albumen (egg white) powder

Leaveners:

- Baking soda, naturally gluten free
- Gluten-free baking powder (some brands contain wheat starch—be sure to read the label)
- Instant yeast
- Carbonated water; cola. (Choose brands that do not contain barley malt. Caramel color, an ingredient found in cola, must be made from corn if sold in the United States.) Do not use diet sodas.

Sweeteners:

- Granulated sugar
- Brown sugar (look for a brand made with molasses, not invert sugar, which may be derived from wheat or barley)
- Powdered sugar
- Sugar substitutes or sugar alcohols (polyols) such as maltitol, sorbitol, mannitol, and sucralose blends designed for baking
- Pure maple syrup
- Molasses
- Corn syrup

Salts:

- Non-iodized salt, kosher salt, or coarse sea salt, depending on recipe
- Gluten-free soy sauce

Vinegars:

- Apple cider, white, balsamic (avoid malt vinegar)

Flavorings:

- Vanilla beans, vanilla extract. (Choose extracts made without barley malt. Caramel coloring sold as an ingredient in U.S. products is made from corn.)
- Chocolate chips, baker's chocolate (check labels to ensure these are gluten free).
- Cocoa powder: natural or Dutch-process, depending on recipe
- Fresh eggs, large size
- Butter, unsalted
- Milk
- Buttermilk
- Cream
- Vegetable oil

also use a dairy-free powdered milk substitute instead of whey, but these substitutes tend to have less protein than whey (see "Readings and Resources," page 247).

As the Autism Network for Dietary Intervention recommends, butter can be replaced with a casein-free margarine. Casein-free milk alternatives are easy to find, but carefully check the label to ensure that the milk substitute you are using does not contain barley malt or other sources of gluten. Cheese products are harder to replace: casein-free versions of cheese don't tend to melt very well. But don't give up. Try various products until you find ones you like.

CHEF COPPEDGE'S FLOUR BLENDS

When considering which ingredients should go into a gluten-free product, it helps to think of what purpose wheat usually serves in regular baking. Wheat contains proteins and starches, which contribute to form the structure of baked goods. So when you eliminate wheat, you need to combine other proteins and starches to perform the same job.

It took years of experimentation to devise five flour blends that meet the needs of most gluten-free baking projects. Blend #1 is the "weakest" blend, most like cake flour in that it is mostly carbohydrates, while blend #5 is the "strongest," highest-protein blend, most like bread flour. Many of the recipes that you'll find later on in the book were developed using a combination of the flour mixes. The gluten-free pie crust recipe, for example, combines Flour Blends #2, #4, and #5.

Once you get comfortable using the flour blends in these recipes, you can adapt some of your own favorite recipes using the five flour blends.

Chef Coppedge's Gluten-Free Flour Blends Ingredients
Each flour blend recipe will fit into a two-quart container.

FLOUR BLEND #1 *(weakest strength; most carbohydrates)*		
Ingredients	Volume	U.S. Weight
White rice flour	1¾ cups	9.5 oz.
Potato starch	2 cups	7.25 oz.
Tapioca starch	1½ cups	7.25 oz.
TOTAL	5¼ cups	1.5 lb.

FLOUR BLEND #2
(second weakest; contains a little protein and fiber from brown rice)

Ingredients	Volume	U.S. Weight
White rice flour	1¾ cups	10 oz.
Brown rice flour	1¼ cups	7 oz.
Potato starch	¾ cup	3 oz.
Tapioca starch	1 cup	4 oz.
TOTAL	4¾ cups	1.5 lb.

FLOUR BLEND #3
(moderately strong; carbohydrate/protein combination)

Ingredients	Volume	U.S. Weight
White rice flour	¾ cup	5.25 oz.
Potato starch	4 cups	14.25 oz.
Guar gum	3½ tablespoons	1.25 oz.
Albumen	½ cup	3.38 oz.
TOTAL	5½ cups	1.5 lb.

FLOUR BLEND #4
(stronger; higher in protein from soy flour)

Ingredients	Volume	U.S. Weight
White rice flour	1½ cups	8 oz.
Tapioca starch	1¾ cups	8 oz.
Soy flour (defatted)	2¼ cups	8 oz.
TOTAL	5½ cups	1.5 lb.

FLOUR BLEND #5
(the strongest; high protein from soy and whey)

Ingredients	Volume	U.S. Weight
White rice flour	1¾ cups	9 oz.
Tapioca starch	1¼ cups	6 oz.
Soy flour (defatted)	1¾ cups	6 oz.
Whey powder	½ cup	3 oz.
TOTAL	5¼ cups	1.5 lb.

Weighing Versus Measuring

A lot of home bakers measure by volume, meaning they use measuring cups. The flour blend recipes given here use measurements based on sweeping the cup into the dry ingredient and leveling off the top with a table knife. For liquids, pour the ingredients into a graduated measuring cup. If you are measuring something sticky, such as honey or maple syrup, coat the inside of the measuring cup first with some gluten-free cooking spray (one that does not contain flour) and the ingredient will easily pour back out.

Professional bakers weigh their ingredients, and they do so in order to get a consistent result. The amount of flour in one cup varies widely: humidity, altitude, and measuring style are all factors that play a role. If you weigh your ingredients, you can be assured that you are getting the same amount each time and, all other factors being equal, a similar result each time.

You can use any type of kitchen scale, but the most accurate ones are calibrated, electronic digital scales (see "Readings and Resources," page 247). Once you are ready to weigh, the same principle applies for dry and liquid ingredients. Know your scale. Read the product manual that came with it and understand how it works. If you don't own a scale, though, don't fret! You'll see that the recipes include weight and volume measurements for most ingredients. Some ingredients have volume measurements only because the amount needed is so small that a scale may not even register a teaspoon of baking soda or instant yeast. Also, when some weights are less than one ounce, the metric weight in grams is given, but a calculator won't be necessary: most scales make these U.S. to metric conversions for you.

Ready, Set, Blend!

A large mixing bowl is the simplest way to blend the flours. When you are first getting started, you may want to weigh or measure your ingredients one at a time in separate containers and then add them to the bowl as you go along. It helps to follow the recipe in order, so you do not forget which ingredient you last measured. Some of the starchy flours look a lot alike, especially to someone new to gluten-free baking. Once all of the dry flour-blend ingredients are together, take a whisk and carefully blend the contents. Take your time and make sure it all gets turned over well. Some people like to put the flours into a large plastic bag, well knotted, and tumble it around. Sift the flour blend and transfer it into a wide-mouthed sealable container, two-quart size or larger. Be sure to attach a label with the contents and date—for example, Flour Blend #5, 10/1/08.

If you are baking frequently, you can store the blends in the cupboard. But to ensure freshness, the best scenario is to make room in your refrigerator or freezer for it. You may wonder whether you really need all five of the flour blends, considering that they take up so much real estate. You can start small, by mixing up the blends you need for one or two recipes. But as you become more proficient, it will make sense to have the whole arsenal at the ready. If you are refrigerating or freezing your blends, take the canisters out when you start assembling all the ingredients, preparing your pans, and preheating the oven. By the time you are ready to use it, the flour blend will have warmed up enough.

EQUIPMENT

Most of the equipment covered here includes things that people who bake a lot already have. If you are new to baking and are only doing it because you have to for dietary reasons, there are many tools and appliances that will make the job easier and more pleasurable. But don't get discouraged by the long list. You can get started with just a few items, and buy new tools and appliances as you need them.

See the "Readings and Resources" section (page 247) for specific brand recommendations and contact information.

Baking Pans

Some of the most important pieces of equipment you need for gluten-free baking are pans with sidewalls. These are necessary because most gluten-free dough is too soft to shape by hand (except for pie crust dough and 1-2-3 pastry dough). The pans you need are dictated by what you are baking. For breads and rolls, try loaf pans, Bundt pans, muffin pans, and miniature loaf pans. For tarts and cheesecakes, you can use springform pans and tart tins or pie pans. Round pans are good for layer cakes, and you will need baking sheets for cookies. For brownies, square and rectangular pans are useful. And if you are going to make English muffins frequently, you will find that English muffin rings make the job easier (instead of making the rings out of foil each time).

If you are using nonstick pans, the gray-colored pans work best because darker pans tend to brown gluten-free items too quickly. If you are using shiny aluminum pans or glass pans, be sure they are well greased so you can get your items out easily. Foil loaf pans and pie tins are good for baking and taking items to parties. And don't shy away from the new flexible silicone bakeware—these baking mats and molds come in interesting shapes and are excellent for gluten-free baking. Baked goods don't adhere to silicone (no need to grease) so cookies slide off easily and delicate items, such as gluten-free pâte à choux éclairs, pop out easily without falling apart. And if your household is not strictly gluten free, it is easy to dedicate some of these molds to gluten-free baking because they take up so little storage space. When using silicone flexi-ware, place the mold or mat on a rigid baking sheet before filling it with dough or batter, and then place them together in the oven.

Papers and Plastics

Parchment paper makes baking a lot easier. It can line a cookie sheet and go right in the oven. Then, after the cookies have cooled, you can easily peel away the paper without breaking the cookies. You can also line the bottom of cake pans with parchment to help prevent sticking.

Disposable plastic piping bags and assorted tips are needed to make spritz cookies, pretzels, and doughnuts. You can also take a plastic storage bag and cut a small hole in the corner.

Waxed paper is useful for storing baked goods. If you make a double batch of pancakes, for example, and freeze half of it, you can separate each pancake with some waxed paper before putting them in a freezer bag. Then when it's breakfast time, you can easily take out the number you need and leave the rest frozen.

Plastic wrap can help keep frozen items from drying out.

Appli(ance) Yourself

As previously mentioned, a kitchen scale is a good investment. They come in a range of prices and sizes. If you already have one, go ahead and use it! But if you are considering purchasing a new one, look for a calibrated, electronic digital scale. If you don't want to use a scale, you will need measuring spoons, and both dry and liquid measuring cups.

For small jobs, sometimes an electric hand mixer is just the thing. But as you bake more and more of your own gluten-free products, you will find that a stand mixer is indispensable. These come in handy when you need to spend five minutes creaming butter and sugar together to get lots of air into the mixture. Instead of giving yourself "mixer elbow" from standing there holding your electric hand mixer, you can walk away and do other things. The paddle attachment and whisk attachments are what you will use most in gluten-free baking. It is also helpful to have an extra mixing bowl, especially if you need to whip egg whites separately and fold them into a batter.

Food processors are great for chopping, shredding, and puréeing. If you don't have one, you can achieve the same goals with kitchen knives, a box grater, and a blender.

A waffle iron is necessary if you want to make waffles. If you are going to make these regularly, look for one with removable plates, which are much easier to clean. To make it easier for yourself, you should have a dedicated gluten-free waffle iron.

A griddle is useful for making pancakes and English muffins. Either an electric or a manual nonstick griddle is fine.

Small fryers are not very expensive and work well for making doughnuts. In households that are not completely gluten free, it is a good idea to dedicate a fryer to gluten-free items.

Microwaves and toaster ovens are not must-haves to achieve your baking goals. However, it makes sense when you are baking gluten-free items to make enough extra to freeze for later use, and microwaves defrost foods quickly. Toaster ovens are very important for households where one person is gluten free but everyone shares the toaster. You can put foil under your items (such as frozen gluten-free waffles) and then flip them over to toast the other side. Then you won't contaminate your food as you might in a regular shared toaster.

Bowls and Utensils

A set of mixing bowls is good to have, ranging from small to extra large. The largest bowl works well for blending flours.

If you plan to make the 1-2-3 cookie/pastry dough, or the pie crust recipe, you will need a rolling pin to roll out the dough. These come with or without handles. Use whatever kind you like best. Cookie cutters are good for making cookies, and the smaller ones can be used to cut out vented shapes in your pie dough.

If you don't own a spatula, you will want to get one. It is needed to scrape down the sides of a mixing bowl, and necessary for getting all of the batter out of the bowl and into the baking pan. Silicone spatulas can tolerate high heat and last longer than rubber spatulas.

Hand whisks are good for blending flours and quickly combining ingredients. Ladles are useful for transferring hot and cold liquid ingredients, such as when you are tempering (gently incorporating a hot liquid into a cooler liquid to gradually raise its temperature) eggs. When making pastry cream, for example, you can use the ladle to add the hot milk and sugar mixture to your eggs to bring them up to temperature.

Wooden chopsticks work well for turning doughnuts in a fryer.

And last but not least, a good set of knives and a plastic or a dedicated wooden gluten-free cutting board makes every cutting and chopping task easier.

Chapter 3

Baking Gluten Free: Tips and Techniques

*P*eople who must live the gluten-free lifestyle know it has a lot of extras that aren't necessarily fun: extra time planning and shopping, extra detective work, and extra will power. But when it comes to gluten-free baking, there is a surprising advantage: once you've done the extra work of blending the gluten-free flours and have cleared the gluten out of your workspace, the actual baking techniques are in some ways easier and less time-consuming. Because there is no gluten to develop, and therefore none to overwork, mixing gluten-free batters and doughs tends to go quickly; you can roll out and reuse pie crust and cookie scraps more than a few times; and in the case of gluten-free bread, there is no prolonged kneading, and only one rise time.

PREPPING: START WITH YOUR OVEN

If the most elaborate thing you've baked recently was a gluten-free frozen pizza, it may be time for you to check whether your oven is heating properly. A simple oven thermometer will tell you whether the temperature you've set on the outside of your oven matches the temperature on the inside. You will need to move the thermometer around in there, too (wearing oven mitts), to see whether some spots are hotter than others. If the temperature is off or you do have hot spots, you will need to have your oven recalibrated. Arrange for a service technician to do this, or check the owner's manual to see whether you can do this yourself. If you'd like, you can leave the thermometer in the oven all the time to keep tabs on whether the temperature remains accurate.

Once your oven is in working order, make setting your oven the first task when you begin a recipe. This will give it time to preheat while you are preparing your pans and assembling the ingredients.

If you have a convection oven, you will want to make sure that the fan is not operating at a high level while baking because too much wind can distort the top of your baked goods, especially delicate ones like sponge cake and angel food cake. Turn the fan off just for the first few minutes of baking to let the product firm up, or set the fan to a lower speed. If neither of those options is possible, you can preheat the convection oven, and then turn it off when you put your pans in the oven. Let your product sit in the residual heat for five to eight minutes, then turn the oven back on to finish baking.

Preparing your pans will involve greasing (or oiling) and dusting (Flour Blend #1 is good for this—it is less gritty than straight rice flour). Most pans benefit from this preparation whether you are using aluminum, glass, nonstick, or flexible silicone bakeware.

What is unique about baking in general is that once your product is in the oven, that's it. You can change certain aspects—e.g., vary the oven temperature, add steam, cover your items with foil, and pour liquid over the top—but you cannot adjust the ingredients that are in there. Preparation, therefore, is important, starting with how you combine your ingredients.

OVEN TEMPERATURES: CONVENTIONAL VS. CONVECTION	
Conventional Oven Temperatures	Convection Oven Temperatures
325°F	300°F
350°F	325°F
375°F	350°F
400°F	375°F
425°F	400°F
450°F	425°F

THE ABCS OF MIXING

The mixing methods used for conventional baking still apply to most gluten-free recipes, with a few adaptations. One piece of advice that applies to all of the methods: use a spatula to frequently scrape down the sides of your mixing bowl as you work, so all of the ingredients are well incorporated.

Straight Mixing

This method can be done by hand or with a mixer. It is used for recipes such as pancakes, quick breads, and some cakes, where a simple combination of wet and dry ingredients works best. Have all your ingredients at room temperature when straight mixing.

1. Combine dry ingredients. Take your flour blend and sift it together with salt and chemical leaveners (baking powder or soda), until evenly distributed. If the recipe calls for guar gum or xanthan gum outside of your premade flour blend, be sure to add these with the dry ingredients, since gums become extremely sticky when wet. Sugar can be added to the dry ingredients in the straight mixing method or added first to the liquid, depending on the recipe.

2. Combine wet ingredients. These may include water, fluid milk products, juice, oil, melted butter, extracts, or liquid sweeteners such as honey or maple syrup (and may include sugar, depending on the recipe's instructions). Whisk together until smooth.

3. Combine dry and wet ingredients. A recipe may instruct you to add all of the dry ingredients at once to the bowl that contains the liquid ingredients, or vice versa. Unlike with wheat-based pancake or muffin recipes, you do not want to leave lumps in a gluten-free batter, so blend until smooth. When you're done mixing, pour the batter into prepared pans and bake right away—so as not to lose leavening power.

Creaming

This method is often used to make moist and dense cakes and cookies. The objective is to create fat-coated air cells in the batter, which expand in the oven. Use a mixer for this, with either the paddle or beater attachment. Creaming by hand with a spoon is not very effective. Ingredients should be at room temperature.

1. Cream the butter and sugar together. In some gluten-free recipes, you will want to cream these together for as long as five minutes to incorporate as much air as possible to make a lighter product. (But this does not apply to all recipes. Some baked goods will collapse if you overaerate, or overcream, so follow individual recipe directions.) A stand mixer is the easiest way to achieve this, but you may also use an electric hand mixer.

2. Add eggs. Do this one at a time and make sure each is well incorporated before you move on to the next. Cold eggs could cause the butter to solidify into hard little pieces, negating all the hard work you've done creating air pockets. If you forget to take your eggs out early enough, try placing them in a bowl of room-temperature water before using them. Then mix them well in a separate container and add them a little at a time to the creamed butter and sugar.

3. Alternate dry and wet ingredients. Sometimes eggs are the only wet ingredient in a recipe. If so, then you would be adding the dry ingredients all at once at this stage, mixing together until smooth. For recipes that include additional liquid ingredients, start by adding a small amount of the dry ingredients to the batter and blend until smooth. Next, blend in a little of the wet ingredients, then continue alternating until everything is well blended.

Rubbing

The rubbing mixing method is used for flaky or crumbly recipes such as pie crust, biscuits, scones, crumb toppings for streusels and crisps, and some cookies. The butter is kept cold to prevent it from completely mixing with the flour. During baking, water in the dough turns to steam, the steam melts the butter, and the water bakes out later, creating the flakiness desired.

1. Combine dry ingredients. Whisk together gluten-free flour blends with salt and chemical leavener if using.

2. Cut fat into the dry ingredients. Keep the butter cold until you are ready to use it, cut it into little cubes, add to the dry ingredients, and toss it around. Then start cutting it in. There are many ways to do this: you can use your hands to rub the butter pieces into the flour, or use a flat handled pastry blending whisk. You could also use a food processor to pulse the butter and dry ingredients together. The recipe will instruct you on what size to leave the fat (e.g., "pea sized"). For crumb topping, you would stop here.

3. Moisten the dough. Next, you will need to moisten the dough with a small amount of cold liquid to get it to hold together. For many recipes, that is the last step.

If you are making pie crust, you will next need to roll it into a ball, cut it in half, flatten it into two disks, and wrap the disks in plastic wrap. It helps to let the dough age in the refrigerator before using it, if time allows. Even just ten minutes in the freezer will make it easier to roll out and manipulate.

Cold Foam

The cold foam mixing method involves whipping eggs (whole, whites, or yolks) and then incorporating them into the batter to add an airy texture. This method is used for waffles, angel food cake, and gluten-free pound cake.

1. Whip the eggs. Use a clean mixing bowl: if there are any traces of oil or fat, egg whites may not expand properly. This is less of an issue for whole eggs. Whip the eggs (with sugar if a recipe calls for it) until they are thick and foamy. Egg whites can increase up to seven times their original volume. Whole eggs and yolks alone can increase up to four times their volume.

2. Fold in the dry ingredients. Work to incorporate the dry ingredients quickly into the foam so you do not lose volume. Gently sprinkle the dry ingredients over the foam and use a spatula to fold in.

3. Add the fat. When adding melted butter to the foam, make sure both the fat and the foam are at room temperature. Temper the fat by folding a small amount of foam batter into it. Then add the tempered fat into the batter, again working quickly to preserve the volume.

Warm Foam

This technique is often used for sponge cake. It requires a lengthy time commitment to achieve the right texture.

1. Whisk eggs and sugar together, only to combine, while heating. Place the eggs and sugar into a bowl or double boiler over simmering water. Whisk as the two heat. (You are just whisking to combine the two at this point, not actually whipping—that comes later.) You will start out with a mucilaginous mixture. As the eggs and sugar heat while you gently whisk, the color will change from yellow to a deep orange, the thick mixture you began with will become watery and frothy, and less of it will stay on your whisk. You will know when it's ready if it looks like defrosted orange juice concentrate. Make sure the temperature is warmer than your body, between 110° and 120°F. What you are doing here is stretching the protein in the eggs, like a pre-exercise stretch, so that the egg protein can withstand the high velocity of whipping without tearing itself.

2. Whip the egg mixture. Place the egg-sugar mixture into a mixing bowl and whip on high speed. If you mark the volume of the mixture on the outside of the bowl to show where your egg mixture started, you will know when it has quadrupled in volume. You should think of the eggs as achieving a "high-water mark" as you might see in a flood. Once the foam has dropped a little from its high point, you need to continue whipping on medium speed until the foam has cooled off, ten to twenty minutes. It will be thick again and light in color.

3. Add flour. Sift your flour blend onto a piece of parchment or waxed paper using a dedicated sifter, to get the lumps out. Then fold the paper and pour the flour into the foam. It will sink to the bottom. Gently fold in the flour by hand or with a spatula.

4. Add the fat. Pour in the melted butter, working quickly as you fold it in, to try not to lose volume.

TIPS FOR MAKING GLUTEN-FREE BREAD

Bread is one of the most complicated items to make gluten free. The premise of regular bread is that you develop the wheat gluten in the dough, which creates a flexible network of strands, which in turn trap carbon dioxide from the yeast to inflate like a balloon. When you use gluten-free flours to make bread, there is no gluten to provide a stretchy network to trap the gas, but you can create a batter with air pockets that serve the same purpose.

The gluten-free bread recipes in this book tend to follow the straight mixing method: first, combine dry ingredients thoroughly, including your instant dry yeast. Next, combine all liquid ingredients. Then add the wet to the dry ingredients, mixing for three minutes or so. If you are adding a garnish or soaked gluten-free grains (such as softened cornmeal, sesame seeds, millet, caraway, or coriander), stir these in just before you assemble the loaf in the pan, or layer them.

Here are ten guidelines for making gluten-free bread, whether you are using the recipes in this book or improvising:

1. Increase hydration. Gluten-free flour blends are drier and more absorbent, so the recipes in this book use more liquid. Carbonated water, even non-diet soda, works wonders in gluten-free bread recipes. The extra bubbles help to lighten the batter, and if you are using non-diet soda, the sugar it contains can provide extra action for the yeast. If you would like to boost the protein in a recipe, you can also add or replace some of the liquid with more eggs.

2. Use the paddle attachment on your mixer, not the bread dough hook. Gluten-free bread doughs have more of a "batter" consistency that does not require kneading. There is no gluten to develop. If the batter is loose, a wire whisk can be used for mixing. A stiff batter will bind inside the whisk. You can also start mixing the dry ingredients using the whip attachment on an electric mixer and switch to the paddle attachment as you mix in the wet.

3. Use a low mixing speed. Since you are working with a thinner batter, rather than an elastic dough, your mixer can operate at a lower speed.

4. Increase the amount of yeast. Since there is no gluten to stretch and trap the gas, the yeast has to work harder, so use more of it. If you are experimenting with your own recipes, start by increasing the amount of yeast by 25 percent.

5. You can use pre-ferment. This is a technique where part of the bread ingredients are mixed ahead of time and allowed to ferment for several hours to develop more flavor and acidity. Among other things, acidity helps improve a baked good's "keeping" ability, which is a welcome benefit since gluten-free products tend to dry out easily. Here's what to do: Take one-third of the gluten-free flour in the recipe, an equal amount of water, and half of the yeast. Mix together and allow to double in volume, which will take about thirty to forty-five minutes. Then proceed with the recipe by combining the remaining ingredients with the pre-ferment.

6. Sourdough can be used, but you must make a starter for yourself that is gluten free. Sourdough starter is a mixture of flour (in this case gluten-free) and water that ferments from wild yeast in the air. You must make it at least three days before using, but once made, it can be used for years if properly fed and maintained. Or you can approximate the sourdough flavor with buttermilk and vinegar (see recipe on page 57).

7. Use pans with side walls. Your gluten-free bread "batter" cannot stand on its own. It will not hold a shape and must be poured into a pan that can support it while it is baking. You will also sometimes have more success if you use smaller loaf pans, rather than large ones. Be sure not to overfill the pan. Make it no more than two-thirds full.

8. Proof in a warm and humid environment. As most bakers say, "the proof is in the proof." What that means is that you are allowing the yeast to "prove itself" in the bread, and a well-leavened product will result. Yeast bread mixtures need humidity and warmth to rise, although gluten-free breads require less humidity because the mixture is wetter. Professional bakers have "proofers"—appliances that provide the perfect environment for bread to rise. These are different from ovens, and you should not try to use your own oven at home to proof your bread.

However, you can set up a proofing atmosphere in your kitchen by finding a warm place for the bread to rise. Or you can use your microwave oven, provided it is large enough. To do this, once your bread has been poured into the pan, set it aside for a moment. Place a graduated, heatproof measuring cup filled with one cup of water in the microwave and heat it until boiling. If there is room in the microwave, carefully push the cup to a back corner, place the bread pan in the center, and close the door. (If there is not enough room, you can gently remove the boiling water, add the pan, then repeat the process a second time to keep the moisture level up in the microwave.) Keep an eye on the pan to see whether the batter is rising properly. This can take between forty and fifty-five minutes, but it could happen earlier or take longer, so it's best to judge for yourself. Take it out when you see a gentle arc at the top of the pan. If the batter is bubbling and has spilled over the sides of the pan, it is overproofed. You may want to throw it out and start over. You could try baking it, but it may have a high alcohol flavor from the over-fermented yeast, which most people don't like. If the flavor is not bad, but the bread looks unattractive and misshapen, you could make bread crumbs out of it.

9. Bake in a moist oven. Professional bakers have ovens that inject steam at the beginning of the baking process, to help the bread rise and prevent the crust from being developed too early. These ovens also vent the steam at the appropriate time toward the end (once proper volume has been achieved) so the bread does not become soggy. Companies are starting to market steam/vent ovens to home bakers (see "Readings and Resources," page 247). But in the meantime, you can reproduce these same effects at home by using some ice cubes and a cast-iron skillet or cookie sheet (one that is warped, or one that you don't mind warping and reusing for this purpose). Place the empty vessel you are using on the bottom rack of the oven when you turn the oven on to preheat. Make sure the top rack is in the middle position so you can place your bread there when it is ready. Once your bread is proofed, put on your oven mitts and place the bread pan on the middle rack in the oven, then, keeping your face back, toss some ice cubes into the hot skillet or baking sheet on the bottom rack and close the door. Voila! You have steam.

To vent toward the end (typically during the last five to eight minutes of baking, once your bread has reached the proper volume), crack open your oven door.

10. Increase baking times and adjust temperature as you go. Gluten-free breads are more dense, so it takes longer to bake them. Start out at a lower temperature—350°—to help prevent the gluten-free bread from overbrowning during the longer baking process. Once the volume is there, increase the temperature by 25° or so to brown at the end. (Or you can bake at the same temperature all along and cover with foil toward the end if the bread is getting too brown).

Once the bread is baked, you can use a thermometer to verify that the bread is done. An internal temperature of 200°F or higher at the center is best. Let the bread rest in the baking pan for five minutes, then remove it from the pan by turning it over and gently tapping on the bottom and sides. Place the bread upright on a cooling screen if you have one.

One final note: Baking bread is both an art and a science. It takes practice, and you will probably have to throw out a few loaves as you learn. Don't give up. Think about where you've succeeded and failed, and apply that knowledge the next time you bake.

QUICK! GET IT INTO THE OVEN! TIPS FOR MAKING QUICK BREADS AND MUFFINS

Quick breads are just that: quick. No fermenting of yeast is involved. The ingredients, which include chemical leaveners, combine to produce carbon dioxide when a catalyst, in this case something wet, is introduced. Then, in the case of double-acting baking powder, a second reaction occurs when heat is introduced, providing another burst of leavening power.

MAKE YOUR OWN BAKING POWDER

Most baking powders available on store shelves today are double acting, meaning that the powder reacts with a catalyst at two separate times to create carbon dioxide—first, when a liquid is added to the dry ingredients; second, when heat from the oven is introduced. All baking powder used to be single acting, and you can make a version of this at home, which is useful if the baking powder you have on hand is not gluten free.

Here is a recipe, by weight and volume.

SINGLE-ACTING BAKING POWDER			
Weight	Volume	Ingredient	Purpose
2 oz.	¼ cup + 2 teaspoons	cream of tartar	the acid
1 oz.	2 tablespoons	baking soda	the alkali
1 oz.	2 tablespoons + 2 teaspoons	starch	the buffer (preventing acid and alkali from reacting before liquid is introduced.

Once you add the liquid catalyst, you need to get the product into the oven right away. Unlike double-acting baking powder, which allows you to work at a more leisurely pace, single-acting baking powder starts working as soon as you add the liquid catalyst.

Most quick bread recipes call for the creaming method: cream butter together with sugar, then add liquid ingredients, and finally add the dry (or alternate adding the last two). Since regular quick breads already take the form of a wet batter (which is the form of most gluten-free recipes) there are not many adjustments to be made, aside from using gluten-free ingredients. Make sure that your baking powder does not contain wheat starch. You can even make your own, single-acting baking powder with just a few ingredients (see page 38).

If you choose to use oil in place of the butter, mix the wet ingredients, then add the dry all at once. The product will not be as aerated and as tender, but it will still be good.

When a quick bread or muffin recipe calls for berries and you want to avoid having the color bleed into your batter, use fresh frozen berries (buy fresh berries and wash them, then place them in the freezer until you're ready to use them). Once you're ready to make the recipe, roughly chop the frozen berries in a food processor, then stir them in just before you scoop the batter into the pan. If you are making banana bread or muffins, use the ripest fruit you can find, which contains more sugar and creates a moister product.

Sanding sugar, a very coarse sugar with crystals that are slightly larger than kosher salt, is something fun to sprinkle on top of muffins before they are baked. It can be found at specialty stores (see "Readings and Resources," 247).

LET IT ROLL: TIPS FOR WORKING WITH GLUTEN-FREE PIE AND COOKIE DOUGH

This book includes a recipe for pie crust that is a gluten-free staple you will use again and again for your holiday favorites, such as pumpkin and apple pie. The recipe does require combining three different flour blends, but once you've done that, the fat and the flours are cut together as you would in a typical pie dough recipe. The result is a gluten-free pie dough you can manipulate, almost like regular, wheat-based pie dough. Since there is no gluten, the gluten-free pie dough is more fragile. Nevertheless, it will roll out easily on a dusted surface and does not require using sheets of plastic or parchment to prevent sticking (you could, however, use these if you want to). The crust also works well for savories such as quiche and Beef Wellington.

3-2-1 Pie Dough

Regular cookies, pies, and tarts don't require a lot of gluten. Classic recipes for pie dough follow a 3-2-1 structure (based on weight, not on volume):

- three parts flour
- two parts fat
- one part cold liquid

The gluten-free pie dough follows roughly the same pattern, with some small adjustments to the structure:

- three parts flour = 3 ounces each of Flour Blends #2, #4, #5, for a total of 9 ounces;
- two parts fat = 5 ounces of butter (a little less fat than the classic wheat recipe);
- one part cold liquid = 4 ounces of cold water (a little more water, because gluten-free flours absorb more liquid)

The three flour blends used here in the gluten-free pie dough recipe provide the right texture. You will be using the rubbing method (as outlined on page 32) to cut the fat into the flours. Mixing a gluten-free pie dough goes faster because there is no gluten matrix with which to contend, although overmixing can adversely affect the texture. Keep the dough cool until you use it. Once you are ready to roll, make sure the fat is evenly distributed; if it is not, work it in. Flour your work surface to provide nice coverage without creating blobs of flour on the dough, and roll out using a pin of your choice, rolling out from the center of the dough into quadrants like those on a clock face.

If you are making a quiche, you will need to parbake, or partially bake, the crust (about ten minutes at 350°F). To do this, place the rolled-out dough over the pie pan and gently pat it into the pan. Flute the edges and discard excess dough from the top. Dock the bottom (use a fork's tines to make tiny little holes) to allow some of the moisture to come out. Cover the bottom of the crust with parchment paper and weigh it down with some dry beans or pie weights to prevent the crust from puffing up in the oven.

For fruit pies, mold the crust to the pan as usual, but do not dock the bottom. Add fruit filling to the raw crust, brush an egg wash along the edge before adding the top crust, then flute the two crusts together by pressing your fingers against the dough. Next, gently cut out a hole in the top to vent. When your apple pie comes out of the oven, you can pour some of the reserved thickening juices (reduced in a saucepan) through the vent hole to fill in gaps after the apples have settled.

1-2-3 Pie and Cookie Dough

For fruit tarts, a sweeter, less flaky crust made from 1-2-3 Cookie Dough is more appropriate (again, based on weight, not on volume):

- one part sugar (cookie dough uses eggs as a liquid)
- two parts fat
- three parts flour
- 1 to 2 eggs, depending on the weight of the flour

Unlike pie dough, which uses the rubbing mixing method, 1-2-3 dough is mixed all at once: cold cubed butter, eggs, gluten-free flours, and sugar are blended together until combined. You don't want to have pieces of fat in the dough, so mix well at the end with your hands. Shape it into a disk, wrap it in plastic, and refrigerate it for a few hours. It must be cold to roll out.

The gluten-free 1-2-3 dough rolls more easily than gluten-free pie dough since it has more sugar and proportionally more fat. Pat the rolled-out dough in a pie pan as you would a regular crust and flute if using it for a cream pie. If you are using a tart pan, pat the dough into the pan, then roll your pin over the top to cut off the scraps. If the side wall is too thin, you may thicken it by pressing in extra dough. A 1-2-3 crust is pre-baked since it is typically filled with pastry cream or custard, and it does not need to be weighted down in the oven. If it starts to bubble while baking, pop the bubbles with a fork. This type of crust is fragile, so if it breaks before you can use it, just crush the pieces and press it into a pan as you would for a cookie crumb crust. Then fill your crust with pastry cream, custard, even store-bought pudding if you wish. To complete a tart, pipe the filling using a pastry bag (see page 44).

To make roll-out cookies with 1-2-3 dough, use the same principle as for a pie crust. Prepare your work surface by lightly dusting with flour, then roll the dough as thick as you wish. Cut out shapes, brush the tops with water or milk, or top with sugar and bake. You may reroll the scraps more than once—the gluten-free dough will stay tender.

TIPS FOR MAKING CAKES

Regular cakes do not rely on flour for structure, but rather on eggs. The eggs in the recipe coagulate, binding all the ingredients together during baking, and are assisted somewhat by the flour in holding the ingredients together and providing texture. So translating a cake into a gluten-free version is generally no more or less complicated than what you'd do for a regular cake recipe. If you are making a gluten-free sponge cake, for example, you will still need to set aside an hour to prepare it, because the lengthy mixing technique is basically the same. When you substitute gluten-free flour blends for wheat flour, you will lose some of the volume, but you can still get a good product.

PLATED DESSERTS: HOW TO CREATE A SHOWSTOPPER

If dessert always seems more elegant at a fine restaurant, that is because it is served "plated." Plating a dessert involves using sauces and garnishes to add color, flavor, and drama to the presentation. Plating can be as simple as adding glaze to a cake or drizzling caramel sauce on ice cream. Or it can be more complex, including several dessert elements with contrasting textures and complementary flavors layered together, such as a gluten-free plated dessert with brownie, short bread, ice cream, tuile, and a sauce of your choice. The sauce can be homemade (see Chapter 6 for recipes), or you can save yourself some time and use something store-bought.

To plate your own desserts at home, try thinking in yin/yang terms: warm versus cold, sweet versus tart, mild versus zingy. Fruit, chocolate, caramel, and custard sauces can add a striking and flavorful effect. If you'd usually pour the sauce over the top of the dessert, try something different: make a pool of chocolate sauce on the serving plate first, dot with caramel sauce, then drag a toothpick through it at even intervals to get a harlequin effect. Place the dessert you are serving, such as cheesecake, on top. Or surround a piece of chocolate cake with droplets of brightly colored fruit sauce. Top with a dollop of whipped cream, a dusting of finely chopped nuts, and a sprig of mint. You could also scatter chocolate shavings or sprinkle on some chocolate powder or powdered sugar. Be creative—just make sure all of your ingredients are gluten free.

One way of getting around the volume problem is to adjust the ingredients or add extra egg whites, as you'll see in the recipe for gluten-free pound cake (page 153).

Classic pound cake is so named for its major ingredients:

One pound of butter,
One pound of sugar,
One pound of eggs, and
One pound of flour.

It is a very dense cake; if you made it using the same proportions, but just substituted gluten-free flour, you'd end up with a solid block good for parking a car on a hill. The gluten-free version of pound cake requires changing the classic ingredients ratio and adding in whipped egg whites at the end it to lighten it up.

For gluten-free pound cake there is a little extra fat, which helps moisten the product, as well as extra sugar, which provides more moisture and makes the pound cake more tender. The proportion of eggs is higher here than in the classic wheat-based recipe to provide more liquid and leavening. And there is more gluten-free flour here, in this case white rice flour, which is very dry and soaks up a lot of liquid. Once you change the proportions of the ingredients, making a gluten-free pound cake involves essentially the same creaming process you'd use for a wheat-based version, except that you are adding meringue (whipped eggs and sugar) as the final step before baking.

The secret to another classic wheat-based recipe, sponge cake, is in the whipping. It is light and dry by definition, and employs the warm foam mixing method (see page 34). The gluten-free version uses the same technique, but the recipe has more carbohydrates and is more dense.

Devil's food cake is super-rich, containing chocolate, cocoa powder, butter, and sour cream (see page 160 for a full list of ingredients). Once you've creamed the ingredients together, the mixture is very thick.

COOKIES AND BROWNIES COOKING TIPS

Most cookie recipes, like cakes, rely on eggs for structure, with the flour there to add some structural assistance and texture. Creaming softened butter together with sugar (see page 32) lightens the mixture and helps the cookies spread out. This is also where things can go wrong in a recipe: if you overaerate during the creaming stage, the fat-coated air cells you've created could collapse, resulting in too much spread. This poses more of a risk with gluten-free flour, since there is no elasticity to help keep the cookies from sliding out. Temperature during the mixing stage is also an important factor. When you add eggs to a creamed butter and sugar mixture, the eggs are supposed to go into the holes of the air cells. If your eggs come straight out of the refrigerator, they will be too cold to perform this role and will instead make the mixture solidify.

The gluten-free spritz cookies, which are designed to be piped, require that butter and eggs be at room temperature. The dough needs to be able to flow through a piping bag, but you don't want it to be too thin because then it won't hold even a simple shape. Professionals have all sorts of tools at their disposal to help dough stay warm, including mixers that can provide a warm water bath. But the easiest thing you can do at home to have success with this recipe or others that call for the butter and eggs to be room temperature is to leave your eggs and butter out on your counter for up to an hour. Then you will quickly get a light and fluffy mixture while creaming.

Using a cookie press for gluten-free spritz cookies is not worth the effort—the shapes are too complex for the dough to hold. But you can get some simple shapes that hold together well enough and look pretty by using a star tip and a pastry bag, or even a plastic storage bag with a corner snipped open a little. Practice making a few test cookies on a piece of parchment first. If they turn out well enough, you can put the parchment onto a cookie sheet and bake. Once you are ready to pipe cookies by the tray, try tacking the parchment to the baking sheet by using a small spritz of cookie batter under each corner. This keeps the paper from sliding around.

Gluten-free drop cookies, including the gluten-free Chocolate-Pecan cookies (recipe on page 109), sometimes need to be flattened before baking. Use a small- to medium-sized scoop to form the cookies. Test bake a few. If they do not flatten by themselves in the oven, take a spatula and help them along.

Brownies are very similar to cookies in that they rely on eggs for structure and the flour adds texture; therefore, it is fairly easy to make gluten-free versions of these. Fudge brownies are dense and not aerated, whereas cake-style brownies are fluffy and use the creaming mixing method to lighten them.

PIPING TECHNIQUES

Sometimes the best tool for a job is a bag—a piping bag, that is. Many of the recipes in this book require piping because gluten-free doughs tend to be too soft to shape with your hands. You can find disposable plastic piping bags in specialty stores, along with a coupler and an array of tips. The coupler allows for a quick interchanging of different sized or shaped tips without having to change bags. If you are going to be baking a lot, it is worth investing in five different types of tips: #2 plain round, #4 plain round, #4 star, #6 plain round, and #6 star. However, there's no harm in using a zipper-style storage bag with a small hole cut in one of the corners. If you have any leftover mixture you need to refrigerate, you can just transfer it to a new plastic bag and store it.

To get the best results when piping anything—whether it is pastry cream or dough for cookies, doughnuts, bagels, or pizza—don't overfill the bag. You want it to be no more than two-thirds full. Start with an empty bag and cut a small hole in the bottom if necessary. Push the coupler base down as far as it can go. Next, fold down the wider top of the bag like a sleeve, then force the mixture you are using down far enough for some of it to come out of the end of the bag. Gather the bag up under the sleeve, unfold it, and twist the top. Attach your tip of choice to the outside of the bag/coupler, then screw on the locking ring.

When you are ready to pipe, you should be holding the top of the bag, where you will squeeze, with your dominant hand, and guiding the tip with the other. If you find that the bag is hard to control when there is a lot of batter or pastry cream in it, you can add a twist in the middle of the bag, then use your dominant hand to both squeeze the bag and guide the tip, with your other hand holding the twist at the top. Otherwise the bag could flop over and spill its contents.

TIPS FOR MAKING SAVORIES

Quiche can be a satisfying and hearty one-dish meal. If you don't have time to make a gluten-free crust, you could always just assemble the ingredients in a well-oiled pan without it. Still, the flakiness of a good pie crust really adds to the pleasure of a quiche. It contrasts nicely with the creaminess of the baked custard and the savory fillings. Earlier in this chapter the subject of preparing crust for quiches was addressed in the pie-baking section (see page 40): you need to dock the bottom of your crust and partially bake it with weights before proceeding with the recipe. Once you have your parbaked crust ready to go, you should first assemble the ingredients dry in the crust. Chopped scallions and/or parsley, sautéed onions, red bell pepper, spinach, and cooked bacon are all popular choices for quiche. Layer those in and top with your choice of cheese. To prevent the crust from becoming soggy, you will want to ladle in the eggs and cream mixture just before you bake it. Try doing this near your oven: you won't have to travel far with the quiche, and will therefore reduce your chances of spilling it. If you do not want to add cheese to your quiche, you could reduce some of the cream and add an extra whole egg to help increase the binding action of the baked custard.

The gluten-free pizza recipe (page 221) uses a soft bread dough that you pipe in a disk shape onto greased parchment paper, or into a greased pie tin (see "Piping Techniques," page 44). You can make your crust any size, but you might like having personal-size 6" crusts. These are easy to handle, and if you make more than you need, the parbaked crusts fit well in your freezer. Once you've piped the crust, let it rest for ten minutes. Then transfer it with the parchment paper onto a baking sheet, or put the greased pie tin into the oven to proof before parbaking at 350°F for ten to twelve minutes. Allow the crusts to cool. You can either freeze the crust at this point, wrapping it well, or go ahead and make your pizza.

Pretzels are salty and crusty, and that is partly because they are dipped into a salty solution before baking (in this gluten-free recipe, a baking soda solution is used). Once in the oven, the solution reacts with sugars in the pretzel dough to create the characteristic hard brown crust. You cannot twist gluten-free pretzel dough because it is too soft to manipulate that way. But a pastry bag will allow you to approximate a pretzel twist, or, easier still, to make pretzel sticks.

Gluten-free bagels must also be piped to achieve their classic ring shape. Then, before baking, they are poached in a simmering solution made with molasses or honey. The poaching liquid for regular bagels contains barley malt, which is off-limits for people on the gluten-free diet.

Finally, there is pasta. This gluten-free recipe uses Flour Blends #3 and #4, eggs, salt, oil, and water to create a mixture that can be rolled into a narrow column and cut into smaller pieces. Or you can roll the mixture into little balls, then elongate them by rolling each ball between your palms. These cook in about a minute and a half in boiling water, usually floating to the top when done. The result is a dense texture and savory flavor similar to gnocchi. These work well with a hearty sauce.

Now, it's time to put on your apron and get started!

WRAPPING, STORING, AND TRAVELING WITH YOUR GLUTEN-FREE GOODS

Gluten-free baked goods tend to dry out easily, so there are special considerations for storing them. One of the best strategies is to bake your items, serve the portions you will be eating that day, and store what remains in the freezer. If you freeze an item the same day, it will retain its freshness better. You will need to make sure it is well wrapped to keep the moisture in and prevent freezer burn, and you will need to make sure each item is separate from its counterparts so you can remove what you need when you need it.

For pancakes, waffles, and cookies, place waxed paper between each one, stack together, and place in a labeled plastic freezer bag. If you know the items will be in the freezer for a while, wrapping the stack tightly with plastic wrap before placing it in the bag will add an extra layer of protection. You can use the same stack-and-wrap method for pizza crusts.

For cupcakes, thick brownies, and pretzels, wrap waxed paper around each one, add a layer of plastic wrap if necessary, then place in a bag.

For cakes, pies, and pie crusts, wrap each one tightly with multiple layers of plastic wrap (use heavy duty freezer wrap if available) before labeling and placing in the freezer. This can apply to loaves of bread, if you are in the habit of freezing the whole loaf and defrosting it for later use. If you need one slice at a time, slice the bread first, separate the slices with waxed paper, then wrap tightly with plastic wrap if necessary and seal in a freezer bag.

When you need to travel with gluten-free items, consider how long you will be in transit. If you will not need the item for several hours, you can take a frozen item and it will be defrosted by the time you arrive at your destination. If you need to ration out your gluten-free goods on a long trip and want them to stay frozen until you can get them into a freezer again, place your items in a rigid cooler with ice packs. This type of container will also help protect fragile goods that are prone to breaking. For air travel, consider checking a suitcase with nonperishable items, or send your food in a package ahead of you. Make sure you will not be violating any customs laws by bringing your foods overseas. It helps to have a doctor's note explaining why you need to carry the food with you.

Chapter 4

Yeast-Raised Breads and Pastries

*S*amuel Taylor Coleridge's poetic line "Water, water, everywhere, nor any drop to drink" could just as easily be applied to bread. When you're on a gluten-free diet, it seems there is an ocean of bread in the world, specifically there to test you: toast for breakfast, sandwiches for lunch, rolls at dinner time, crackers for snacks. Who can blame you if you think gluten-free bread comes in two types: dense and rubbery or dry and crumbly. Sure, it's safe to eat, but why bother?

Let the sad scenario end here. This book's recipes, flour blends, and techniques make it possible to bake and eat bread you will enjoy. It takes time and effort to make good bread, and that does not change when you switch to gluten-free ingredients. Mixing goes more quickly, and there's only one rise cycle, but you will still need to put all of your senses to work, and add a good dose of intuition. The process takes awhile, so make sure you give yourself enough time to be relaxed about it.

Once you've done the work, there's a lot to look forward to. Toast up some mock rye and eat it with your eggs. Make a sandwich with a couple of slices of multigrain. Serve dinner with a nice sourdough, or a lean French-style loaf—you can even make some rolls, if you prefer. Bake some egg bread and turn it into French toast the next morning.

All of the other breakfast classics are now on the table as well: doughnuts, cinnamon buns, English muffins, and even bagels. Bagels made with wheat are poached in a barley malt bath, but molasses serves the same purpose in the gluten-free version. You will get a product that is crusty and chewy, perfect for any time of day. Set aside a morning when you don't have to be rushed, and be sure you have enough extra to freeze. Then you can pull something special out at the last minute during the week and heat it up in your toaster oven or microwave. Now you're sailing in first class!

Focaccia

While this bread is free of gluten, it is full of everything needed to recreate an Italian favorite. In this bread dough, rosemary, basil, and oregano are combined with olive oil to create a flavor truly reminiscent of the Mediterranean.

YIELD: ONE 9" PAN (EIGHT SERVINGS)

1¼ teaspoons	Instant yeast
½ teaspoon (dried), ½ bunch fresh	Rosemary
½ teaspoon (dried), ½ bunch fresh	Basil
½ teaspoon (dried), ½ bunch fresh	Oregano
½ teaspoon	Salt
2 cups (12 oz.)	Flour Blend #1
½ cup (3 oz.)	Flour Blend #3
1¼ cups (10 oz.)	Sparkling water, room temperature
⅓ cup	Olive oil
¼ teaspoon	White vinegar
As needed	Olive oil, for garnish
1¾ tablespoons	Coarse salt

1. Blend the dry ingredients and herbs in a mixer bowl. Add all the wet ingredients and mix with a paddle for 5 minutes on medium speed.
2. Place dough into one 9" pie pan brushed liberally with olive oil.
3. Cover and proof in a warm, humid environment for 30 to 40 minutes.
4. Bake in a preheated 385ºF oven for 30 to 35 minutes or until golden brown.
5. Remove from the pan and place on a cooling rack. Brush with olive oil and sprinkle with coarse salt.

NUTRITIONAL INFORMATION PER SERVING

SERVING SIZE: 1 slice	SODIUM: 610mg	DIETARY FIBER: 1g
CALORIES: 280cal	TOTAL CARBOHYDRATE: 39g	PROTEIN: 2g
TOTAL FAT: 9g		

Lean Bread

This recipe offers a gluten-free version of a simple lean dough. Lean doughs are characteristically low in fat and sugar, examples of which are seen in crusty French breads and pizza dough. Before shaping and baking, you may add herbs, spices, grated cheese, or other additional ingredients of your choice to create variations on the standard recipe.

YIELD: TWO STANDARD 8" × 4" × 2¾" LOAVES OR 20 ROLLS (20 SERVINGS)

2⅔ cups (1 lb.)	Flour Blend #3
3 cups (1 lb.)	Flour Blend #5
1 tablespoon	Salt
3 tablespoons (24 g)	Guar gum
2⅓ tablespoons	Instant yeast
3½ cups (28 oz.)	Sparkling water
6 ea.	Egg whites

1. Thoroughly combine flour blends, salt, guar gum, and yeast.
2. In a separate bowl, combine sparkling water and egg whites and then add the wet to the dry ingredients.
3. Mix, using a paddle for 4 minutes on low speed or until smooth.
4. Just before shaping, consider stirring in your favorite additional ingredients—e.g., grated cheese, herbs, raisins, vegetables, fruits, or spices. Layer some of the filling as you assemble the roll or loaf.
5. Scoop the mixture into greased baking cups for rolls or loaf pans for bread loaves, filling about two-thirds full.
6. Proof the shaped product in a warm, humid environment for 40 to 55 minutes (for a reminder on how to proof, see page 36).
7. Bake in a preheated 375°F oven with some steam/moisture. Bake rolls for 15 minutes and breads for 45 to 55 minutes.

8. Once the bread has risen to the top of the pan, vent the oven (if applicable; usually just necessary in professional ovens) during the last 5 to 8 minutes. The product should be firm at the center with an internal temperature of 200°F. You can test this with a meat thermometer. If the bread is not at the correct temperature, bake for 5 minutes more.

9. Remove from the oven and unmold onto cooling racks.

NUTRITIONAL INFORMATION PER SERVING		
SERVING SIZE: 1 slice	SODIUM: 370mg	DIETARY FIBER: 4g
CALORIES: 160cal	TOTAL CARBOHYDRATE: 37g	PROTEIN: 8g
TOTAL FAT: 0g		

When properly mixed, the dough should have a tacky, spreadable consistency.

Allow the dough to proof until doubled in volume before baking.

Mock Rye

WITH ONIONS BREAD

After one bite, you will agree that there is nothing mock about the bold flavor of this bread. The presence of caramelized onions in the dough offers a touch of savory sweetness; made into rolls or cut as slices off a loaf, this bread makes a dramatic splash when added to any breadbasket.

YIELD: TWO STANDARD 8" × 4" × 2¾" LOAVES OR 20 ROLLS (20 SERVINGS)

¼ cup	Vegetable oil
1 cup (1 ea.)	Onion, diced ¼" thick
2⅔ cups (1 lb.)	Flour Blend #3
3 cups (1 lb.)	Flour Blend #5
1 tablespoon	Salt
4 tablespoons (1 oz.)	Guar gum
3 tablespoons	Instant yeast
3½ cups (28 oz.)	Sparkling water
¾ cup	Vegetable oil
3⅓ teaspoons	White vinegar

1. Heat ¼ cup of vegetable oil in a pan and sauté the onions over medium heat until caramelized. Set aside.
2. Thoroughly combine flour blends, salt, guar gum, and yeast.
3. In a separate bowl, combine sparkling water, vegetable oil, and white vinegar, then pour into dry ingredients.
4. Mix, using a paddle for 4 minutes on low speed or until smooth.
5. Gently stir in onions by hand until evenly distributed.
6. Scoop mixture into greased baking cups or a loaf pan, filling about two-thirds full.
7. Proof the shaped product in a warm, humid environment for 40 to 45 minutes.
8. Bake in a preheated 375°F oven with some steam/moisture. Bake rolls for 15 minutes or loaves for 45 to 50 minutes.

9. Once product has risen to the top of the pan, vent the oven (if applicable; usually just necessary in professional ovens) during the last 5 to 8 minutes. The product should be firm at the center with an internal temperature of 200°F. If the bread is not the correct temperature, bake for 5 minutes more.

10. Remove from oven and unmold onto cooling racks.

NUTRITIONAL INFORMATION PER SERVING		
SERVING SIZE: 1 slice	**SODIUM:** 490mg	**DIETARY FIBER:** 4g
CALORIES: 210cal	**TOTAL CARBOHYDRATE:** 35g	**PROTEIN:** 7g
TOTAL FAT: 6g		

Mock Rye Bread

Specifically designed gluten-free flour blends combine with other ingredients to create the flavor of rye bread without the gluten. Grilled or toasted, slathered with Russian dressing and piled high with corned beef, sauerkraut, and Swiss cheese, this mock rye bread makes for a perfect Reuben.

YIELD: TWO STANDARD 8" × 4" × 2¾" LOAVES OR 20 ROLLS (20 SERVINGS)

2⅔ cups (1 lb.)	Flour Blend #3
3 cups (1 lb.)	Flour Blend #5
1 tablespoon	Salt
3 tablespoons	Instant yeast
½ cup	Caraway seeds
3½ cups (28 oz.)	Sparkling water
½ cup	Vegetable oil
3 teaspoons	White vinegar

1. Thoroughly combine all dry ingredients.
2. In a separate bowl, combine all liquids and then pour into dry ingredients.
3. Mix, using a paddle for 4 minutes on low speed or until smooth.
4. Scoop mixture into two greased loaf pans, about two-thirds full.
5. Proof the shaped product in a warm, humid environment for 40 to 45 minutes.
6. Bake in a preheated 375°F oven with some steam/moisture for 45 to 50 minutes.
7. Once product has risen to the top of the pan, vent the oven (if applicable; usually just necessary in professional ovens) and continue baking for 5 to 8 minutes.
8. The bread should be firm at the center with an internal temperature of 200°F. If the bread is not at the correct temperature, bake for 5 minutes more.
9. Remove from oven and unmold onto cooling racks.

NUTRITIONAL INFORMATION PER SERVING

SERVING SIZE: 1 slice	**SODIUM:** 490mg	**DIETARY FIBER:** 3g
CALORIES: 200cal	**TOTAL CARBOHYDRATE:** 33g	**PROTEIN:** 7g
TOTAL FAT: 6g		

Multigrain Soaker

Before adding seeds to bread dough, a soaker is created; soakers involve simply letting the seeds soak in and absorb hot water before being added. The soaking of seeds tenderizes them so they are more pleasing to eat and hydrates them so they do not pull moisture away from the dough during baking.

YIELD: 1¾ CUPS (15 OZ.)

¼ cup (1.5 oz.)	Yellow cornmeal
¼ cup	Flaxseed
¼ cup	Caraway seeds
¼ cup	Sesame seeds
1¼ cups (10 oz.)	Water, boiling

1. Combine the cornmeal, flaxseed, caraway seeds, and sesame seeds.
2. Pour the boiling water over the mixture.
3. Cover with plastic wrap and allow to cool in refrigerator for 1 hour.
4. Prior to use, allow soaker to come to room temperature.

Note: To store, keep in airtight container and store in refrigerator for up to one week or keep frozen for up to one month.

NUTRITIONAL INFORMATION OMITTED DUE TO VARIANCE OF USE.

Multigrain Bread

Treat yourself well by eating this bread. Both tasty and health-conscious, this recipe calls for a multi-grain soaker made from flax, caraway, and sesame seeds. Prepare your morning toast or lunchtime sandwiches using this bread and both your body and taste buds will thank you.

YIELD: THREE STANDARD 8" × 4" × 2¾" LOAVES OR 30 ROLLS (30 SERVINGS)

2⅔ cups (1 lb.)	Flour Blend #3
3 cups (1 lb.)	Flour Blend #5
1 tablespoon	Salt
4 tablespoons (1 oz.)	Guar gum
4 tablespoons	Instant yeast
3½ cups (28 oz.)	Sparkling water
6 ea.	Egg whites
1½ cups (12 oz.)	Multigrain soaker (page 55)

1. Combine Flour Blend #3, Flour Blend #5, salt, guar gum, and yeast and whisk together thoroughly. In a separate bowl combine the sparkling water and egg whites and mix.
2. Add the wet ingredients and the soaker to the dry ingredients in a bowl and mix, using a paddle, until smooth.
3. Scoop the mixture into greased baking cups or loaf pans, filling about two-thirds full.
4. Proof the portioned dough in a warm, humid environment for 1 hour.
5. Bake in a preheated 375°F oven with some steam/moisture. Bake rolls for 15 minutes, loaves for 45 to 55 minutes.
6. Once the bread has risen to the top of the pan and is a rich golden brown, vent the oven (if applicable; usually just necessary in professional ovens) for the remaining 5 to 8 minutes. The bread should be firm at the center with an internal temperature of 200°F. If the bread is not the correct temperature, bake for 5 minutes more.
7. Remove from oven and unmold onto cooling screens.

NUTRITIONAL INFORMATION PER SERVING

SERVING SIZE: 1 slice	SODIUM: 510mg	DIETARY FIBER: 5g
CALORIES: 190cal	TOTAL CARBOHYDRATE: 37g	PROTEIN: 9g
TOTAL FAT: 2g		

Sourdough

Turn the famed crusty San Francisco classic into a classic of your own with this recipe for sourdough bread. The tangy, moist white bread can be made into loaves or rolls; if desired, add your choice of topping to the dough before shaping and baking.

YIELD: TWO STANDARD 8" × 4" × 2¾" LOAVES OR 20 ROLLS (20 SERVINGS)

1½ tablespoons	Salt
½ cup (4 oz.)	Sugar
2¼ cups (13.5 oz.)	Flour Blend #1
2 cups + 1 tablespoon (13 oz.)	Flour Blend #3
3 tablespoons	Instant yeast
3 ea.	Eggs
1 cup (2 sticks) (8 oz.)	Butter, melted
3 cups (24 oz.)	Buttermilk
4 tablespoons	White vinegar

1. Thoroughly combine salt, sugar, flour blends, and yeast.
2. Mix in all remaining ingredients using a whip for 4 minutes on low speed.
3. Just before shaping, consider stirring in your favorite additional ingredients—e.g., grated cheese, herbs, raisins, vegetables, fruits, or spices.
4. Scoop mixture into greased baking cups or loaf pans, filling pans about two-thirds full.
5. Proof the shaped product in a warm, humid environment for 30 to 45 minutes.
6. Bake in a preheated 375°F oven with some steam/moisture. Bake rolls for 15 minutes, loaves for 45 to 55 minutes.
7. Once product has risen to the top of the pan, vent the oven (if applicable; usually just necessary in professional ovens) during the last 5 to 8 minutes. The product should be firm at the center with an internal temperature of 200°F. If the bread is not the correct temperature, bake for 5 minutes more.
8. Remove from oven and unmold onto cooling screens.

NUTRITIONAL INFORMATION PER SERVING

SERVING SIZE: 1 slice	SODIUM: 630mg	DIETARY FIBER: 2g
CALORIES: 260cal	TOTAL CARBOHYDRATE: 40g	PROTEIN: 6g
TOTAL FAT: 10g		

Sourdough-Multigrain

Sourdough bread gets a makeover in this multigrain version of the gluten-free standard recipe. Made with a soaker that includes flax, caraway, and sesame seeds, the final product, which can be in loaf or roll form, is a unique blend of earthy sweetness paired with strong bite. Serve this bread as is in a basket or use it to boost your lunchtime sandwich.

YIELD: TWO STANDARD 8" × 4" × 2¾" LOAVES OR 20 ROLLS (20 SERVINGS)

1⅓ cups (8 oz.)	Flour Blend #3
3 cups (1 lb.)	Flour Blend #5
4½ teaspoons	Salt
¾ cup (6 oz.)	Sugar
3 tablespoons (24 g)	Guar gum
5 tablespoons	Instant yeast
3 ea.	Eggs
3 cups (24 oz.)	Buttermilk
2 teaspoons	White vinegar
1½ cups (12 oz.)	Multigrain soaker (page 55)

1. Thoroughly combine flour blends, salt, sugar, guar gum, and yeast.
2. In a separate bowl, combine eggs, buttermilk, and white vinegar.
3. Combine liquid ingredients, dry ingredients, and soaker. Mix, using a paddle for 4 minutes on low speed or until smooth.
4. Scoop mixture into greased baking cups or a loaf pan, filling about three-fourths full.
5. Proof the shaped product in a warm, humid environment for 60 to 70 minutes.
6. Bake in a preheated 375°F oven with some steam/moisture. Bake rolls for 15 minutes, breads for 45 to 55 minutes.
7. Once product has risen to the top of the pan, vent the oven (if applicable; usually just necessary in professional ovens) during the last 5 to 8 minutes. The product should be firm at the center with an internal temperature of 200°F. If the bread is not the correct temperature, bake for 5 minutes more.
8. Remove from oven and unmold onto cooling racks.

NUTRITIONAL INFORMATION PER SERVING		
SERVING SIZE: 1 slice	SODIUM: 650mg	DIETARY FIBER: 5g
CALORIES: 200cal	TOTAL CARBOHYDRATE: 40g	PROTEIN: 9g
TOTAL FAT: 3g		

Jalapeño-Cheddar Cheese Bread

Make a statement with this spicy bread. Chopped jalapeño peppers are kept in check by the addition of grated cheddar to create a flavor that is both fiery and bold. Serve this bread as an accompaniment to a meal and it won't go unnoticed.

YIELD: TWO STANDARD 8" × 4" × 2¾" LOAVES OR 20 ROLLS (20 SERVINGS)

5¾ cups (2 lb.)	Flour Blend #5
4 teaspoons	Salt
2 teaspoons (6 g)	Guar gum
⅓ cup (2.7 oz.)	Sugar
3 tablespoons	Instant yeast
4 cups (32 oz.)	Water
½ cup (2.5 oz.)	Jalapeño peppers, chopped
1 cup (4.7 oz.)	Cheddar cheese, grated

1. Thoroughly combine all dry ingredients.
2. Add water.
3. Mix, using a paddle for 6 minutes on low speed.
4. Just before shaping, stir in peppers and cheese.
5. Scoop mixture into greased baking cups or loaf pans.
6. Proof the shaped product in a warm, humid environment for 1 hour.
7. Bake in a preheated 350°F oven with some steam/moisture. Bake rolls for 15 minutes, breads for 1 hour.
8. Once proper volume is achieved, vent the oven (if applicable; usually just necessary in professional ovens) and continue baking for 5 to 8 minutes. The product should be firm at the center with an internal temperature of 200°F. If the bread is not the correct temperature, bake for 5 minutes more.

NUTRITIONAL INFORMATION PER SERVING		
SERVING SIZE: 1 slice	SODIUM: 680mg	DIETARY FIBER: 3g
CALORIES: 200cal	TOTAL CARBOHYDRATE: 39g	PROTEIN: 9g
TOTAL FAT: 2.5g		

Beer Bread

The rich yeasty flavor characteristic of beer bread is recreated in this recipe with the addition of a sorghum-based gluten-free beer. It's hearty and delicious with a meal, or as sandwich bread.

YIELD: TWO STANDARD 8" × 4" × 2¾" LOAVES OR 20 ROLLS (20 SERVINGS)

2⅔ cups (1 lb.)	Flour Blend #3
3 cups (1 lb.)	Flour Blend #5
2½ teaspoons	Salt
3 tablespoons (24 g)	Guar gum
1 tablespoon	Instant yeast
2½ cups (20 oz.)	Sparkling water
1½ cups (12 oz.)	Sorghum-based gluten-free beer*
8 ea.	Egg whites

* Sorghum-based gluten-free beer available at any well-stocked beer store, or see "Readings and Resources" section.

1. Thoroughly combine flour blends, salt, guar gum, and yeast.
2. In a separate bowl, combine remaining ingredients, then add to dry ingredients.
3. Mix, using a whip for 4 minutes on low speed or until smooth.
4. Just before shaping, consider stirring in your favorite additional ingredients—e.g., grated cheese, herbs, raisins, vegetables, fruits, or spices. Layer some of the filling as you assemble the roll or loaf.
5. Scoop mixture into greased baking cups or loaf pans, filling about two-thirds full.
6. Proof the shaped product in a warm, humid environment for 40 to 55 minutes.
7. Bake in a preheated 375°F oven with some steam/moisture. Bake rolls for 15 minutes, breads for 45 to 55 minutes.
8. Once product has risen to the top of the pan, vent the oven (if applicable; usually just necessary in professional ovens) and continue baking for 5 to 8 minutes.
9. The product should be firm at the center with an internal temperature of 200°F. If the bread is not the correct temperature, bake for 5 minutes more.
10. Remove from oven and unmold onto cooling racks.

NUTRITIONAL INFORMATION PER SERVING

SERVING SIZE: 1 slice   SODIUM: 330mg   DIETARY FIBER: 4g
CALORIES: 170cal   TOTAL CARBOHYDRATE: 35g   PROTEIN: 8g
TOTAL FAT: 0g

Egg Bread

Made with the addition of egg yolks, this bread is slightly sweet with a golden hue. Moist and tender, egg bread shines at breakfast, and is delicious spread with fruit preserves or turned into French toast.

YIELD: TWO APPROX. 8½" × 4½" × 2½" LOAVES OR 12 TO 14 ROLLS (12 TO 14 SERVINGS)

3 cups (1 lb.)	Flour Blend #5
2 teaspoon	Salt
1 tablespoon	Instant yeast
½ cup (4 oz.)	Sugar
2 teaspoons (6 g)	Guar gum
6 ea.	Egg yolks
⅓ cup	Oil
1¾ cups (14 oz.)	Sparkling water

1. Combine flour blend, salt, yeast, sugar, and guar gum in mixing bowl. In a separate bowl, combine egg yolks, oil, and sparkling water.
2. Add liquids to dry ingredients and mix with a whip or paddle for 4 minutes on medium speed.
3. Place in greased baking cups or loaf pan and proof in a warm, humid environment, covered, for 40 to 50 minutes.
4. Bake at 325°F for 50 to 60 minutes, or until sides begin to pull away from the pan and the internal temperature is 200°F. If the bread is not the correct temperature, bake for 5 minutes more.
5. Unmold from pan immediately and cool on a rack.

NUTRITIONAL INFORMATION PER SERVING

SERVING SIZE: 1 slice	**SODIUM:** 310mg	**DIETARY FIBER:** 2g
CALORIES: 160cal	**TOTAL CARBOHYDRATE:** 25g	**PROTEIN:** 5g
TOTAL FAT: 6g		

Soft Rolls

(OR ENRICHED BREAD IN LOAF FORM)

This soft roll will challenge you to find an occasion for which they aren't perfectly suited. Eaten plain, sweet, or savory, this recipe is sure to become a staple in any gluten-free baker's kitchen.

YIELD: THREE APPROX. 8" × 4½" × 2¾" LOAVES OR 24 ROLLS (24 SERVINGS)

5¾ cups (2 lb.)	Flour Blend #5
1 tablespoon + 1 teaspoon	Salt
⅓ cup (2.7 oz.)	Sugar
3 tablespoons (24 g)	Guar gum
2 tablespoons	Instant yeast
3½ cups (28 oz.)	Water
2 ea.	Eggs
¾ cup (6 oz.)	Butter, melted

1. Thoroughly combine flour blend, salt, sugar, and guar gum. Blend in yeast.
2. Mix together the water, eggs, and butter, then add to the dry mixture. Mix, using a paddle for 6 minutes on low speed.
3. Just before shaping, consider stirring in your favorite additional ingredients (approximately ½ cup)—e.g., grated cheese, herbs, raisins, vegetables, fruits, or spices.
4. Scoop mixture into greased baking cups or loaf pans.
5. Proof the shaped product in a warm, humid environment for 40 to 55 minutes.
6. Bake in a preheated 350°F oven with some steam/moisture. Bake rolls for 15 minutes, breads for 50 to 60 minutes.
7. Once proper volume is achieved, vent the oven (if applicable; usually just necessary in professional ovens) and continue baking during last 5 to 8 minutes. The product should be firm at the center with an internal temperature of 200°F. If the bread is not the correct temperature, bake for 5 minutes more.
8. Remove from oven, rest in pan for 5 minutes, then unmold onto cooling racks.

NUTRITIONAL INFORMATION PER SERVING

SERVING SIZE: 1 slice (or roll) SODIUM: 520mg DIETARY FIBER: 3g
CALORIES: 200cal TOTAL CARBOHYDRATE: 32g PROTEIN: 7g
TOTAL FAT: 7g

Cinnamon Raisin Bread

Swirled in a gluten-free dough, raisins and cinnamon combine to create a well-loved breakfast bread. Finish the bread with a classic vanilla icing, or, for an earthy sweetness, a warm honey glaze; either will enhance a bread that is sure to be a positive start to any day.

YIELD: TWO STANDARD 8" × 4" × 2¾" LOAVES (20 SERVINGS)

3 cups (1 lb.)	Flour Blend #5
2 teaspoons	Salt
2 tablespoons	Instant yeast
1 cup (8 oz.)	Sugar
1 tablespoon (8 g)	Guar gum
6 ea.	Egg yolks
½ cup (4 oz.)	Butter, melted
1¾ cups (14 oz.)	Sparkling water
1 cup (6 oz.)	Raisins (dark or golden)
2 teaspoons	Cinnamon

1. Combine the flour blend, salt, yeast, sugar, and guar gum in a mixing bowl using a whisk.
2. In a separate bowl, combine the egg yolks, butter, and sparkling water. Blend the wet into the dry ingredients and mix until smooth.
3. Stir in the cinnamon and raisins gently to achieve a swirled or marbled effect.
4. Scoop mixture into greased 8" × 4" × 2¾" loaf pans, filling about two-thirds full.
5. Proof the bread in a warm, humid environment for 40 to 55 minutes.
6. Bake in a preheated 350°F oven, with steam, for 45 to 55 minutes.
7. Once the bread has risen to the top of the pans, vent the oven (if applicable; usually just necessary in professional ovens) and continue baking for 5 to 8 minutes. The bread should be firm at the center with an internal temperature of 200°F. If the bread is not the correct temperature, bake for 5 minutes more.
8. Remove from oven and unmold onto cooling racks.

NUTRITIONAL INFORMATION PER SERVING

SERVING SIZE: 1 slice	SODIUM: 320mg	DIETARY FIBER: 2g
CALORIES: 210cal	TOTAL CARBOHYDRATE: 42g	PROTEIN: 5g
TOTAL FAT: 6g		

Naan

A variety of bread that hails from Central and Southern Asia, naan is perhaps most commonly associated today with Indian cuisine. Similar in texture, shape, and flavor to pita bread, naan is best served hot, its outside browned and crisp from grilling or sautéing in olive oil.

YIELD: 15 2" × 4" FLATBREADS

4 tablespoons (2 oz.)	Plain yogurt
1 ea.	Egg
¼ cup (2 oz.)	Butter, melted
2 cups (16 oz.)	Water, lukewarm (90°F)
3 tablespoons	Instant yeast
2 tablespoons (1 oz.)	Sugar
2 teaspoons	Salt
4¼ cups (1 lb. 12 oz.)	Flour Blend #5
½ cup	Olive oil

1. Combine the yogurt, egg, butter, and water and mix to blend.
2. In a separate bowl, combine the yeast, sugar, salt, and flour blend and thoroughly whisk together. Add the liquid mixture.
3. Mix, using a paddle on medium speed for 2 to 4 minutes, until smooth.
4. Using a pastry bag with a #6 plain tip, pipe dough onto parchment paper in 2" × 4" rectangles, allowing at least 1" of space between each rectangle.
5. Proof in a warm, humid environment for 25 to 30 minutes.
6. Bake in a preheated 325°F oven for 10 to 12 minutes or until light golden brown.
7. Remove from oven and allow to cool on a cooling rack.
8. Right before serving bread, fry in hot olive oil until browned on both sides, or lightly toast or grill.

NUTRITIONAL INFORMATION PER SERVING

SERVING SIZE: 1 slice	SODIUM: 450mg	DIETARY FIBER: 3g
CALORIES: 230cal	TOTAL CARBOHYDRATE: 42g	PROTEIN: 9g
TOTAL FAT: 4g		

After piping the naan onto a sheet tray, lightly wet your hand and smooth the top of the dough out.

The baked naan should have a relatively smooth top and be evenly golden brown in color.

Bagels

YIELD: 20 4" BAGELS

2⅔ cups (1 lb.)	Flour Blend #3
3½ cups (1 lb. 3 oz.)	Flour Blend #5
1½ tablespoons	Salt
4 tablespoons (1 oz.)	Guar gum
3 tablespoons	Instant yeast
4 cups (32 oz.)	Water, room temperature
3 ea.	Egg whites
4 cups (32 oz.)	Water
3 tablespoons (2.25 oz.)	Molasses or honey

1. Combine flour blends, salt, guar gum, and yeast and blend thoroughly.
2. In a separate bowl, combine 4 cups of water and egg whites and whisk to combine.
3. Blend the wet ingredients into the dry, mixing until completely smooth.
4. Cut 6" × 6" squares of parchment paper and lightly spray each with pan spray. Neatly arrange the parchment squares on a cookie sheet, laying them flat to cover the surface.
5. Fill a pastry bag with the bagel dough, and cut a 1" diameter opening in the small end.
6. Pipe a 4" diameter bagel into each greased parchment paper square. Freeze uncovered for at least two hours, or overnight.
7. For the poaching liquid, combine 4 cups of water and molasses or honey in a large pot, bring to a simmer over moderate heat, and stir occasionally to completely dissolve the sweetener.
8. Remove a frozen bagel from the parchment paper and, using a slotted spoon, place into the simmering liquid.
9. Poach for 1 minute, or until the bagel floats to the surface. Remove the bagel from the liquid with the slotted spoon and place into a bowl of ice water.
10. Remove from ice water and place onto parchment-paper-lined cookie sheet. If using seeds, coat bagels in seeds before the surface dries.
11. Bake in a preheated 425°F oven for approximately 15 minutes.

NUTRITIONAL INFORMATION PER SERVING

SERVING SIZE: 1 bagel   **SODIUM:** 510mg   **DIETARY FIBER:** 4g
CALORIES: 180cal   **TOTAL CARBOHYDRATE:** 40g   **PROTEIN:** 8g
TOTAL FAT: 0g

Bialys

Bialys are yeast-leavened rolls with an indentation in the center most commonly filled with onions. Sprinkled with poppy seeds, these onion-topped bialys are best eaten warmed with either butter or cream cheese.

YIELD: EIGHT 3" × 4" BIALYS

1⅓ cups (8 oz.)	Flour Blend #3
1⅓ cups (8 oz.)	Flour Blend #5
2 teaspoons	Salt
¾ teaspoon (2 g)	Guar gum
1 tablespoon	Instant yeast
2 cups (16 oz.)	Water, room temperature
2 ea.	Egg whites
1 cup (2 oz.)	Spanish onions, medium dice
¼ cup	Vegetable oil
⅛ cup	Poppy seeds

1. Thoroughly combine flour blends, salt, guar gum, and yeast.
2. In a separate bowl, combine water and egg whites, and then pour into dry ingredients. Mix, using a whip for 4 minutes on low speed or until smooth.
3. Cut parchment into 6" × 6" squares and spray with pan spray.
4. Place dough into a pastry bag and cut a 1¼" diameter opening in the small end. Pipe into oval shapes, one per parchment paper square. Freeze uncovered for at least 4 hours, or overnight.
5. Bring bialys to room temperature.
6. Combine chopped onions, oil, and poppy seeds. Make an indentation in the center of each bialy, approximately 1" × 2". Place 1 tablespoon of the onion mixture in the indentation.
7. Bake for approximately 15 minutes, with steam, at 400°F. Then turn oven down to 350°F and bake another 5 minutes.
8. Remove from oven and place on a cooling rack.

NUTRITIONAL INFORMATION PER SERVING		
SERVING SIZE: 1 bialy	SODIUM: 620mg	DIETARY FIBER: 4g
CALORIES: 270cal	TOTAL CARBOHYDRATE: 43g	PROTEIN: 10g
TOTAL FAT: 8g		

Soft Pretzels

Salted or without; the decision is yours with this recipe that brings a favorite on-the-go snack to your own oven. Eat these gluten-free soft pretzels plain or serve them with your choice of dipping sauces.

YIELD: FIVE - SIX 3" × 6" PRETZELS

Pretzels:

1⅓ cups (8 oz.)	Flour Blend #3
1⅓ cups (8 oz.)	Flour Blend #5
1¼ teaspoons	Salt
5 teaspoons (15 g)	Guar gum
4 teaspoons	Instant yeast
¼ cup (2 oz.)	Sugar
1¾ cups (14 oz.)	Water
2 ea.	Egg whites
¼ cup (2 oz.)	Butter or margarine, melted, or vegetable oil

Dipping:

2 cups (16 oz.)	Water, warm
3 tablespoons	Baking soda
2 tablespoons	Coarse salt

1. Preheat oven to 400° F.
2. Thoroughly combine flour blends, salt, guar gum, yeast, and sugar.
3. In a separate bowl, combine water, egg whites, and melted butter or oil, then pour the wet into the dry ingredients.
4. Mix, using a paddle for 4 minutes on low speed or until smooth.
5. Line pans with parchment and spray parchment with pan spray.
6. Place dough in a pastry bag and cut a ¾" diameter hole in the small end. Pipe into pretzels 3" long by 6" wide.
7. Freeze, uncovered, for two hours, or overnight.

8. For dipping, combine warm water and baking soda. Dip the frozen pretzels into the baking soda and water mixture.

9. Place the dipped pretzel onto an ungreased baking sheet.

10. Garnish with coarse salt.

11. Bake for approximately 18 minutes in a 400°F oven.

NUTRITIONAL INFORMATION PER SERVING		
SERVING SIZE: 1 pretzel	SODIUM: 1100mg	DIETARY FIBER: 8g
CALORIES: 500cal	TOTAL CARBOHYDRATE: 75g	PROTEIN: 17g
TOTAL FAT: 8.5g		

English Muffins

Whether they are spread with jam, sandwiched with eggs, or simply topped with a dab of butter, English muffins are a breakfast classic. Whatever your preference for preparation, this gluten-free recipe makes moist muffins perfect for piling up or for eating plain. For a reduced-fat, lower-calorie option, replace the milk with sparkling water.

YIELD: FIVE 4" × 1" MUFFINS

1 cup (6 oz.)	Flour Blend #1
¾ cup (5 oz.)	Flour Blend #3
2 teaspoons	Salt
1 teaspoon	Instant yeast
2 teaspoons (8.5 g.)	Sugar
1 ea.	Egg
1¼ cups (10 oz.)	Milk, warmed to 80°–100° F*
4 tablespoons (2 oz.)	Butter or margarine, melted or vegetable oil

*Any type of milk: skim, 2%, soy, or even buttermilk for a tangier "sour" flavor

1. Combine the dry ingredients in a mixing bowl. In a separate bowl, combine the wet ingredients. Blend the wet into the dry ingredients, using a whip on medium speed for 2 minutes or until smooth.
2. Scoop into heavily sprayed tins or ring molds. If you don't have ring molds, you can use cleaned-out tuna cans with the tops and bottoms removed instead.
3. Allow to proof for 30 to 45 minutes.
4. Bake with steam in a preheated 400°F oven for 20 minutes or until done.

NUTRITIONAL INFORMATION PER SERVING

SERVING SIZE: 1 muffin	SODIUM: 630mg	DIETARY FIBER: 2g
CALORIES: 400cal	TOTAL CARBOHYDRATE: 69g	PROTEIN: 8g
TOTAL FAT: 13g		

Cinnamon-Raisin English Muffins

The addition of raisins and a hint of cinnamon sweeten up the standard English muffin in this gluten-free recipe. Toast these juicy raisin-packed muffins and serve them simply with butter for a pleasing addition to your breakfast.

YIELD: EIGHT 4" × 1" MUFFINS

1¼ cups + 2 teaspoons (½ lb.)	Potato starch
¾ cup + 2 tablespoons (¼ lb.)	Brown rice flour
½ teaspoon (1.5 g)	Guar gum
2 teaspoons	Salt
¾ teaspoon	Instant yeast
1 tablespoon (0.5 oz.)	Sugar
1 ea.	Egg
1½ cups (12 oz.)	Milk, warmed
4 tablespoons (2 oz.)	Butter, melted
⅓ cup (2 oz.)	Raisins, dark
1 teaspoon	Cinnamon

1. Combine the dry ingredients in a mixing bowl. In a separate bowl, combine the wet ingredients. Blend the wet into the dry ingredients, using a whip on medium speed for 2 minutes or until smooth.
2. Thoroughly mix in raisins, followed by a gentle swirling-in of the cinnamon.
3. Scoop into heavily sprayed tins or ring molds.
4. Allow to proof for 30 to 45 minutes.
5. Bake with steam at 425°F for 20 minutes or until done.

NUTRITIONAL INFORMATION PER SERVING

SERVING SIZE: 1 muffin	**SODIUM:** 810mg	**DIETARY FIBER:** 2g
CALORIES: 340cal	**TOTAL CARBOHYDRATE:** 58g	**PROTEIN:** 5g
TOTAL FAT: 11g		

Multigrain English Muffins

Start your day off by doing something right for your heart and your stomach with these healthy and flavorsome multigrain English muffins. The fiber-rich soaker of flax, caraway, and sesame seeds elevates a simple muffin to new heights of texture, flavor, and nutrition. Serve these muffins toasted with butter or use them to create breakfast sandwiches of your choice.

YIELD: 10 4" × 1" MUFFINS

2 cups (11.5 oz.)	Flour Blend #2
¾ cup + 2 tablespoons (6 oz.)	Flour Blend #3
1 tablespoon	Salt
2 tablespoons	Instant yeast
1 teaspoon (8.5 g.)	Sugar
2 cups (16 oz.)	Milk, warmed to 80°–100°F
½ cup	Vegetable oil
⅔ cup (6 oz.)	Multigrain soaker (page 55)

1. Combine flour blends, salt, yeast, and sugar in mixing bowl. In a separate bowl, combine warmed milk and vegetable oil.
2. Add wet ingredients and soaker to dry ingredients. Mix using a paddle until smooth.
3. Prepare a cookie sheet with ring molds and coat the base of each ring mold with gluten-free cooking spray. Scoop the mix into the molds.
4. Allow to proof for at least 45 minutes. Or the muffins can be proofed, slowly, in the refrigerator overnight: oil the top of each muffin, cover tops with parchment paper, and store in the refrigerator; remove from refrigerator while oven is preheating.
5. Bake with steam at 425°F for 20 minutes or until done.

NUTRITIONAL INFORMATION PER SERVING		
SERVING SIZE: 1 muffin	SODIUM: 750mg	DIETARY FIBER: 3g
CALORIES: 290cal	TOTAL CARBOHYDRATE: 42g	PROTEIN: 7g
TOTAL FAT: 12g		

Doughnuts

These doughnuts are the gluten-free version of a well-loved breakfast treat. Fried and sprinkled with sugar then eaten still-warm, or cooled and saved for later, these doughnuts make the perfect companion to any cup of coffee.

YIELD: 20 3" DOUGHNUTS

1⅓ cups (8 oz.)	Flour Blend #3
1½ cups (8 oz.)	Flour Blend #4
1¼ tablespoons (10 g)	Guar gum
¾ cup (6 oz.)	Sugar
1 tablespoon	Baking powder
3 tablespoons	Instant yeast
1¼ cups (10 oz.)	Milk, warmed
¾ cup (6 oz.)	Butter, melted
3 ea.	Egg yolks
As needed	Powdered sugar, for garnish
As needed	Granulated sugar, for garnish
As needed	Cinnamon sugar, for garnish

1. Mix together the flour blends, guar gum, sugar, baking powder, and yeast.
2. In a separate bowl, mix together the milk, melted butter, and egg yolks. Add to the dry ingredients. Blend with a mixer for about 4 minutes or until completely smooth.
3. Allow the dough to rest, covered, for 20 minutes. Place dough in a pastry bag with a ½" opening. Pipe out into doughnut-shaped pieces onto 5" × 5" parchment squares.
4. Proof the doughnuts for 20 minutes in a warm, humid environment.
5. Fry the doughnuts in 300°F oil for 5 to 6 minutes.
6. While still warm, garnish doughnuts with powdered or granulated sugar (plain or cinnamon).

NUTRITIONAL INFORMATION PER SERVING

SERVING SIZE: 1 doughnut	SODIUM: 60mg	DIETARY FIBER: 1g
CALORIES: 310cal	TOTAL CARBOHYDRATE: 25g	PROTEIN: 5g
TOTAL FAT: 22g		

Almond Stollen

This traditionally German, breadlike cake is commonly eaten during the Christmas season. Its characteristic fruity sweetness comes from the addition of candied citrus peel and golden raisins; in this recipe, the earthy richness is lent from the almonds added to the dough as well as the filling. While stollen is a staple at many a Christmas table, it is sure to please when served any time of the year.

YIELD: ONE 9" PIE TIN LOAF (10 SERVINGS)

Pre-ferment

½ cup (3 oz.)	Flour Blend #5
½ teaspoon	Instant yeast
¼ cup (2 oz.)	Milk, heated to 80°F

Filling

4 tablespoons (2 oz.)	Almond paste
¼ cup (2 oz.)	Sugar
1 ea.	Egg white

Final Dough

1 tablespoon + 1 teaspoon (23 g)	Sugar
¼ teaspoon	Vanilla extract
⅓ cup (3 oz.)	Butter, melted
All (All)	Pre-ferment
⅓ cup (2 oz.)	Flour Blend #5
Pinch	Salt
¼ cup	Candied lemon/orange peel
¼ cup (1.5 oz.)	Golden raisins
¼ cup (1.25 oz.)	Almond slivers

Finishing

½ cup (4 oz.)	Clarified butter
¼ cup (2 oz.)	Sugar
¼ cup (1.25 oz.)	Powdered sugar, sifted

Pre-ferment:

1. Mix with an electric mixer all pre-ferment ingredients for 2 minutes or until smooth. Cover and allow to ferment at room temperature for 30 minutes.

Filling:

1. Mix filling ingredients together using paddle on low speed. Roll into a log. Keep covered and at room temperature. Set aside.

Final Dough:

1. Mix together sugar, vanilla, and butter
2. Add pre-ferment, flour blend, and salt. Mix until semi-smooth, 2 minutes on low speed and 2 minutes on medium speed. Allow to ferment 30 minutes.
3. Add candied peel, raisins, and almonds. Mix just until incorporated. Divide into two equal sections (one "base," one "cover"); shape the base to fit into a greased 9" pie tin to make a disk shape. If necessary, use a small amount of Flour Blend #1 to prevent dough sticking to your hands. Roll almond filling log into a disk and insert on top of base, leaving a ½" edge along outside of base.
4. Place cover piece on top of the filled base. Press down to conform to pie tin.
5. Final proof for 15 to 20 minutes.
6. Bake for 375°F for 20 to 25 minutes.

Finishing procedure:

1. Right after baking, remove any burnt nuts and fruit from the surface and liberally brush surface with clarified butter.
2. Allow to cool for 30 minutes, then coat liberally with sugar.
3. Two hours later or the next day, sugar the stollen with powdered sugar.

Note: You can use gluten-free marzipan in place of almond paste for filling.

NUTRITIONAL INFORMATION PER SERVING		
SERVING SIZE: 1 slice	SODIUM: 140mg	DIETARY FIBER: 2g
CALORIES: 390cal	TOTAL CARBOHYDRATE: 42g	PROTEIN: 5g
TOTAL FAT: 23g		

Pecan Cinnamon Buns

This recipe for cinnamon buns creates a bun sure to make any morning sweeter. Topped with sugary pecans and sweetened with a touch of honey, these buns are also baked with ice cubes, the steam from which aids in creating an ultra-moist product you'll want to wake up to.

YIELD: 12 2" × 1½" BUNS

1¼ teaspoons	Instant yeast
½ cup (4 oz.)	Sugar
1½ cups (9 oz.)	Flour Blend #3
1½ cups (9 oz.)	Flour Blend #2
2 tablespoons	Guar gum
1½ cups (12 oz.)	Milk
2 ea.	Eggs
1 teaspoon (7 g)	Honey
6 tablespoons (3 oz.)	Butter, melted
One recipe	Cinnamon Smear (page 78)
	Pan Smear (page 78)
½ cup (2.5 oz.)	Pecan halves (raw), chopped
½ teaspoon	Salt
¼ cup (2 oz.)	Egg Wash (page 197)

Dough:

1. Mix yeast, sugar, flour blends, and guar gum together.
2. In a separate bowl, mix milk, eggs, honey, and melted butter together.
3. Combine wet into dry ingredients and mix with a paddle until smooth.
4. Refrigerate dough for 1 hour.
5. Put cast-iron skillet into cold oven and heat with oven (refer to steaming technique, page 37)

Cinnamon buns:

1. Roll out dough to 16" × 8" rectangle and spread with cinnamon smear. Seal the edge nearest you with egg wash.
2. Roll up into one long log and cut into 1½" to 2" pieces.
3. Place into a 9" × 9" cake pan that has been prepared with pan smear and sprinkled with chopped pecans.

4. Proof in a warm, humid environment until doubled in bulk, about 75 minutes.
5. Add 1 to 2 ice cubes to skillet, to bake as ice produces steam.
6. Bake in a 375°F oven.
7. Bake for approximately 30 minutes
8. Allow pan to cool for 3 minutes. Using oven mitts, put the heat-resistant plate over the baking pan and then turn the two upside down. Carefully remove baking pan, to display baked-pecan/smear-coated buns.

NUTRITIONAL INFORMATION PER SERVING		
SERVING SIZE: 1 bun	SODIUM: 260mg	DIETARY FIBER: 2g
CALORIES: 375cal	TOTAL CARBOHYDRATE: 55g	PROTEIN: 6g
TOTAL FAT: 17g		

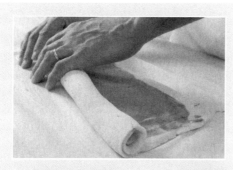

When properly mixed, the dough should have a tacky, spreadable consistency.

Allow the dough to proof until doubled in volume before baking.

Cinnamon Smear

Add some spice to your breakfast with the addition of cinnamon. This cinnamon smear isn't only for cinnamon buns; try it on a piece of gluten-free toast, pancakes, or waffles.

2 tablespoons (1 oz.)	Butter
3 tablespoons (1.5 oz.)	Light brown sugar, packed
1 teaspoon	Cinnamon
1 teaspoon (8.5 g)	Corn syrup, light
1 ea.	Egg, beaten
¼ teaspoon	Vanilla extract

1. Melt the butter and allow to cool to 90°F.
2. Add light brown sugar, cinnamon, and corn syrup.
3. Mix until smooth.
4. Mix in egg and vanilla extract.

NUTRITIONAL INFORMATION OMITTED DUE TO VARIATION OF USE.

Pan Smear

Pan smear is used to prevent baked goods from sticking to a pan; this recipe adds brown sugar and vanilla extract for sweetness. The addition of sugar in the smear will create a golden, caramelized bottom to cinnamon buns and other baked products.

¼ cup (2 oz.)	Light brown sugar
2 tablespoons (1 oz)	Unsalted butter
3 tablespoons (2.7 oz.)	Light corn syrup
¼ teaspoon	Vanilla extract
Pinch	Salt

1. Cream the butter and sugar.
2. Add the corn syrup, vanilla, and salt.

NUTRITIONAL INFORMATION OMITTED DUE TO VARIATION OF USE.

Chapter 5

Quick Breads

*P*eople who must follow the gluten-free diet represent a cross-section of the population: they can be of any ethnicity or from any geographic region; they can be young, old, or in-between; they can be accomplished bakers or novice water-boilers. If you fall into the last category, you can relax a little. The gluten-free quick bread recipes in this chapter will be a great place for you to start.

Quick breads are so named because they are made with chemical leaveners (meaning baking soda or baking powder), or with eggs, which work much faster than yeast to puff up baked goods. Many of the recipes use either the straight mixing method or the creaming method, which don't take much time. Banana bread is a classic example of a quick bread—if you follow the recipe, it's hard to go wrong, especially if you use over-ripe bananas. You will find gluten-free banana bread in the following pages, along with recipes for gluten-free quick breads made with pumpkin, zucchini, and even cherry and strawberry. You can make mini loaves or pour the batter into muffin tins so you have smaller portions that freeze well.

You can also put a spin on some of the classic muffin recipes. Make gluten-free corn muffins and mix in some jalapeños and cheese, or add some lemon zest to your blueberry muffins. You will find other gluten-free muffin recipes here that are sure to become new favorites, including apple spice, orange cranberry, lemon poppy seed, walnut, and double chocolate.

A lot of hearty goods also fit under the quick breads umbrella, including scones and biscuits. These are made with the rubbing mixing method, where you cut the fat into the gluten-free flour. If you miss having real buttermilk biscuits, here's your chance. And if the idea of scones makes your mouth water, you can make them sweet with fruit or savory, whatever suits your taste.

Pancakes and waffles are also considered quick breads, and the recipes in this book will make it easy to turn out these breakfast classics gluten free. The big difference between pancakes and waffles is that you add whipped egg whites to the waffles to make them fluffy (and, of course, use a waffle iron to make them). Make sure that your waffle iron is GF-dedicated. You will also want to double-check your baking powder, since some brands contain wheat starch.

There are also some special occasion recipes: next time St. Patrick's Day rolls around (or any other time you feel like it), you can enjoy a slice of Irish soda bread. And if it's been years since you've been able to have funnel cake when everyone else at the fairground is enjoying it, you can now make a gluten-free version at home.

Banana Bread

Have bananas that are just too ripe to eat? This version of a classic recipe is the perfect place to put them to work. Moistened using mashed bananas and a drop of sour cream, this bread is naturally sweet and nutty, a perfect addition to any breakfast table or breadbasket.

YIELD: ONE STANDARD 8" × 4" × 2¾" LOAF (10 SERVINGS)

¾ cup (6 oz.)	Butter, softened
1 cup (8 oz.)	Sugar
1 ea.	Egg
1⅓ cups (8 oz.)	Flour Blend #3
½ teaspoon	Baking soda
½ teaspoon	Baking powder
1 cup (6.5 oz.)	Bananas, mashed
2 tablespoons (1.2 oz.)	Sour cream
¾ cup (3.75 oz.)	Walnuts, chopped

1. Preheat oven to 350°F.
2. Cream together softened butter and sugar until light and fluffy.
3. Add egg gradually and scrape down bowl.
4. In a separate bowl, combine dry ingredients. Add all dry ingredients to wet ingredients at once; mix until just combined.
5. Add the mashed bananas and sour cream to batter and mix until just combined.
6. Fold in chopped nuts by hand.
7. Pour batter into a greased and lined loaf pan.
8. Bake for 55 to 60 minutes, or until a skewer inserted near the center of the loaf comes out clean.

NUTRITIONAL INFORMATION PER SERVING

SERVING SIZE: 1 slice	**SODIUM:** 230mg	**DIETARY FIBER:** 2g
CALORIES: 380cal	**TOTAL CARBOHYDRATE:** 44g	**PROTEIN:** 5g
TOTAL FAT: 22g		

Cherry Bread

Ruby-colored cherries folded into cinnamon-sprinkled dough create a vibrant and uniquely flavored gluten-free fruit bread evocative of summertime. Serve this bread in the morning with tea or as a sweet ending to your outdoor dinners.

YIELD: ONE STANDARD 8" × 4" × 2¾" LOAF (10 SERVINGS)

1¾ cups (8 oz.)	Dried cherries, chopped
1 cup (8 oz.)	Water, boiling
½ cup (3 oz.)	Flour Blend #2
1 cup + 2 tablespoons (6 oz.)	Flour Blend #4
Pinch	Salt
3½ teaspoons	Baking powder
¼ teaspoon	Cinnamon
¼ cup (2 oz.)	Sugar
½ cup + 2 tablespoons	Vegetable oil
½ cup + 2 tablespoons (5 oz.)	Buttermilk
6 ea.	Eggs

1. Preheat oven to 375°F.
2. Combine chopped dried cherries with boiling water and set aside until cool. Drain liquid off and set aside.
3. Combine flour blends, salt, baking powder, cinnamon, and sugar thoroughly.
4. In a separate bowl, combine oil, buttermilk, and eggs thoroughly.
5. Add dry ingredients to wet ingredient mixture and blend completely until smooth.
6. Fold soaked dried cherries into batter. Pour into oiled loaf pan.
7. Bake for 30 minutes, or until a skewer inserted near the center of the loaf comes out clean.

NUTRITIONAL INFORMATION PER SERVING

SERVING SIZE: 1 slice	SODIUM: 280mg	DIETARY FIBER: 3g
CALORIES: 350cal	TOTAL CARBOHYDRATE: 41g	PROTEIN: 8g
TOTAL FAT: 17g		

Mango Bread

This recipe is an island party in a bread. Exotically flavored with fresh mangoes, richly sweet dark raisins, and light shredded coconut, this summertime-suited quick bread will create a tropical paradise in your home.

YIELD: ONE STANDARD 8" × 4" × 2¾" LOAF (10 SERVINGS)

½ cup (3 oz.)	Flour Blend #2
1 cup + 2 tablespoons (6 oz.)	Flour Blend #4
Pinch	Salt
3½ teaspoons	Baking powder
¼ teaspoon	Cinnamon
¼ cup (2 oz.)	Sugar
¼ cup	Vegetable oil
½ cup + 2 tablespoons (5 oz.)	Buttermilk
6 ea.	Eggs
1½ cups (12 oz.)	Mangoes, chopped
½ cup (3 oz.)	Dark raisins
⅓ cup (1 oz.)	Shredded coconut

1. Preheat oven to 375°F.
2. Combine flour blends, salt, baking powder, cinnamon, and sugar thoroughly.
3. In a separate bowl, combine oil, buttermilk, and eggs thoroughly.
4. Add dry ingredients to wet ingredient mixture, blend completely until smooth.
5. Fold in mangoes, raisins, and coconut. Pour into greased loaf pan.
6. Bake for 40 minutes, or until a skewer inserted near the center of the loaf comes out clean.

NUTRITIONAL INFORMATION PER SERVING

SERVING SIZE: 1 slice	SODIUM: 280mg	DIETARY FIBER: 2g
CALORIES: 260cal	TOTAL CARBOHYDRATE: 37g	PROTEIN: 8g
TOTAL FAT: 10g		

Pumpkin Bread

Let this quick-bread favorite spice up your season. It is no trick that this pumpkin bread—sprinkled with cinnamon and iced with cream cheese frosting—is one sweet treat. As an alternative to the iced bread, consider using the dough to create gluten-free pumpkin muffins.

YIELD: ONE STANDARD 8" × 4" × 2¾" LOAF OR 10 MUFFINS (10 SERVINGS)

1 cup (8 oz.)	Sugar
½ cup + 1 tablespoon	Canola oil
2 ea.	Eggs
1 cup (8½ oz.)	Pumpkin, canned, solid pack (about half of one 15 oz. can)
¾ cup + 2 tablespoons (5 oz.)	Flour Blend #5
1 tablespoon	Cinnamon
1¼ teaspoons	Baking soda
¼ teaspoon	Salt
One recipe	Cream Cheese Frosting (page 170)

1. Preheat oven to 350°F.
2. Mix sugar, oil, eggs, and pumpkin with whisk until fully combined.
3. Add in flour blend, cinnamon, baking soda, and salt.
4. Mix by hand until fully combined (approximately 30 seconds).
5. Pour into sprayed and lined loaf pan and bake for 50 to 60 minutes for bread, 15 minutes for muffins, or until a skewer inserted in the center comes out clean.
6. Cool for 5 minutes, then unmold onto rack and cool completely.
7. Ice with cream cheese frosting.

NUTRITIONAL INFORMATION PER SERVING
(without Cream Cheese Frosting)

SERVING SIZE: 1 slice	**SODIUM:** 535mg	**DIETARY FIBER:** 2g
CALORIES: 360cal	**TOTAL CARBOHYDRATE:** 46g	**PROTEIN:** 5g
TOTAL FAT: 19g		

Doughnuts, page 73

Pecan Cinnamon Buns, page 76

Pancakes, page 99

Quickbreads, from back to front: Pumpkin, page 84, and Banana Bread, page 81

Linzer Cookies, page 120

Éclairs, page 139

Chocolate-Pecan Cookies, page 109

Lean Dough Rolls, page 50

Pumpkin Raisin Bread

With rich hues of burnt orange and deep brown, a slice of this raisin-speckled pumpkin bread is the just the thing to serve as fall leaves begin changing their color. Eat it as is or top with cream cheese frosting for an extra touch of sweetness.

YIELD: ONE STANDARD 8" × 4" × 2¾" LOAF (10 SERVINGS)

1 cup (8 oz.)	Sugar
¼ cup + 3 tablespoons	Canola oil
2 ea.	Eggs
1 cup (8½ oz.)	Pumpkin, canned, solid pack
¾ cup + 2 tablespoons (5 oz.)	Flour Blend #5
2 teaspoons	Cinnamon
1½ teaspoons	Baking soda
½ teaspoon	Salt
½ cup (3 oz.)	Dark raisins
As needed	Cream Cheese Frosting, optional (page 170)

1. Preheat oven to 350°F.
2. Mix sugar, oil, eggs, and pumpkin with whisk until combined.
3. Combine flour blend, cinnamon, baking soda, salt, and raisins. Add to wet ingredients, mixing by hand until fully combined.
4. Pour into a sprayed and lined loaf pan. Bake for 30 to 40 minutes, or until a skewer inserted in the center comes out clean.
5. Cool for 5 minutes, then unmold onto a cooling rack and cool completely.
6. Ice with cream cheese frosting if desired.

NUTRITIONAL INFORMATION PER SERVING
(without Cream Cheese Frosting)

SERVING SIZE: 1 slice	SODIUM: 270mg	DIETARY FIBER: 2g
CALORIES: 270cal	TOTAL CARBOHYDRATE: 41g	PROTEIN: 4g
TOTAL FAT: 11g		

Strawberry Bread

Strawberries continue to prove their versatility as they sweeten up this gluten-free quick bread. Full of the berry flavor familiar to and loved by so many, this bread will charm breakfast tables and dessert plates alike.

YIELD: ONE STANDARD 8" × 4" × 2¾" LOAF (10 SERVINGS)

1¾ cups (8 oz.)	Dried strawberries, chopped
1 cup (8 oz.)	Boiling water
½ cup (3 oz.)	Flour Blend #2
1 cup + 2 tablespoons (6 oz.)	Flour Blend #4
Pinch	Salt
1 tablespoon	Baking powder
¼ teaspoon	Cinnamon
¼ cup (2 oz.)	Sugar
½ cup + 2 tablespoons	Vegetable oil
½ cup + 2 tablespoons (5 oz.)	Buttermilk
6 ea.	Eggs

1. Preheat oven to 375°F.
2. Combine chopped dried strawberries with boiling water; set aside until cool. Drain liquid off and set aside.
3. Combine flour blends, salt, baking powder, cinnamon, and sugar thoroughly.
4. In a separate bowl, combine oil, buttermilk, and eggs thoroughly.
5. Add dry ingredients to wet ingredient mixture, and blend completely until smooth.
6. Fold in soaked dried strawberries. Pour into oiled loaf pan.
7. Bake for 30 minutes, or until a skewer inserted near the center of the loaf comes out clean.

NUTRITIONAL INFORMATION PER SERVING

SERVING SIZE: 1 slice	SODIUM: 280mg	DIETARY FIBER: 3g
CALORIES: 360cal	TOTAL CARBOHYDRATE: 46g	PROTEIN: 8g
TOTAL FAT: 17g		

Zucchini Bread

Give the grill a rest and introduce zucchini to the sweeter side of the kitchen. This gluten-free quick bread recipe uses shredded zucchini as the main ingredient to create a baked good that is a healthy treat. Go ahead—ask for seconds.

YIELD: ONE STANDARD 8" × 4" × 2¾" LOAF (10 SERVINGS)

¾ cup (5 oz.)	Flour Blend #3
1 cup (8 oz.)	Sugar
¼ cup + 3 tablespoons	Canola oil
2 ea.	Eggs
2 cups (10 oz.)	Zucchini, shredded
2 teaspoons	Cinnamon
2½ teaspoons	Baking powder
1 teaspoon	Salt

1. Preheat oven to 350°F.
2. Combine all dry and wet ingredients in a mixing bowl, and blend completely until smooth.
3. Pour into a greased and lined loaf pan and bake for about 1 hour, or until a skewer inserted near the center of the loaf comes out clean.
4. Cool completely, then unmold.

NUTRITIONAL INFORMATION PER SERVING

SERVING SIZE: 1 slice	**SODIUM:** 330mg	**DIETARY FIBER:** 2g
CALORIES: 240cal	**TOTAL CARBOHYDRATE:** 34g	**PROTEIN:** 3g
TOTAL FAT: 11g		

Apple Spice Muffins

Served for breakfast or as a coffee-time accompaniment, these muffins just may change the way in which you get your "apple a day."

YIELD: EIGHT 4 OZ. MUFFINS

1½ cups (7 oz.)	Granny Smith apples
1 ea.	Egg
½ cup (4 oz.)	Sugar
1 cup + 2 tablespoons (7 oz.)	Flour Blend #3
1 teaspoon	Baking powder
½ teaspoon	Baking soda
½ teaspoon	Cinnamon
¼ teaspoon	Nutmeg
¼ teaspoon	Allspice
⅛ teaspoon	Salt
¼ cup (2 oz.)	Orange juice
¼ cup	Canola oil
½ teaspoon	Vanilla extract
¼ cup + 2 tablespoon (3 oz.)	Buttermilk

1. Preheat oven to 350°F.
2. Cut the apples into a small dice and set aside.
3. Beat the egg until light and foamy. Gradually add the sugar and whisk until completely combined.
4. Sift together the dry ingredients. In a separate bowl, mix together the orange juice, oil, vanilla, and buttermilk.
5. Blend dry ingredients into the egg mixture. Add the wet ingredients and mix until completely combined. Fold in the diced apples.
6. Scoop mix into muffin cups (either paper-lined or sprayed).
7. Bake for 25 to 30 minutes. Cool on a rack for 10 minutes before unmolding.

NUTRITIONAL INFORMATION PER SERVING

SERVING SIZE: 1 muffin	SODIUM: 220mg	DIETARY FIBER: 2g
CALORIES: 220cal	TOTAL CARBOHYDRATE: 34g	PROTEIN: 4g
TOTAL FAT: 8g		

Walnut Muffins

The warm, bold flavor of walnuts is the focus of this gluten-free recipe. Spiced with a touch of cinnamon, these regal nut muffins are wholesome and comforting, the perfect snack to curl up with on a fall or winter day.

YIELD: SIX 4 OZ. MUFFINS

1 cup + 2 tablespoons (6.5 oz.)	Flour Blend #2
1 teaspoon	Baking powder
½ cup (4 oz.)	Butter
¾ cup (6 oz.)	Sugar
⅛ teaspoon	Salt
¼ cup + 1 tablespoon (2.5 oz.)	Skim milk
2 ea.	Eggs
1 teaspoon	Cinnamon
1 cup (5 oz.)	Walnuts, chopped

1. Preheat oven to 350°F.
2. Sift flour blend and baking powder. Set aside.
3. Cream butter, sugar, and salt on medium speed. Blend in the skim milk.
4. Add the eggs to butter mixture in increments.
5. Add sifted flour mixture and cinnamon; mix on low speed until combined.
6. Add walnuts and mix until fully incorporated, but do not overmix.
7. Scoop into muffin cups, filling three-fourths full, and bake for 20 to 30 minutes, until tops are golden and spring back when touched.

NUTRITIONAL INFORMATION PER SERVING

SERVING SIZE: 1 muffin	SODIUM: 160mg	DIETARY FIBER: 2g
CALORIES: 530cal	TOTAL CARBOHYDRATE: 58g	PROTEIN: 8g
TOTAL FAT: 33g		

Orange Cranberry Muffins

The perfect balance of sweet citrus and tangy berry is achieved in these colorful gluten-free muffins. Cranberries, fresh or frozen, add both a kick to the flavor and a pop to the appearance of a muffin that is sure to liven up any breakfast table.

YIELD: 12 4 OZ. MUFFINS

½ cup + 2 tablespoons (3.5 oz.)	Flour Blend #2
¾ cup + 1 tablespoon (4.5 oz.)	Flour Blend #4
1 teaspoon	Baking powder
½ cup (4 oz.)	Butter
¾ cup (6 oz.)	Sugar
⅛ teaspoon	Salt
¼ cup	Heavy cream
2 ea.	Eggs
3 tablespoons (1.5 oz.)	Orange juice, fresh
1⅓ tablespoons	Orange zest, fresh
¾ cup (4 oz.)	Cranberries (fresh or frozen), chopped

1. Preheat oven to 350°F.
2. Sift flour blends and baking powder; set aside.
3. Cream butter, sugar, and salt on medium speed. Blend in the cream.
4. Combine eggs and juice and add to butter mixture in increments.
5. Add sifted flour mixture; mix on low speed until combined.
6. Add zest and cranberries and mix until fully incorporated, but do not overmix.
7. Scoop into muffin cups, filling three-fourths full. Bake for 20 to 30 minutes, until tops are golden and spring back when touched.

NUTRITIONAL INFORMATION PER SERVING

SERVING SIZE: 1 muffin	SODIUM: 75mg	DIETARY FIBER: less
CALORIES: 230cal	TOTAL CARBOHYDRATE: 28g	than 1g
TOTAL FAT: 12g		PROTEIN: 4g

Corn Muffins

Golden-topped corn muffins are a breadbasket staple. Traditionally sweet, these corn muffins are also a complementary base for the addition of savory items such as grated cheese, cooked bacon, or jalapeño peppers. Prepared as you wish, this recipe yields moist muffins that are enjoyably versatile.

YIELD: 12 4 OZ. MUFFINS

1½ cups (12 oz.)	Buttermilk
4 ea.	Eggs
¾ cup	Vegetable oil
2¾ cups (15 oz.)	Flour Blend #4
⅔ cup (4 oz.)	Yellow cornmeal
¾ cup (6 oz.)	Sugar
2½ teaspoons	Salt
1 tablespoon	Baking powder
5 ea. (1.5 oz.)	Jalapeños, seeded and diced
½ cup (2.3 oz.)	Cheese, grated

1. Preheat oven to 375°F.
2. Whisk together buttermilk, eggs, and oil in a mixing bowl. In a separate bowl, combine flour blend, cornmeal, sugar, salt, and baking powder.
3. Add the dry ingredients to the wet ingredients, whisking until smooth.
4. Fold in peppers and cheese.
5. Transfer batter into oiled muffin pans and fill three-fourths full.
6. Bake for 20 to 25 minutes, or until golden brown and firm in the center.

NUTRITIONAL INFORMATION PER SERVING

SERVING SIZE: 1 muffin	**SODIUM:** 660mg	**DIETARY FIBER:** 4g
CALORIES: 410cal	**TOTAL CARBOHYDRATE:** 50g	**PROTEIN:** 11g
TOTAL FAT: 19g		

Double Chocolate Muffins

When a little bit of chocolate just isn't enough, turn to these double chocolate muffins to get your fill. Crowded with chocolate chips, both bittersweet and semisweet, these golden-topped muffins come together in a snap to create a rich and tasty treat.

YIELD: SIX 4 OZ. MUFFINS

1 cup + 2 tablespoons (6.5 oz.)	Flour Blend #2
1 teaspoon	Baking powder
½ cup (4 oz.)	Butter
½ cup + 2 tablespoons (5 oz.)	Sugar
Pinch	Salt
¼ cup + 1 tablespoon	Whipping cream
2 ea.	Eggs
½ cup	Semisweet chocolate chips
⅓ cup	Bittersweet chocolate chips

1. Preheat oven to 375°F.
2. Sift flour blend and baking powder; set aside.
3. Cream butter, sugar, and salt on medium speed.
4. Blend together cream and eggs and add to butter mixture in increments, scraping bowl after each addition.
5. Add sifted flour mixture; mix on low speed until combined.
6. Add chocolate chips and mix until fully incorporated, but do not overmix.
7. Scoop into muffin cups and bake for 20 to 30 minutes, until tops are golden and spring back when touched.

NUTRITIONAL INFORMATION PER SERVING

SERVING SIZE: 1 muffin	SODIUM: 660mg	DIETARY FIBER: 3g
CALORIES: 640cal	TOTAL CARBOHYDRATE: 42g	PROTEIN: 11g
TOTAL FAT: 20g		

Lemon Poppy Seed Muffins

Lemon Poppy Seed muffins are a bright and zesty start to the day. Golden yellow and speckled with dark poppy seeds, these muffins are densely packed with fresh, edgy citrus flavor.

YIELD: FIVE 4 OZ. MUFFINS

¾ cup (4.4 oz.)	Flour Blend #2
½ teaspoon	Baking powder
5 tablespoons (2.5 oz.)	Butter
¼ cup + 2 tablespoons (3 oz.)	Sugar
Pinch	Salt
2 ea.	Eggs
1 tablespoon	Corn oil
1 tablespoon (0.5 oz.)	Lemon juice
2 tablespoons	Lemon zest
1 tablespoon + 1 teaspoon	Poppy seeds

1. Preheat oven to 375°F.
2. Sift flour blend and baking powder together and set aside.
3. Cream butter, sugar, and salt together until light and fluffy.
4. In a separate bowl, combine the eggs, oil, and juice. Add to the creamed mixture in three additions, scraping bowl after each addition.
5. Add the sifted flour mixture and mix until just combined.
6. Add the zest and poppy seeds and mix until just incorporated, being careful not to overmix.
7. Scoop into muffin cups and bake for 20 to 30 minutes, or until tops are golden and spring back when lightly touched.

NUTRITIONAL INFORMATION PER SERVING

SERVING SIZE: 1 muffin SODIUM: 290mg DIETARY FIBER: less
CALORIES: 310cal TOTAL CARBOHYDRATE: 36g than 1g
TOTAL FAT: 18g PROTEIN: 4g

Blueberry Muffins

The summer months bring us blueberries aplenty. What better use to make of the juicy berry but everyone's favorite muffin in a gluten-free version. This recipe uses fresh or dried blueberries mixed in a simple batter to produce muffins that just may disappear as quickly as they are made . . .

YIELD: SIX 4 OZ. MUFFINS

¾ cup (4.4 oz.)	Flour Blend #2
¼ cup + 1 tablespoon (1.8 oz.)	Flour Blend #3
⅓ cup (2 oz.)	Flour Blend #4
1 teaspoon	Baking powder
⅓ cup + 1 tablespoon (3.17 oz.)	Sugar
Pinch	Salt
1 ea.	Egg
2 ea.	Egg whites
⅓ cup	Canola oil
½ cup (2.5 oz.)	Blueberries, frozen or fresh

1. Preheat oven to 350°F.
2. Combine all wet and dry ingredients until well blended.
3. Bake in lined and greased muffin tins for 10 to 15 minutes, or until tops are golden and spring back when lightly touched or a skewer inserted in the top comes out clean.
4. Let cool, then unmold.

NUTRITIONAL INFORMATION PER SERVING

SERVING SIZE: 1 muffin
CALORIES: 330cal
TOTAL FAT: 15g

SODIUM: 270mg
TOTAL CARBOHYDRATE: 47g

DIETARY FIBER: less than 1g
PROTEIN: 6g

Irish Soda Bread

This traditional Irish bread substitutes baking soda for yeast, with buttermilk to help activate the soda for leavening; the top of the loaf is characteristically scored with a cross. The Irish would tell you that soda bread is an appropriate accompaniment to any meal of the day, from breakfast to dinner. This recipe adds dried currants and caraway seeds for variation.

YIELD: ONE 8" ROUND LOAF (SIX SERVINGS)

2 cups (10.5 oz.)	Flour Blend #4
¾ teaspoon	Baking powder
½ teaspoon	Salt
3 tablespoons (1.5 oz.)	Butter, cold
¼ cup + 1 tablespoon (2.5 oz.)	Sugar
⅔ cup (4 oz.)	Dried currants
1 tablespoon	Caraway seeds
1 cup (8 oz.)	Buttermilk
1 ea.	Egg
½ teaspoon	Baking soda

1. Preheat oven to 350°F.
2. Sift together the flour blend, baking powder, and salt. Rub in the cold butter.
3. Add the sugar, currants, and caraway seeds to the flour mixture and toss to combine. Make a well in the center and set the bowl aside.
4. In a separate bowl, combine the buttermilk, egg, and baking soda.
5. Pour the wet ingredients into the well in the dry ingredient bowl. Stir until just combined.
6. Turn the dough out onto a lightly floured board. Shape into an 8" round loaf without kneading the dough.
7. Move the dough to a greased round cake pan and score the top with an X.
8. Bake for 40 minutes or until the top is nicely browned.

NUTRITIONAL INFORMATION PER SERVING

SERVING SIZE: 1 slice	SODIUM: 450mg	DIETARY FIBER: 5g
CALORIES: 330cal	TOTAL CARBOHYDRATE: 63g	PROTEIN: 11g
TOTAL FAT: 7g		

Scones

Fancy up your tea or coffee with this recipe for gluten-free buttermilk scones. While these scones call for the addition of soaked fruit, the possibilities for variety are vast; consider adding spices, nuts, chocolate chips, or savory items such as grated cheese to create scones to your liking.

YIELD: SIX SCONES

1⅓ cups (8 oz.)	Flour Blend #1
1 cup (5.75 oz.)	Flour Blend #2
½ teaspoon	Salt
3 tablespoons (1.5 oz.)	Sugar
1 tablespoon	Baking powder
2 ea.	Eggs
¼ cup + 3 tablespoons (3.5 oz.)	Buttermilk
⅝ cup	Heavy cream
¾ cup	Soaked fruit, optional
¼ cup (2 oz)	Simple syrup, optional (for soaking fruit)
As needed	Egg Wash (page 197)
	or
⅓ cup (2 oz.)	Flour Blend #1
⅓ cup (2.7 oz.)	Sugar

1. Preheat oven to 400°F.
2. Sift flour blends, salt, sugar, and baking powder together.
3. In a separate bowl, combine eggs, buttermilk, and heavy cream.
4. Mix wet ingredients into dry ingredients until combined.
5. Incorporate soaked fruit if desired.
6. Portion out with a large ice cream scoop and place on a parchment-lined baking sheet.
7. Top with either the egg wash or ⅓ cup Flour Blend #1 and ⅓ cup granulated sugar.
8. Bake for 15 to 17 minutes or until golden brown on edges.

NUTRITIONAL INFORMATION PER SERVING

SERVING SIZE: 1 scone	**SODIUM:** 370mg	**DIETARY FIBER:** 1g
CALORIES: 320cal	**TOTAL CARBOHYDRATE:** 59g	**PROTEIN:** 4g
TOTAL FAT: 9g		

Buttermilk Biscuits

A homage to Southern cooking, these buttermilk biscuits are food for the soul. Serve these biscuits, cooked to a golden brown, with honey or jam, or smother them with gravy for a heartier breakfast fare.

YIELD: 12 2½" × 1¾" BISCUITS

1½ cups (9 oz.)	Flour Blend #2
1⅓ cups (8 oz.)	Flour Blend #3
1 tablespoon (8 g)	Guar gum
1 teaspoon	Salt
¼ cup	Baking powder
½ cup (3 oz.)	Sugar
2 ea.	Eggs
2¾ cups (22 oz.)	Buttermilk
8 tablespoons (1 stick) (4 oz.)	Butter, melted
¼ cup (2 oz.)	Egg Wash (page 197)

1. Preheat oven to 350°F.
2. Mix flour blends, guar gum, salt, baking powder, and sugar together in a mixing bowl. In a separate bowl, mix eggs, buttermilk, and melted butter together.
3. Add wet ingredients to dry ingredients, and mix together by hand.
4. Using a #12 scoop or shaping by hand (2½" diameter and 1¾" high), portion onto a parchment-lined sheet pan or scoop into a greased muffin tin. Brush with egg wash.
5. Bake for 12 to 15 minutes or until lightly browned.

NUTRITIONAL INFORMATION PER SERVING

SERVING SIZE: 1 biscuit	SODIUM: 710mg	DIETARY FIBER: 2g
CALORIES: 260cal	TOTAL CARBOHYDRATE: 42g	PROTEIN: 6g
TOTAL FAT: 9g		

Funnel Cake

This recipe brings the carnival to your kitchen. Fairground style, fried in spirals and sprinkled with powdered sugar, this funnel cake hints of amusement park nostalgia and promises to leave you happily sticky-fingered.

YIELD: 10 3"- TO 4"-WIDE CAKES

¾ cup + 2 tablespoons (6 oz.)	Flour Blend #3
3 tablespoons (1.5 oz.)	Sugar
1 teaspoon	Baking soda
¾ teaspoon	Baking powder
½ teaspoon	Salt
1 ea.	Egg
½ cup (4 oz.)	Milk
2 cups	Vegetable oil
2 teaspoons (5 g)	Powdered sugar

1. Combine the dry ingredients in a medium mixing bowl. Add the egg and milk and whisk until smooth.
2. Heat ¼" (2 cups or more) oil in a small shallow pot to about 375°F.
3. Pipe the batter directly into the hot oil, keeping tip-end of pastry bag out of the hot oil! Starting in small spirals, getting larger as you move outward, move back and forth over the circles to form desired shape.
4. Cook until golden brown, turning over once.
5. Drain on paper towels; dust with powdered sugar as desired.

NUTRITIONAL INFORMATION PER SERVING

SERVING SIZE: 1 cake	SODIUM: 310mg	DIETARY FIBER: less than 1g
CALORIES: 490cal	TOTAL CARBOHYDRATE: 17g	
TOTAL FAT: 46g		PROTEIN: 3g

Pancakes

Settle in on Sunday morning with a stack of these gluten-free, griddle-cooked pancakes. They're deliciously comforting eaten plain, butter-moistened and smothered in maple syrup; you may also consider adding nuts, chocolate chips, or fruit fillings and toppings to create whatever type of pancake suits the morning.

YIELD: SIX SERVINGS

1⅓ cups (7.7 oz.)	Flour Blend #5
½ tablespoon	Baking powder
½ teaspoon	Salt
½ cup (4 oz.)	Sugar
2 ea.	Eggs
¼ cup (2 oz.)	Butter, melted
¾ cup (6 oz.)	Milk

1. Mix together dry ingredients in a mixing bowl. In a separate bowl, mix together wet ingredients.
2. Pour wet ingredients into dry ingredients and mix together until completely combined.
3. If batter is too thick, add additional water or milk to thin to correct consistency.
4. Cook on oiled griddle.

NUTRITIONAL INFORMATION PER SERVING

· ·

SERVING SIZE: 1 pancake   SODIUM: 370mg   DIETARY FIBER: 2g
CALORIES: 300cal   TOTAL CARBOHYDRATE: 47g   PROTEIN: 9g
TOTAL FAT: 10g

Heat up the iron; this waffle batter brings back a standard breakfast staple in a gluten-free version as good as any waffle to come before. Serve them beside eggs and bacon—or alone, showcased with nuts, a fruit topping, or chocolate chips and whipped cream. However you plate them, these waffles are sure to please.

YIELD: FOUR SERVINGS

1⅓ cups (7.7 oz.)	Flour Blend #5
½ tablespoon	Baking powder
½ teaspoon	Salt
½ cup (4 oz.)	Sugar
2 ea.	Eggs
¼ cup (2 oz.)	Butter, melted
¾ cup (6 oz.)	Milk
2 ea.	Egg whites

1. Mix together flour blend, baking powder, salt, and sugar in a mixing bowl. In a separate bowl, mix together eggs, melted butter, and milk.
2. Pour wet ingredients into dry ingredients and mix together until completely combined.
3. Whip egg whites to medium peaks.
4. Temper egg whites by adding one-third of the batter to the egg whites and mixing together gently.
5. Fold tempered whites into remaining batter.
6. Bake in oiled waffle iron until no more steam comes out of iron.

NUTRITIONAL INFORMATION PER SERVING

. . . .

SERVING SIZE: 1 waffle **SODIUM:** 580mg **DIETARY FIBER:** 3g

CALORIES: 450cal **TOTAL CARBOHYDRATE:** 68g **PROTEIN:** 15g

TOTAL FAT: 16g

Chapter 6

Cookies, Brownies,
and Pastries

*C*ookies hold a special place in many hearts, perhaps because they evoke childhood memories of happy times during the holidays. Taking a bite of a cookie made from your grandmother's recipe can send you hurtling back in time to when you were in elementary school and she was still spry and bustling around the kitchen. If you've tried converting your favorite family recipes into gluten-free versions and had mixed results, you can look forward to starting some new traditions with the recipes in this book.

Gluten-free 1-2-3 Cookie Dough (see page 103) can be rolled out, cut into shapes, and decorated just as you would regular roll-out cookie dough, but it also works well as a tart crust. Many of the other favorites you've been missing can be found in the pages that follow. How about chocolate-chip pecan, peanut butter, triple chocolate, macaroons, and shortbread? Yes, yes, yes, yes, and yes!

Looking for something elegant? You'll find recipes for gluten-free Linzer cookies and spritz cookies. A cookie press doesn't work for gluten-free spritz cookies, because the batter is too soft to hold a complicated shape, but you can still achieve some beautiful looking rosettes, shells, and figure eights by using a piping bag. Place a dollop of jam in the center and you'll be ready for afternoon tea. Or, if you prefer coffee, you can make some gluten-free biscotti, regular or double chocolate, to dunk in your cup, as well as some delicious cream cheese rugelach.

Pull out all the stops with gluten-free pecan diamonds. Other special recipes include Mexican wedding cookies, whoopie pies, toffee bars, and hip hugger bars. If you can get your hands on some gluten-free oats, you can look forward to oatmeal cookies. Make sure your oats come from a source that guarantees they are uncontaminated—in other words, not grown near wheat crops or processed near wheat (see "Readings and Resources," page 247).

And then, of course, there is the 800-pound gorilla in the room: brownies. Can't stop thinking about fudge brownies? You've got 'em, gluten free. You'll also find cream cheese brownies, chocolate peanut butter brownies, and blondies. The choice is yours, for a change.

1-2-3 Cookie Dough

Roughly one part sugar, two parts butter, and three parts gluten-free flour blend, this cookie dough is indeed "easy as one, two, three." Use this dough as a base for fruit tarts, or roll it out to make cut-out cookies that can be sprinkled or colored with food dye for holiday celebration.

YIELD: 12 SERVINGS (14 OUNCES)

½ cup (4 oz.)	Butter, cold
¼ cup (2 oz.)	Sugar
1¼ cups (7 oz.)	Flour Blend #2
1 ea.	Egg, room temperature

1. Cut the butter into 1" cubes.
2. Combine all ingredients in a bowl. Mix (by hand or with a paddle) until thoroughly combined.
3. Wrap the dough in plastic or waxed paper.
4. Refrigerate for at least 1 hour before use. Depending on the application, it can be held in the refrigerator for two weeks or even frozen for up to two months.

NUTRITIONAL INFORMATION PER SERVING

SERVING SIZE: 1 cookie or 1 oz. of dough
CALORIES: 140cal

TOTAL FAT: 8g
SODIUM: 5mg
TOTAL CARBOHYDRATE: 16g

DIETARY FIBER: 0g
PROTEIN: 1g

Shortbread

Following the classic recipe ratio of one part sugar to two parts butter to three parts flour, this gluten-free shortbread formula creates cookies that are crumbly, buttery, and sweet. Following the tradition of Scotland and other areas of Europe, you can use this recipe to make shortbread in your own home; eat the cookies plain or dunk them into a cup of tea.

YIELD: SIX SERVINGS

¼ cup (2 oz.)	Butter, cold
⅛ cup (1 oz.)	Sugar
½ cup (3 oz.)	Flour Blend #2
1 ea.	Egg, room temperature
As needed	Egg Wash (page 197)
As needed	Sugar, for garnish

1. Cut the butter into 1" cubes.
2. In a bowl, combine all ingredients except egg wash and sugar for garnish.
3. Mix (by hand or with a paddle) until thoroughly combined.
4. Wrap the dough in plastic or waxed paper. Refrigerate for 1 to 2 hours before use.
5. When ready to bake, preheat oven to 350°F.
6. Roll out dough to ¼" thick, place into a 6" pie tin, and trim.
7. Cut shapes into dough (triangles, quarters, strips, etc.), brush with egg wash, and sprinkle with sugar.
8. Bake for about 15 minutes or until edges are golden brown.

NUTRITIONAL INFORMATION PER SERVING

SERVING SIZE: 1 cookie	SODIUM: 10mg	DIETARY FIBER: 0g
CALORIES: 150cal	TOTAL CARBOHYDRATE: 16g	PROTEIN: 2g
TOTAL FAT: 9g		

Ice Cream Sandwiches

Pair your favorite nutty, chocolaty cookie with ice cream, and you'll have a delicious treat that will win raves from all who try it. Don't be afraid to try different cookies to be the "bread" of your sandwich—you'll eventually find your favorite combination.

YIELD: FOUR SANDWICHES

1 cup	of your favorite gluten-free ice cream, softened
One recipe	Chocolate-Pecan Cookies (see page 109)

1. Spread ¼ cup of the ice cream in between two cookies. Wrap each in plastic and place in the freezer for about 1 hour, or until firm, before serving.

NUTRITIONAL INFORMATION PER SERVING

SERVING SIZE: 1 sandwich	**SODIUM:** 270mg	**DIETARY FIBER:** 5g
CALORIES: 640cal	**TOTAL CARBOHYDRATE:** 74g	**PROTEIN:** 10g
TOTAL FAT: 18g		

Biscotti

Slide one of these crisp elongated cookies onto a saucer and you've got the quintessential companion to your coffee cup. In this recipe the Italian dipping cookie is flavored with almond, vanilla, and hazelnut; the finished biscotti are well suited for dipping into coffee, tea, or even wine.

YIELD: TWO 12" LOGS (24 SERVINGS)

1¼ cups (5.4 oz.)	Almond flour
¾ cup + 2 tablespoons (6 oz.)	Flour Blend #3
2 teaspoons	Baking powder
¾ cup (6 oz.)	Sugar
⅔ cup (3 oz.)	Gluten-free bread crumbs
¾ cup (3.75 oz.)	Almonds, whole with skin
¾ cup (3.75 oz.)	Hazelnuts, whole with skin
½ teaspoon	Vanilla extract
½ teaspoon	Almond extract
2 tablespoons (1 oz.)	Orange juice
3 ea.	Eggs

1. Preheat oven to 370°F.
2. In a mixing bowl, combine almond flour, flour blend, baking powder, sugar, bread crumbs, and nuts.
3. Add vanilla and almond extracts, orange juice, and whole eggs, and mix on low speed until just combined.
4. On a lightly floured work surface, shape the dough into a log 3" to 4" wide by ½" thick.
5. Place the log on a sheet tray, allowing enough room to accommodate spread.
6. Bake log at 370°F for 20 minutes or until the log is firm to the touch. Remove from oven and allow to cool for 5 minutes. Reduce oven temperature to 300°F.
7. Cut the log into slices ½" to ¾" wide and place cut sides up on the baking sheet.
8. Bake a second time at 300°F for about 25 minutes or until biscotti are dry in the center.

Short dough can be used for a variety of applications and should have a smooth texture and pliable consistency.

Double Chocolate Biscotti

These crisp Italian cookies take your favorite coffee drink from ordinary to extraordinary.

YIELD: TWO 12" LOGS (24 SERVINGS)

3 ea.	Eggs
¾ teaspoon	Vanilla extract
1 cup + 3 tablespoons (7.25 oz.)	Flour Blend #3
¼ cup (2 oz.)	Cocoa powder
1½ teaspoons	Baking soda
Pinch	Salt
1¼ cup (10 oz.)	Sugar
1 tablespoon	Instant coffee
1 cup	Chocolate chips
1 cup (5 oz.)	Hazelnuts, chopped, toasted, and cooled
2 cups	White chocolate chips

1. Preheat oven to 350°F. Lightly whisk together eggs and vanilla. Set aside.

2. Combine remaining ingredients, except white chocolate, in mixer bowl. With paddle attachment, slowly add egg mixture on low speed. Mix until dough just comes together. Scrape bowl to fully incorporate dry ingredients.

3. On a lightly floured work surface, divide dough into two equal portions and spread out onto sheet tray to form two logs.

4. Place logs on a sheet tray, allowing enough room for spread. Press down 3" wide × ½" high, and 12" long, using cold water on hands.

5. Bake logs at 350°F about 20 minutes, until the tops are cracked and no longer wet-looking. Cool logs to room temperature.

6. Decrease oven temperature to 325°F. Cut logs into slices 1" thick.

7. Place them, cut side up, on a sheet tray. After 10 minutes in the oven, flip biscotti onto other side. Bake until dry and firm, about 25 minutes.

8. Melt white chocolate. Once cooled, dip biscotti lengthwise into the chocolate, allowing chocolate to come halfway up the biscotti.

9. Place biscotti, chocolate side down, on a sheet tray and allow to set.

NUTRITIONAL INFORMATION PER SERVING

SERVING SIZE: 1 biscotti	SODIUM: 175mg	DIETARY FIBER: 1.5g
CALORIES: 180cal	TOTAL CARBOHYDRATE: 27g	PROTEIN: 3.5g
TOTAL FAT: 7.5g		

Chocolate-Pecan Cookies

Grab an extra large glass of milk for this nutty treat. Here, the standard chocolate-chip cookie is upgraded as chocolate chips are paired with pecans, creating a recipe for a cookie that has both sweetness and crunch.

YIELD: NINE 1.5 OZ. COOKIES

¼ cup (2 oz.)	Butter, softened
¼ cup (2 oz.)	Sugar
¼ cup (2 oz.)	Brown sugar
¼ teaspoon	Baking soda
¼ teaspoon	Baking powder
¼ teaspoon	Salt
⅛ cup (1 oz.)	Water
1 ea.	Egg
½ teaspoon	Vanilla extract
¾ cup (4 oz.)	Flour Blend #4
½ cup (2.5 oz.)	Pecan pieces
½ cup	Semisweet chocolate chips

1. Preheat oven to 375°F.
2. Cream the butter, sugar, brown sugar, baking soda, baking powder, and salt together until light and fluffy, scraping down the side of the bowl as needed.
3. Add the water, egg, and vanilla and blend until just incorporated, scraping down the side of the bowl as needed.
4. Add flour blend to the creamed mixture, blending until just combined.
5. Blend in the pecan pieces and chocolate chips.
6. Scoop out cookies using a small- to medium-sized scoop. Gently flatten tops of cookies with your hand.
7. Bake for 10 to 12 minutes or until center is set.

NUTRITIONAL INFORMATION PER SERVING		
SERVING SIZE: 1 cookie	SODIUM: 120mg	DIETARY FIBER: 2g
CALORIES: 250cal	TOTAL CARBOHYDRATE: 30g	PROTEIN: 4g
TOTAL FAT: 14g		

Peanut Butter Cookies

There is no shortage of flavor in this recipe for peanut butter cookies. Peanut butter lends the characteristically full, sweet, nutty taste while the addition of chopped raw peanuts gives these sugary cookies a hint of salty, authentic crunch.

YIELD: 16 COOKIES

½ cup (4 oz.)	Butter
½ cup - 1 tablespoon (3.3 oz.)	Brown sugar, packed
⅓ cup (2.7 oz.)	Sugar
½ tablespoon	Salt
½ tablespoon	Baking soda
½ cup (5 oz.)	Peanut butter
1 ea.	Egg
½ cup + 1 tablespoon (3.4 oz.)	Flour Blend #1
½ cup (3 oz.)	Flour Blend #3
⅓ cup (1.66 oz.)	Peanuts, raw, roughly chopped

1. Preheat oven to 350°F.
2. Cream butter, sugars, salt, and baking soda together until smooth.
3. Blend in the peanut butter.
4. Blend in the egg.
5. Sift together the flour blends and add to the mixture until just combined.
6. Add the chopped peanuts.
7. Line a cookie sheet with parchment paper. Portion into 1 oz. balls and place on the prepared pan.
8. Bake for 13 minutes or until golden brown.

NUTRITIONAL INFORMATION PER SERVING

SERVING SIZE: 1 cookie	SODIUM: 340mg	DIETARY FIBER: less than 1g
CALORIES: 195cal	TOTAL CARBOHYDRATE: 19g	PROTEIN: 4g
TOTAL FAT: 11g		

Triple Chocolate Cookies

These cookies take chocolate seriously and satisfy the palates of even the most intense chocolate lovers.

YIELD: 22 COOKIES

1 cup (6 oz.)	White rice flour
1 cup (4.4 oz.)	Almond flour
2½ tablespoons (21 g)	Cocoa powder
¼ teaspoon	Baking powder
¼ teaspoon	Salt
2 ea.	Eggs
¾ teaspoon	Vanilla extract
2 teaspoons	Instant coffee powder
5 tablespoons (2.5 oz.)	Butter
⅔ cup (5.5 oz.)	Brown sugar, packed
½ cup (4 oz.)	Sugar
2 cups	Bittersweet chocolate, melted
1½ cups	Semisweet chocolate chips

1. Preheat oven to 325°F.
2. Sift together rice flour, almond flour, cocoa powder, baking powder, and salt.
3. Beat eggs, vanilla extract, and instant coffee powder together and set aside.
4. Cream butter and sugars together until light and fluffy.
5. Add the melted chocolate all at once to the creamed butter and sugar mixture and mix until just combined.
6. Blend in the egg mixture, scraping down the side of the bowl as necessary.
7. Add dry ingredients and blend just until fully incorporated.
8. Fold in the chocolate chips.
9. Line a cookie sheet with parchment paper. Scoop out the cookies onto the pan.
10. Bake for 12 to 15 minutes; rotate the pan 180° half way through baking.
11. Transfer to wire racks to cool.

NUTRITIONAL INFORMATION PER SERVING

SERVING SIZE: 1 cookie	SODIUM: 50mg	DIETARY FIBER: 2g
CALORIES: 260cal	TOTAL CARBOHYDRATE: 34g	PROTEIN: 4g
TOTAL FAT: 15g		

Black & White Cookies

Known to New Yorkers as a bake shop classic, it is the contrasting icing on these boldly recognizable cookies that, in this recipe, turns a simple sugar cookie into a cookie with attitude.

YIELD: 12 COOKIES

½ cup (4 oz.)	Butter, softened
½ cup (4 oz.)	Sugar
¾ teaspoon	Vanilla extract
2 ea.	Eggs
2 ea.	Egg yolks
2 tablespoons (1 oz)	Milk
¼ cup (1.5 oz.)	Flour Blend #1
¾ cup + 2 tablespoon (6 oz.)	Flour Blend #3
1 teaspoon	Baking powder
¼ teaspoon	Salt
½ teaspoon	Lemon zest
As needed	Black and white cookie frosting: Recipe follows, but store-bought is an option as long as it is gluten-free.

1. Preheat oven to 350°F.
2. Cream butter, sugar, and vanilla together in a large bowl until light and fluffy. Scrape down the side of the bowl as needed.
3. Beat in eggs and yolks one at a time, scraping down the side of the bowl as needed for full incorporation.
4. Gradually add the milk, mixing until thoroughly blended.
5. In a separate bowl, sift together the flour blends, baking powder, and salt. Add lemon zest.
6. Add flour mixture slowly to the creamed mixture, mixing until just combined.
7. Line a cookie sheet with parchment paper. Scoop cookies using an ice cream scoop leveled at the top, placing them approximately 2" apart on the cookie sheet. Dampen hands and lightly flatten the cookies.
8. Bake for 15 minutes, or until the center springs back when lightly touched.

9. Leave the cookies on the sheet for 5 minutes before transferring to wire cooling rack to cool completely.
10. Frost with half black frosting and half white frosting when cool.

BLACK AND WHITE FROSTING:

White frosting:

⅓ cup (2.7 oz.)   Simple syrup
1 cup (5 oz.)   Powdered sugar

1. Combine simple syrup and powdered sugar; stir until well combined.

Black frosting:

½ cup (4 oz.)   Simple syrup
½ cup + 1 tablespoon   Semisweet chocolate chips
2 tablespoons (0.5 oz.)   Powdered sugar

1. Warm simple syrup, and stir in chocolate chips until completely melted.
2. Allow to cool slightly, and then stir in powdered sugar until fully incorporated.

NUTRITIONAL INFORMATION PER SERVING		
SERVING SIZE: 1 cookie (with frosting)	SODIUM: 112mg	DIETARY FIBER: 1g
	TOTAL CARBOHYDRATE: 54g	PROTEIN: 4g
CALORIES: 320cal		
TOTAL FAT: 12g		

Trail Mix Cookies

Packed with protein and fiber, these cookies will make people reminiscent of hiking in the outdoors. The chocolate chips make these cookies hard to resist, and will become a new family favorite.

YIELD: 15 COOKIES

8 tablespoons (4 oz.)	Butter, room temperature
1 cup (8 oz.)	Natural cane sugar
3 ea.	Eggs, room temperature
⅛ teaspoon	Baking soda
Pinch	Salt
⅛ teaspoon	Vanilla extract
⅓ cup (2 oz.)	Flour Blend #1
¼ cup (1.5 oz.)	Flour Blend #3
⅓ cup (2 oz.)	Flour Blend #4
1 cup (6 oz.)	Almond flour
½ cup (2.5 oz.)	Dried fruits
¼ cup (1.25 oz.)	Raw nuts, chopped
¼ cup	Chocolate chips

1. Preheat oven to 375°F.
2. Cream the butter and sugar together until light and fluffy.
3. Blend in one egg at a time, scraping down the sides of the bowl as necessary.
4. Sift together the baking soda, salt, and flours. Add all at once to the egg mixture and mix until just combined.
5. Mix in the dried fruits, nuts, and chocolate chips just until combined.
6. Portion into 2 oz. balls and place the cookies onto a sheet tray; lightly press the top of the dough to flatten out the cookies.
7. Bake for 10 to 12 minutes, until the cookies are golden brown.

NUTRITIONAL INFORMATION PER SERVING

SERVING SIZE: 1 cookie	SODIUM: 40mg	DIETARY FIBER: 2g
CALORIES: 280cal	TOTAL CARBOHYDRATE: 32g	PROTEIN: 6g
TOTAL FAT: 16g		

Coconut Macaroons

Traditionally made without flour, these coconut cookies are deliciously dense, bite-sized drops of golden sweetness. For added flavor and visual appeal, the cooked and cooled macaroons may be half-dipped in melted chocolate.

YIELD: 12 COOKIES

6 ea.	Egg whites
2 cups (16 oz.)	Sugar
5¾ cups + 1 tablespoon (1 lb. 6 oz.)	Dried coconut
2 teaspoons	Vanilla extract
2 cups	Semisweet chocolate, chopped (optional)

1. Preheat oven to 350°F.
2. Combine egg whites and sugar in a mixing bowl.
3. Heat the mixture over a pan of barely simmering water, stirring constantly with a spoon, until mixture reaches 120°F. Make sure sugar is dissolved, then remove bowl from heat.
4. Add coconut and vanilla and blend well.
5. Line a cookie sheet with parchment paper. Shape the cookie dough into balls about 2 ounces each (about the size of a quarter) and place on the prepared pan.
6. Bake for 20 minutes until lightly browned. Do not overbake—the centers should be moist. Allow to cool completely.
7. Optional: Melt the chocolate in a bowl set over a pan of barely simmering water. Dip the bottoms of the cookies in the chocolate, and place on a clean piece of parchment paper. Set aside until chocolate is firm.

NUTRITIONAL INFORMATION PER SERVING

WITHOUT CHOCOLATE:

SERVING SIZE: 1 cookie	SODIUM: 25mg	DIETARY FIBER: 5g
CALORIES: 290cal	TOTAL CARBOHYDRATE: 32g	PROTEIN: 3g
TOTAL FAT: 19g		

WITH CHOCOLATE:

CALORIES: 600cal	SODIUM: 50mg	DIETARY FIBER: 10g
TOTAL FAT: 39g	TOTAL CARBOHYDRATE: 65g	PROTEIN: 6g

Mexican Wedding Cookies

Commonly found during holiday times or on special occasions, these buttery melt-in-your-mouth cookies are sugar-coated delights. Full of walnuts and tossed with sugar after cooling, these white bites are cause for celebration themselves.

YIELD: 25 COOKIES

½ cup (4 oz.)	Butter
1 cup (5 oz.)	Powdered sugar
¼ teaspoon	Vanilla extract
¼ teaspoon	Rum
⅔ cup (4.5 oz.)	Flour Blend #3
¾ cup (3.75 oz.)	Walnuts, chopped

1. Preheat oven to 350°F.
2. Cream together butter and ¼ cup sugar.
3. Add vanilla extract and rum.
4. Add Flour Blend #3 and walnuts. Mix until incorporated.
5. Scoop with a #100 scoop or roll into 1" balls and place on sheet pan.
6. Bake for about 15 to 20 minutes.
7. When cool, toss in remaining powdered sugar.

NUTRITIONAL INFORMATION PER SERVING

SERVING SIZE: 1 cookie SODIUM: 10mg DIETARY FIBER: 0g
CALORIES: 90cal TOTAL CARBOHYDRATE: 9g PROTEIN: 1g
TOTAL FAT: 6g

Spritz Cookies

Spritz cookies are formed from a thicker dough that is piped, rather than scooped or rolled, onto a pan. Using a piping bag, you can form these cookies into various shapes, from simple circles to whimsical stars. When garnished with chocolate, nuts, or fruit, spritz cookies make a perfect accompaniment to an afternoon cup of tea, or a morning mug of coffee.

YIELD: 36 COOKIES

½ cup (4 oz.)	Butter, room temperature
½ cup (4 oz.)	Sugar
1 ea.	Egg, room temperature
1 ea.	Egg white, room temperature
1 cup (6 oz.)	White rice flour
½ cup (3 oz.)	Flour Blend #3
⅓ cup	Raspberry jam

1. Preheat oven to 375°F.
2. Cream butter and sugar together until light and fluffy.
3. Blend in the egg and egg white, scraping down the side of the bowl as necessary.
4. Mix flours into the mixture just until combined.
5. Line a cookie sheet with parchment paper. Fit a piping bag with a #6 star tip, folding over the top of the bag to form a cuff. Fill the pastry bag with the cookie dough. Pipe the batter into shapes the size of a quarter onto the prepared cookie sheet.
6. Garnish the center of each cookie with a small dollop of jam.
7. Bake for approximately 10 minutes or until lightly golden brown.

Note: Shapes can be circular, shells or stars.

NUTRITIONAL INFORMATION PER SERVING

SERVING SIZE: 1 cookie	SODIUM: 10mg	DIETARY FIBER: 0g
CALORIES: 70cal	TOTAL CARBOHYDRATE: 11g	PROTEIN: 1g
TOTAL FAT: 3g		

Pizzelles

Pizzelles, also known as Italian waffle cookies, are pressed in a pizzelle iron (similar to a waffle iron) and hand-held over hot heat to bake. Most irons feature a pattern that is imprinted onto the cookie, usually a snowflake, which makes these a popular treat during the winter holidays.

YIELD: 12 COOKIES

2 tablespoons + ½ teaspoon (1.2 oz.)	Margarine
2 tablespoons (1 oz.)	Sugar
1 ea.	Egg
½ ea.	Lemon (zest and juice)
½ cup (3 oz.)	Flour Blend #3
¼ teaspoon	Baking powder
Pinch	Salt
1 tablespoon	Anise seeds

1. Cream together margarine and sugar.
2. Add egg and mix in well.
3. Add lemon zest and juice.
4. Add Flour Blend #3, baking powder, and salt; mix until just combined.
5. Mix in anise seeds.
6. Drop a teaspoonful of the pizzelle dough onto a pizzelle hot iron sprayed with cooking spray.
7. Press the cookie dough in the iron.
8. Remove the pressed cookie onto a flat surface to cool. Stack to store.

NUTRITIONAL INFORMATION PER SERVING

SERVING SIZE: 1 cookie	**SODIUM:** 190mg	**DIETARY**
CALORIES: 80cal	**TOTAL CARBOHYDRATE:** 12g	**FIBER:** Less than 1g
TOTAL FAT: 3.5g		**PROTEIN:** 2g

Chocolate Crinkles

Chocolate takes center stage in these fudge-filled cookies. They are rolled in powdered sugar before cooking; as they bake, their dark chocolate insides begin to peek through cracks, or crinkles, that form in the white coating. Simple and attractive, these contrasting cookies appeal to both the eye and the taste buds.

YIELD: 24 COOKIES

¼ cup	Unsweetened chocolate chips
¼ cup	Vegetable oil
1 cup (8 oz.)	Sugar
2 ea.	Eggs
1 teaspoon	Vanilla extract
1 cup (6.25 oz.)	Flour Blend #3
1 teaspoon	Baking powder
¼ teaspoon	Salt
½ cup (2.5 oz.)	Powdered sugar

1. Melt chocolate over a double boiler.
2. Mix chocolate, oil, and sugar until combined.
3. Add eggs one at a time, mixing well after each, and scraping the bowl down with each addition. Then add vanilla and mix until combined.
4. Add Flour Blend #3, baking powder, and salt.
5. Place dough, covered or wrapped in plastic, in the refrigerator for at least 2 hours (overnight preferred).
6. When ready to bake, preheat oven to 350°F.
7. Scoop out 30g portions (the size of a quarter) and roll in the powdered sugar. Place on a parchment-lined cookie tray, ½ inch apart.
8. Bake for 8 to 10 minutes.

NUTRITIONAL INFORMATION PER SERVING

SERVING SIZE: 1 cookie   **SODIUM:** 60mg   **DIETARY FIBER:** less than 1g
CALORIES: 110cal   **TOTAL CARBOHYDRATE:** 19g   **PROTEIN:** 2g
TOTAL FAT: 4g

Linzer Cookies

A variation of one of Austria's most famous desserts, these Linzer cookies offer simple beauty paired with complex flavor. With the addition of ground nuts to the batter, the finished Linzer cookie, sandwiched around a dollop of fruit jam, is both warmly nutty and brightly sweet.

YIELD: 20 SANDWICHES (20 SERVINGS)

3½ tablespoons (1.75 oz.)	Butter
2½ tablespoons (1.5 oz.)	Sugar
⅛ teaspoon	Salt
¼ cup (23 g)	Hazelnuts, finely ground
⅛ cup (11 g)	Almonds, finely ground
1 ea.	Egg yolk
⅛ teaspoon	Vanilla extract
⅓ cup + 1 tablespoon (2.5 oz.)	Flour Blend #2
5 tablespoons	Raspberry jam, seedless
½ cup (2.5 oz)	Powdered sugar, sifted

1. Cut the butter into one-inch cubes and, using a mixer with paddle attachment, combine all ingredients (except the flour, jam, and powdered sugar) until smooth.
2. Sift the flour blend and blend into the mixture, mixing until just until incorporated.
3. Wrap the dough tightly in plastic wrap and chill for a minimum of 2 hours before using.
4. When ready to bake, preheat oven to 375°F.
5. Roll out the dough on a gluten-free floured surface to ⅛" thickness.
6. Using a round 1½" cookie cutter, cut out 20 circles of dough for the bottoms of the sandwiches. Using a fluted 1½" cookie cutter, cut out 20 more for the tops. Cut a ¾" hole in the center of the fluted dough circles (you can re-roll the insides or bake them on their own for extra cookies).
7. Bake for 15 to 20 minutes or until very lightly browned.

8. Place the cookie tray on wire cooling racks and allow to cool completely before assembling.
9. When cool, place a quarter-sized amount of jam onto base cookie.
10. Dust the top cookies with sifted powdered sugar, and place the top cookies onto the jam-filled bottom cookies.

NUTRITIONAL INFORMATION PER SERVING		
SERVING SIZE: 2 cookies with jam	TOTAL FAT: 3g	DIETARY FIBER: 0g
	SODIUM: 17mg	PROTEIN: 0.5g
CALORIES: 75cal	TOTAL CARBOHYDRATE: 12g	

Cut the middle out of half the linzer cookies to create a space for the filling to shine through once the cookies are sandwiched together.

Tuile

These thin cookies, flavored with a touch of almond, are commonly used as a decorative element to plated desserts, though they are equally delicious eaten plain with coffee or tea. While still warm after baking, tuiles may be pressed into cups, wrapped around tubes, or shaped in any other fashion to produce a hardened cookie with dimension.

YIELD: 36 COOKIES

½ cup + 1 tablespoon (2.75 oz.)	Powdered sugar
⅓ cup (2.25 oz.)	Flour Blend #3
3 ea.	Egg whites
3 tablespoons (1.5 oz.)	Butter, melted
1 teaspoon	Vanilla extract
½ teaspoon	Almond extract

1. Preheat oven to 375°F.
2. Combine sugar and Flour Blend #3.
3. Slowly add the egg whites, in parts, scraping when necessary.
4. Add butter, vanilla, and almond extract; mix until just combined.
5. Spread into a 2" × 3" triangle stencil onto a buttered and floured parchment-lined pan or use a nonstick silicone baking mat. Repeat as dough allows.
6. Bake for 4 to 5 minutes until light brown around the edges. They may be shaped while still warm around the outside of a coffee cup.

NUTRITIONAL INFORMATION PER SERVING

SERVING SIZE: 1 tuile	SODIUM: 10mg	DIETARY FIBER: 0g
CALORIES: 25cal	TOTAL CARBOHYDRATE: 4g	PROTEIN: 1g
TOTAL FAT: 1g		

Sand Cookies

Originating in Normandy, these cookies are named after sand because of their crumbly, delicate texture. They are usually cut into round shapes with fluted edges, but this is certainly not a requirement—for even more fun, try sandwiching two with some chocolate or hazelnut spread.

YIELD: EIGHT COOKIES

1 ea.	Hard-boiled egg yolk
6 tablespoons + 1 teaspoon (3.3 oz.)	Butter
3 tablespoons (21 g)	Powdered sugar
1 tablespoon + 1 teaspoon (8.5 g)	Almond flour
½ cup + 1 tablespoon (3.4 oz.)	Flour Blend #3
½ teaspoon	Baking powder
⅛ teaspoon	Salt
As needed	Egg Wash (page 197)

1. Preheat oven to 350°F.
2. Hard-boil the egg. When cool, separate the white from the yolk and pass the yolk through a sieve. Reserve.
3. Cream the butter and the sugar until smooth, but do not overmix.
4. Add the cooked yolk.
5. Add the rest of the ingredients to the butter, sugar, and yolk and mix well.
6. Roll out the dough to ¼" thick and cut with a 2.25" round cookie cutter.
7. Apply egg wash to the top of the cookies. Let dry and apply egg wash a second time.
8. Using a fork, make two criss-cross imprints on top of the cookie.
9. Bake for 7 minutes, or until you can just pick up the cookie and it has no color.

NUTRITIONAL INFORMATION PER SERVING

SERVING SIZE: 1 cookie	**SODIUM:** 65mg	**DIETARY FIBER:** less than 1g
CALORIES: 147cal	**TOTAL CARBOHYDRATE:** 11g	
TOTAL FAT: 11g		**PROTEIN:** 2g

Whoopie Pie

This oversized cream-filled chocolate cake sandwich is a crowd-pleasing favorite traditionally found both in Amish farmer's markets and Pennsylvania Dutch cuisine as well as in bakeries across the New England area. Serve this gluten-free version of the fluffy comfort treat and you just may have your happy guests shouting, "Whoopie!"

YIELD: THREE SANDWICHES (THREE SERVINGS)

Cake:

4½ tablespoons (2.5 oz.)	Butter
½ cup + 1 tablespoon (4.5 oz.)	Sugar
1 ea.	Egg
¼ cup (2 oz.)	Cocoa powder
1 teaspoon	Salt
1 teaspoon	Baking powder
¼ cup + 1 tablespoon (2.5 oz.)	Coffee, brewed
⅓ cup + 1 tablespoon (2.5 oz.)	Flour Blend #1
⅓ cup (2.25 oz.)	Flour Blend #3
¼ cup + 1 tablespoon (2.5 oz.)	Buttermilk

Filling:

11 tablespoons (5.5 oz.)	Butter
1½ cups (7.5 oz.)	Powdered sugar
3 tablespoons (1 oz.)	Pasteurized egg white
½ tablespoon	Vanilla extract
⅛ cup (1 oz.)	Milk, warm

Cake:

1. Preheat oven to 350°F.
2. Cream together butter and sugar.
3. Add the egg in increments, scraping down the side of the bowl when necessary.
4. Sift together cocoa powder, salt, baking powder, coffee, and flour blends, then add slowly to the butter mixture, scraping down the side of the bowl when necessary.

5. Add the buttermilk and mix until everything is combined.
6. Scoop batter onto a parchment-lined sheet pan with a #20 scoop.
7. Sprinkle tops with granulated sugar.
8. Bake for 12 to 15 minutes. Cool.

Filling:
1. Cream together butter and powdered sugar with a paddle.
2. Add in the other ingredients until combined.
3. Spread one-third of the filling onto 3 cookies, then top with the other 3 to make sandwiches.

NUTRITIONAL INFORMATION PER SERVING

SERVING SIZE: 1 sandwich (with filling)
CALORIES: 1220cal
TOTAL FAT: 66g

SODIUM: 1020mg
TOTAL CARBOHYDRATE: 95g

DIETARY FIBER: 6g
PROTEIN: 11g

Cream Cheese Rugelach

Rugelach, a traditional Jewish pastry, is formed into a customary cylindrical shape; choose whatever jam you would like to create the perfect pastry for your taste.

YIELD: 16 COOKIES

6 tablespoons (3 oz.)	Cream cheese
6 tablespoons (3 oz.)	Butter
¼ cup (2 oz.)	Sugar
2 ea.	Eggs
1½ cups (8 oz.)	Flour Blend #4
2 tablespoons	Cinnamon
½ cup	Jam

1. Cream together cream cheese, butter, and sugar for three minutes.
2. Add remaining ingredients except for jam. Rest 30 minutes uncovered, in refrigerator.
3. When ready to bake, preheat oven to 350°F. Divide dough into two pieces.
4. Roll out each piece to a ¼"-thick round and spread a thin even layer of jam on top.
5. Cut into 8 triangular pieces, and roll each triangular piece into a croissant shape.
6. Transfer each rolled piece onto a parchment-lined baking sheet.
7. Bake for 25 to 30 minutes or until golden brown.

NUTRITIONAL INFORMATION PER SERVING

SERVING SIZE: 1 cookie	**SODIUM:** 30mg	**DIETARY FIBER:** less than 1g
CALORIES: 160cal	**TOTAL CARBOHYDRATE:** 21g	
TOTAL FAT: 7g		**PROTEIN:** 4g

Shape the rugelach by cutting a circle of dough into wedges and rolling the wedges up into a croissant shape.

Pecan Diamonds

Pecan pie goes bite-sized in this recipe for pecan diamonds. Bars cut from a pie, these diamond-shaped treats are piled with honey and brown sugar sweetened pecan pieces, all together creating small cookies with big flavor.

YIELD: ONE 8" PIE TIN, APPROX. 20 DIAMONDS (20 SERVINGS)

One-half recipe (7 oz.)	1-2-3 Cookie Dough, uncooked (page 103)
½ cup (3.75 oz.)	Light brown sugar
4 tablespoons (2 oz.)	Butter
⅛ cup	Heavy cream
3 tablespoons (2.25 oz)	Honey
1 cup (5 oz.)	Pecan pieces

1. Preheat oven to 375°F.
2. Roll out cookie dough to cover a 8" fluted tart pan, with approximately ⅛" thickness of crust bottom and side edges. Parbake for 6 minutes. After removing the pan, reduce the oven temperature to 350°F.
3. Combine sugar, butter, heavy cream, and honey in a heavy-bottomed saucepot and bring to a boil while stirring.
4. Simmer, without stirring, until the mixture reaches 240°F.
5. Once mixture comes to 240°F, add nuts and gently stir.
6. Remove saucepot from heat and spread mixture evenly in the prebaked shell. Place pie tin on a cookie sheet pan to catch any mixture that boils over during baking.
7. Bake at 350°F for 25 to 30 minutes, or until the mixture bubbles evenly across the surface and crust is brown on the edges.
8. When cool, cut into 1" × 1" diamonds.

NUTRITIONAL INFORMATION PER SERVING

SERVING SIZE: 1 diamond	SODIUM: 5mg	DIETARY FIBER: less than 1g
CALORIES: 150cal	TOTAL CARBOHYDRATE: 15g	
TOTAL FAT: 10g		PROTEIN: 1g

Cream Cheese Brownies

The marriage of chocolate and cream cheese in this recipe results in a brownie that is ultra-moist and uniquely creamy. The finished swirl of the chocolate-chip-laden cream cheese filling through the dark cake base makes for a simple and elegant version of an old favorite.

YIELD: ONE 9" × 9" PAN (NINE SERVINGS)

Cream Cheese Filling:

⅔ cup (5.6 oz.)	Cream cheese, softened
⅔ cup (4.25 oz.)	Flour Blend #1
¼ cup (2 oz.)	Sugar
2 ea.	Eggs
¼ teaspoon	Salt
¾ cup	Semisweet chocolate chips

Black Bottom Cake:

2 tablespoons (21 g)	Flour Blend #1
½ cup (3 oz.)	Flour Blend #4
½ cup (3 oz.)	Flour Blend #5
1½ tablespoons (13 g)	Cocoa powder
½ cup (4 oz.)	Sugar
1 teaspoon	Baking soda
½ teaspoon	Salt
¾ cup (6 oz.)	Water
1¾ teaspoons	White vinegar
¾ teaspoon	Vanilla extract

Filling:

1. Blend the cream cheese, Flour Blend #1, sugar, eggs, and salt.
2. Carefully fold in chocolate chips and set the mixture aside.

Cake:

1. Preheat oven to 375°F.
2. Line a 9" × 9" baking pan with parchment paper; spray with pan spray and dust with Flour Blend #1.
3. Combine Flour Blends #4 and #5, cocoa powder, sugar, baking soda, and salt and blend.
4. Add the water, white vinegar, and vanilla extract to the dry ingredients. Blend using a whisk until completely combined.
5. Pour the batter into the prepared pan. Drop heaping tablespoons of cream cheese mixture evenly over top of cake batter. Swirl with knife to create a marbled effect.
6. Bake for 35 to 40 minutes, or until a knife inserted near the center of the brownies comes out with only a few moist crumbs. Allow to cool.

NUTRITIONAL INFORMATION PER SERVING

SERVING SIZE: 1 brownie   SODIUM: 370mg   DIETARY FIBER: 2g
CALORIES: 330cal   TOTAL CARBOHYDRATE: 52g   PROTEIN: 6g
TOTAL FAT: 13g

Fudge Brownie

The only thing this classic brownie recipe is missing is the gluten. Chocolaty and packed with walnuts, these simple, chewy, and moist brownies are just as brownies should be.

YIELD: ONE 9" × 9" PAN (NINE SERVINGS)

2 tablespoons (21 g)	Flour Blend #1
½ cup	Unsweetened chocolate chips
12 tablespoons (6 oz.)	Butter
3 ea.	Eggs
1 cup + 2 tablespoons (9 oz.)	Sugar
1 teaspoon	Vanilla extract
¼ cup (1 oz.)	Flour Blend #4
½ cup (2.5 oz.)	Walnuts

1. Preheat oven to 375°F.
2. Spray a 9" × 9" pan with cooking spray and dust it with Flour Blend #1.
3. Melt the chocolate and butter together in a bowl set over simmering water, blending gently. Allow to cool until just warm.
4. Combine the eggs, sugar, and vanilla in a mixer bowl. Beat using a wire whisk until thick and light in color, about 4 minutes, scraping down the side of the bowl as needed during mixing.
5. Blend one-third of the egg mixture into the chocolate-butter mixture.
6. Blend the chocolate mixture into the remaining egg mixture, scraping down the side of the bowl as necessary.
7. Add the flour blend and nuts, blending gently. The batter will be very wet.
8. Pour into prepared pan.
9. Bake for about 45 to 50 minutes, or until a crust forms but the product is still moist in the center. Allow to cool completely in the pan before cutting and unmolding.

NUTRITIONAL INFORMATION PER SERVING

SERVING SIZE: 1 brownie	SODIUM: 25mg	DIETARY FIBER: less than 1g
CALORIES: 440cal	TOTAL CARBOHYDRATE: 40g	
TOTAL FAT: 29g		PROTEIN: 6g

Blondies

Rather than using chocolate, these soft golden cookie bars put vanilla and brown sugar to work. With brownie-like consistency and hints of a butterscotch flavor, these blondies incorporate nuts to complement the rich flavor and to add interest to the finished texture of the product.

YIELD: ONE 9" × 9" PAN (12 SERVINGS)

1½ cups (11.6 oz.)	Brown sugar, divided
½ cup (4 oz.)	Butter
⅛ cup (1 oz.)	Water
2 ea.	Eggs
¼ teaspoon	Vanilla extract
⅓ cup (2 oz.)	Flour Blend #1
¾ cup + 2 tablespoons (6 oz.)	Flour Blend #3
¼ teaspoon	Baking powder
1½ cup (7.5 oz.)	Walnut pieces

1. Preheat oven to 350°F.
2. Heat 1 cup brown sugar, butter, and water until dissolved; set aside to cool.
3. Beat eggs, ½ cup brown sugar, and vanilla for 10 minutes.
4. Add sugar mixture to egg mixture and mix thoroughly.
5. In a separate bowl, sift together flour blends and baking powder.
6. Mix sifted flour mixture into wet mixture.
7. Add 1 cup of walnuts.
8. Spread into a greased and lined pan. Top with ½ cup of nuts.
9. Bake for 30 to 40 minutes until golden brown.

NUTRITIONAL INFORMATION PER SERVING

SERVING SIZE: 1 brownie   **SODIUM:** 55mg   **DIETARY FIBER:** 2g
CALORIES: 360cal   **TOTAL CARBOHYDRATE:** 44g   **PROTEIN:** 6g
TOTAL FAT: 20g

Chocolate Peanut Butter Brownie

This is no ordinary brownie. Flavored with melted chocolate, cocoa powder, and chocolate chips, the addition of a smooth peanut butter topping makes this chocolate-rich brownie an ultra-decadent treat worthy of indulging.

YIELD: ONE 9" × 9" PAN (NINE SERVINGS)

6 tablespoons (3 oz.)	Butter, softened
⅝ cup (5 oz.)	Sugar
½ teaspoon	Salt
2 ea.	Eggs
1½ teaspoons	Vanilla extract
½ cup	Chocolate, melted
¼ cup (1.5 oz.)	Flour Blend #1
1 tablespoon + ¼ teaspoon (11 g)	Cocoa powder
2 tablespoons	Chocolate chips
2 tablespoons (21 g)	Flour Blend #1 for dusting

Peanut Butter Topping:

2 tablespoons (1 oz.)	Butter, softened
½ cup (5 oz.)	Peanut butter
2 tablespoons (1 oz.)	Sugar
1 ea.	Egg

1. Preheat oven to 375°F.
2. Cream together the butter, sugar, and salt until light and fluffy. Scrape down the side of the bowl as needed.
3. Gradually add the eggs and vanilla, beating until completely incorporated and scraping down the side of the bowl as needed. Blend in the melted chocolate.
4. In a separate bowl, mix together Flour Blend #1 and cocoa powder. Add the dry ingredients to the creamed mixture, blending until just combined.
5. Blend in the chocolate chips.
6. Lightly grease a 9" × 9" baking pan and lightly dust with Flour Blend #1. Spread the batter into the prepared pan and set aside.
7. For the peanut butter topping, cream the butter, peanut butter, and sugar together until light and fluffy, scraping down the side of the bowl as needed.

8. Gradually add the egg, scraping down the side of the bowl as needed.

9. Spoon or pipe the peanut butter mixture on top of the brownie batter and swirl gently together with a knife, creating a marbled effect.

10. Bake for 18 to 20 minutes. Allow to cool completely before cutting and unmolding.

NUTRITIONAL INFORMATION PER SERVING

. . . .

SERVING SIZE: 1 brownie   SODIUM: 210mg   DIETARY FIBER: 2g

CALORIES: 350cal   TOTAL CARBOHYDRATE: 35g   PROTEIN: 6g

TOTAL FAT: 23g

Hip Hugger Bars

These bar cookies are rugged and layered in sweetness. The recipe incorporates oats both for texture and for an additional old-fashioned, wholesome flavor that, sandwiched around a gloriously gooey center of milky chocolate, makes these bars something not to be missed!

YIELD: ONE 9" × 9" BAKING PAN (NINE SERVINGS)

Filling:

½ cup	Sweetened condensed milk
½ cup + 1 tablespoon	Semisweet chocolate chips
1 tablespoon (0.5 oz.)	Butter, softened
¼ teaspoon	Vanilla extract

Cookies:

¼ teaspoon	Salt
¼ teaspoon	Baking soda
⅓ cup (2 oz.)	Flour Blend #2
¼ cup (1 oz.)	Flour Blend #4
3 tablespoons (1.5 oz.)	Butter
⅓ cup (2.7 oz.)	Brown sugar, packed
1 ea.	Egg
¼ teaspoon	Vanilla extract
½ cup (2 oz.)	Old-fashioned oats, gluten free
2 tablespoons (21 g)	Flour Blend #1

1. Preheat oven to 350°F.
2. For the filling, combine the condensed milk, chocolate chips, butter, and vanilla in a small saucepan.
3. Stir over medium heat until fully melted and blended. Set aside.
4. For the cookies, combine salt, baking soda, and flour blends in a small bowl and blend together with a whisk. Set aside.
5. In a separate bowl, cream butter and brown sugar together until smooth.
6. Add egg and vanilla gradually, scraping down the side of the bowl as necessary.
7. Add the dry ingredient mixture to the creamed mixture and blend until just combined. Stir in the oats.

8. Lightly grease a 9" × 9" baking dish and flour with Flour Blend #1. Using lightly moistened hands, press two-thirds of the cookie mixture evenly into the bottom of the prepared pan.

9. Spread the chocolate mixture over the top of the cookie mixture.

10. Taking small pieces of the remaining one-third of the cookie mixture, press them onto the top of the chocolate filling. There will not be enough to cover the entire surface and some chocolate will show.

11. Bake for about 20 minutes or until the top is lightly browned. Allow to cool completely before cutting and unmolding.

NUTRITIONAL INFORMATION PER SERVING

SERVING SIZE: 1 bar	**SODIUM:** 130mg	**DIETARY FIBER:** 2g
CALORIES: 250cal	**TOTAL CARBOHYDRATE:** 36g	**PROTEIN:** 4g
TOTAL FAT: 11g		

Toffee Bars

Butter, brown sugar, and vanilla combine in this recipe to create a rich toffee flavor. A hint of cinnamon in the batter highlights the toffee's warm golden taste. Complemented by the final addition of melted chocolate chips and toasted almonds, these toffee bars are perfectly decadent.

YIELD: ONE 9" × 9" BAKING PAN (NINE SERVINGS)

1 cup (8 oz.)	Butter, softened
1 cup (7.75 oz.)	Brown sugar, packed
1 ea.	Egg yolk
2 teaspoons	Vanilla extract
1½ cups (9 oz.)	Flour Blend #3
¼ teaspoon	Salt
½ teaspoon	Cinnamon
2 tablespoons (21 g)	Flour Blend #1
½ cup + 1 tablespoon	Semisweet chocolate chips
½ cup (2.5 oz.)	Sliced almonds, toasted

1. Preheat oven to 350°F.
2. Cream butter and brown sugar together until light and fluffy.
3. Blend in egg yolk and vanilla, scraping down the side of the bowl as necessary.
4. In a separate bowl, sift together flour blend, salt, and cinnamon. Blend the sifted flour mixture into the wet ingredients until just combined.
5. Lightly grease a 9" × 9" baking dish and dust with Flour Blend #1. Spread the batter in the prepared pan in an even layer.
6. Bake for 20 to 25 minutes, or until edges are golden brown and center is somewhat firm.
7. Remove the product from the oven, sprinkle on the chocolate chips, and return to the oven just until the chocolate is completely melted, about 5 minutes.
8. Spread the chocolate evenly and sprinkle with the toasted almonds.
9. Allow the product to cool in the pan completely before cutting and unmolding.

NUTRITIONAL INFORMATION PER SERVING

SERVING SIZE: 1 bar	SODIUM: 135mg	DIETARY FIBER: 4g
CALORIES: 500cal	TOTAL CARBOHYDRATE: 54g	PROTEIN: 8g
TOTAL FAT: 31g		

Cannoli Shells

The foundation of the famous Sicilian pastry, this recipe for gluten-free cannoli shells creates a fried tube that is sweet and crisp; once cooked and cooled, begging to be filled with the traditional milky rich cannoli cream, these bite-sized pastries may not last long . . .

YIELD: 14 SHELLS

¼ cup (1.5 oz.)	Flour Blend #1
¼ cup + 1 tablespoon (1.65 oz.)	Flour Blend #2
¼ cup + 1 tablespoon (1.65 oz.)	Flour Blend #3
¼ cup (2 oz.)	Whole milk
¼ cup (2 oz.)	Sparkling water
½ teaspoon	Fresh orange peel
1 teaspoon	Vanilla extract
¼ teaspoon	Cinnamon
½ tablespoon (7 g)	Sugar
2 tablespoons (21 g)	Flour Blend #1
2 cups (16 oz.)	Canola oil, for frying
As needed	Egg Wash (page 197)

1. Mix all dry and wet ingredients (except egg wash and Flour Blend #1) together with a paddle or by hand.
2. Roll out dough to ⅛" thick and cut to a 3" to 4" diameter using Flour Blend #1 for dusting. Pierce the dough round twice with a fork.
3. Wrap dough around the cannoli tube (a round, open metal tube) and glue edges together with egg wash.
4. Place tubes into a fryer at 350°F for 2½ minutes.
5. Remove tubes from dough and fry for another 1 minute at 350°F.
6. Let cool.

NUTRITIONAL INFORMATION PER SERVING

SERVING SIZE: 1 shell	SODIUM: 10mg	DIETARY FIBER: 0g
CALORIES: 180cal	TOTAL CARBOHYDRATE: 8g	PROTEIN: 1g
TOTAL FAT: 16g		

Cannoli Filling

Exceptionally light and creamy, Impastada ricotta cheese is the ideal choice for this Italian pastry filling. Sweetened with sugar, vanilla, and a hint of orange zest, this delicate cheese mixture when contained in a crisp outer shell is sensational.

YIELD: ENOUGH FOR APPROX. 14 SHELLS

3 cups (1 lb.)	Impastada ricotta cheese
½ cup (2.5 oz.)	Powdered sugar
2 teaspoons	Vanilla extract
½ teaspoon	Orange zest
14 ea.	Cannoli Shells (see page 137)

1. Mix together all ingredients except for shells.
2. Fill a pastry bag with filling.
3. Fill shells with filling (about 1.14 oz. or about ¼ cup each shell).

NUTRITIONAL INFORMATION PER SERVING

SERVING SIZE: 1.14 oz.	SODIUM: 25mg	DIETARY FIBER: 0g
CALORIES: 70cal	TOTAL CARBOHYDRATE: 5g	PROTEIN: 4g
TOTAL FAT: 4g		

Éclairs

Éclairs are a delicious staple in many French patisseries and you can easily make them a staple in your own home! Pâte à choux is piped into an oblong shape, then baked and filled with a smooth sweet pastry cream before being topped with a thin layer of chocolate ganache.

YIELD: SIX ÉCLAIRS

One recipe	Pâte à Choux, baked into éclair shells (page 228)
One-half recipe (14 oz.)	Pastry Cream (page 140)
One-half recipe	Chocolate Ganache (page 141)

1. After the shells have completely cooled, slice each in half lengthwise.
2. Fill a pastry bag fitted with a large (#4) star tip with the pastry cream. Using the tip of a paring knife, create two holes 1" apart along the bottom of the shell. Pipe the pastry cream into each hole, until the shell feels heavy and full.
3. Dip the éclair shell tops in warm chocolate ganache and place on top of the pâte à choux shell bottom. Place in refrigerator for 15 minutes before serving.

NUTRITIONAL INFORMATION PER SERVING		
SERVING SIZE: 1 pâte à choux shell with pastry cream and chocolate ganache	CALORIES: 400cal TOTAL FAT: 25g SODIUM: 280mg TOTAL CARBOHYDRATE: 38g	DIETARY FIBER: 2g PROTEIN: 8g

Pate a choux, the dough used to make the éclair shell, should have a smooth, spreadable consistency before baking.

Pastry Cream

This recipe creates a smooth sweet pastry cream, with a texture, flavor, and subtly rich color that make it an ideal standard filling. From éclairs to the traditional cream puff, this pastry cream is an essential element in the completion of countless puff pastry recipes.

YIELD: APPROXIMATELY 3 CUPS (28 OUNCES)

3 ea.	Egg yolk
2 cups (16 oz.)	Milk, divided
½ cup (4 oz.)	Sugar, divided
5 tablespoons (1.5 oz.)	Cornstarch
3 tablespoons (1.5 oz.)	Butter
½ teaspoon	Vanilla extract

1. Whisk together the eggs, ½ cup milk, ¼ cup sugar, and the cornstarch in a medium bowl. Set aside.
2. Combine remaining milk and remaining sugar in a saucepan and bring to a boil over moderate heat.
3. Add approximately one-fourth of the heated milk mixture to the egg mixture, adding it in four parts and whisking constantly to combine.
4. Add the egg-milk mixture to the remaining simmering milk mixture in the saucepan on the stove all at once; continue whisking until it comes to a boil and begins to thicken. Remove the pan from the heat.
5. Stir in the butter and vanilla extract.
6. Pour the pastry cream into a wide shallow pan and cover surface with plastic wrap, pressing it to the surface of the cream to prevent the formation of a skin.
7. Allow the pastry cream to cool completely in the refrigerator before using as a filling for pastries such as pâte à choux puffs or éclairs.
8. Stir or whisk cooled cream before using.

NUTRITIONAL INFORMATION PER SERVING		
SERVING SIZE: 2 tablespoons (1 oz.)	TOTAL FAT: 2.5g	DIETARY FIBER: 0g
	SODIUM: 15mg	PROTEIN: 1g
CALORIES: 50cal	TOTAL CARBOHYDRATE: 6g	

Chocolate Ganache

Ganache is a French term that refers to a smooth combination of chocolate and heavy cream. As with the Sacher cake, ganache is often used as an icing or glaze; it is also a common filling for cakes and other pastries, or can be chilled and scooped to create truffles.

YIELD: 12 OUNCES

½ cup	Heavy cream
1¼ cups	Bittersweet chocolate chips

1. In a small pot, bring the cream to a boil.
2. Remove from heat and pour over the chocolate chips in a medium bowl; allow to sit undisturbed for 30 to 60 seconds to soften the chocolate.
3. Stir in small vigorous circles in the center until the chocolate has combined with the cream, then stir in larger circles until completely combined.

NUTRITIONAL INFORMATION PER SERVING

SERVING SIZE: 1 oz. SODIUM: 5mg DIETARY FIBER: 1g
CALORIES: 121cal TOTAL CARBOHYDRATE: 12g PROTEIN: 1g
TOTAL FAT: 8.5g

Bread Pudding

These puddings will warm you through and through. With a little chocolate and a cinnamon rum sauce to finish, this recipe makes a dessert that is both maturely rich and feel-good cozy.

YIELD: ONE 9" × 9" PAN (NINE SERVINGS)

2½ cups (8 oz.)	Gluten-free Egg Bread (page 61), cut into 1" cubes
4 tablespoons (2 oz.)	Butter, melted
½ cup	Semisweet chocolate chips
1⅛ cups	Half-and-half
½ cup (4 oz.)	Sugar
3 ea.	Eggs
2 ea.	Egg yolks
1 tablespoon	Vanilla extract
Pinch	Salt
1 tablespoon (14 g)	Brown sugar
½ cup (4 oz.)	Cinnamon Rum Sauce (page 148)

1. Heavily grease pan.
2. Put cut egg bread in a bowl. Pour ¼ cup of melted butter over the bread and toss to coat. Add chocolate chips and set aside.
3. Prepare custard by combining the half-and-half, sugar, eggs, egg yolks, vanilla, and salt in a bowl and whisking to combine. Transfer to baking pan.
4. Let bread soak in custard for 30 minutes, pressing the bread down into the liquid occasionally. At this point, the pudding can be covered and refrigerated for one day, if desired.
5. When ready to bake, preheat oven to 350°F.
6. Sprinkle product with brown sugar.
7. Bake until puffed, brown, and set in the center, about 20 minutes.
8. Cool for 1 hour. Serve while still warm with Cinnamon Rum Sauce.

NUTRITIONAL INFORMATION PER SERVING

SERVING SIZE: 1 piece	SODIUM: 340mg	DIETARY FIBER: 1g
CALORIES: 350cal	TOTAL CARBOHYDRATE: 37g	PROTEIN: 6g
TOTAL FAT: 20g		

Apple Turnovers

If you enjoy warm apple pie, then you are sure to love these apple turnovers, which are basically convenient single servings of the American favorite—pastry cream is a sweet twist on the classic. These pair well with a dollop of whipped cream or vanilla ice cream.

YIELD: FOUR TURNOVERS

One recipe (24 oz.)	3-2-1 Pie Dough, uncooked (page 195)
⅓ cup (2.7 oz.)	Brown sugar
⅓ cup (2 oz.)	Flour Blend #1
1 teaspoon	Cinnamon
5 cups (1 lb. 8 oz.)	Apples, tart, peeled and cut into small dice or 1½ cups dried apples
½ cup (4.7 oz.)	Pastry Cream (page 140)
As needed	Egg Wash (page 197)

1. Preheat oven to 375°F.
2. Divide the pie dough into four equal parts. On a work surface lightly dusted with flour, roll out each portion into an 8"-diameter circle.
3. Whisk together the brown sugar, Flour Blend #1, and cinnamon. Toss together with the diced apples and mix in the pastry cream.
4. Divide the filling evenly among the four circles of dough, placing it in the center of each. Lightly brush the edges of each circle with egg wash.
5. Fold over each of the dough circles to completely encase the filling. Crimp the edge of each turnover with the tines of a fork.
6. Lightly brush the top of each turnover with egg wash and cut vents in the top with a sharp paring knife.
7. Place the turnovers on a baking sheet lined with a piece of parchment and bake for 20 to 30 minutes or until the crust is golden brown.

NUTRITIONAL INFORMATION PER SERVING

SERVING SIZE: 1 turnover **SODIUM:** 105mg **DIETARY FIBER:** 6g
CALORIES: 860cal **TOTAL CARBOHYDRATE:** 126g **PROTEIN:** 13g
TOTAL FAT: 37g

Apple Strudel

Strudels are usually associated with Austrian cuisine, and this recipe is no different. The dough is made in the way strudel dough was originally made, spread so thinly that it is transparent. Purists believe the dough should be so thin that a newspaper can be read through it. Just remember to be very gentle with this fragile dough.

YIELD: 4 SERVINGS

Strudel batter:

2 tablespoons (17 g)	Flour Blend #3
2 tablespoons (17 g)	Flour Blend #5
⅛ cup + 1½ teaspoons (1.25 oz.)	Water
pinch	Salt
1 teaspoon	Vegetable oil

Filling:

1½ cups (7 oz.)	Apples, peeled, cored and thinly sliced
¼ cup (1.2 oz.)	Gluten-free bread crumbs
½ teaspoon	Cinnamon
2 tablespoons (21 g)	Raisins
⅛ cup + 1 tablespoon (1.5 oz.)	Granulated sugar

Finishing:

5 tablespoons (2.5 oz.)	Melted butter
1 tablespoon (14 g)	Sugar
1 tablespoon (7 g)	Powdered sugar

1. Preheat oven to 375°F.
2. In a bowl, mix all of the batter ingredients together using a rubber spatula until smooth.
3. In a separate bowl, mix all filling ingredients together until well combined. Reserve.
4. Lay a silicone baking mat directly on the table and spread the batter into a thin transparent layer about 10½" × 10½".

5. Pre-bake the dough in the oven at for 3 minutes or until it releases from the silicone mat. If there are any holes or thin spots, patch them with a little more batter and put the tray back in the oven for one more minute.

6. Carefully remove the dough from the silicone mat and transfer the sheet of dough onto a piece of parchment paper or aluminum foil.

7. Lay the filling on the dough and cut away the excess dough, leaving a one-inch border.

8. Brush the edges of the dough with melted butter. Fold the border inward and roll the strudel up.

9. Finish by brushing with the melted butter and sprinkling with sugar.

10. Using the parchment paper (or foil) underneath, transfer the strudel to a sheet pan lined with parchment paper.

11. Bake in a 400°F oven for 15 to 17 minutes until the exterior takes on some brown color on either end.

12. Let the strudel cool and dust it with powdered sugar before slicing into 2-inch wide pieces and serving.

NUTRITIONAL INFORMATION PER SERVING		
SERVING SIZE: 1 slice (approximately 7 oz.) CALORIES: 173cal	TOTAL FAT: 6g SODIUM: 144mg TOTAL CARBOHYDRATE: 27g	DIETARY FIBER: 2g PROTEIN: 3g

Plated Dessert

(BLACK BOTTOM CAKE WITH CHERRY COMPOTE)

Assume the role of pastry chef by assembling this simple plated dessert that will showcase your work, making it appear as impressive as it tastes. With attention to color, texture, and height, you can present a finished plated dessert that will rival the professionals'.

YIELD: ONE PLATE (DUPLICATE AS NEEDED FOR NUMBER OF GUESTS)

1 cookie	Shortbread (page 104)
1 square	Cream Cheese Brownie (page 128)
1 scoop	Ice cream (any gluten-free ice cream of your choosing)
As needed	Fruit Compote (page 147)
1 piece	Tuile (page 122)

1. Place shortbread on a plate and top with the slightly warmed brownie.
2. Add a scoop of ice cream.
3. Top with some compote and garnish with a tuile.

NUTRITIONAL INFORMATION PER SERVING

SERVING SIZE: 1 plate	SODIUM: 459mg	DIETARY FIBER 4g
CALORIES: 1005cal	TOTAL CARBOHYDRATE: 141g	PROTEIN: 13g
TOTAL FAT: 31g		

Fruit Compote

Raspberries, blueberries, cherries . . . take your pick of frozen berries to cook with cornstarch and water, thickening to produce a slightly sweetened fruit compote. Serve this fruit compote along with cakes, ice cream, pancakes, or even savory cooked meats to add complementary flavor and color to your dishes.

YIELD: 12 TWO-OUNCE SERVINGS

2 cups (11 oz.)	Frozen berries, any kind, brought to room temperature
1 tablespoon (14 g)	Sugar
1 tablespoon (8.5 g)	Cornstarch
¼ cup (2 oz.)	Juice/water

1. Drain and reserve juices of berries.
2. Combine berries and sugar.
3. In a separate bowl, combine cornstarch and berry juice.
4. Add cornstarch mixture to berries and cook over low heat until thickened.
5. Remove one-third of the mixture and purée.
6. Add puréed portion back to the mixture; stir to combine.

NUTRITIONAL INFORMATION PER SERVING

SERVING SIZE: 2 oz.	SODIUM: 39mg	DIETARY FIBER: 2g
CALORIES: 369cal	TOTAL CARBOHYDRATE: 56g	PROTEIN: 1g
TOTAL FAT: 0g		

Cinnamon Rum Sauce

Dark and rich in color and flavor, the aroma of this sauce as it cooks is nearly as indulgent as the flavor of it once finished. The full, brown-sugar-cinnamon-spiced rum flavor is the perfect complement to bread puddings; if desired, this sauce may also be served with vanilla sponge cake, pound cake, or pumpkin bread.

YIELD: APPROXIMATELY 2¼ CUPS (10 OUNCES)

½ cup (4 oz.)	Butter
½ cup (3.75 oz.)	Dark brown sugar
½ teaspoon	Cinnamon
Pinch	Salt
¼ cup (2 oz.)	Dark rum
¼ teaspoon	Vanilla extract

1. Melt butter in a small saucepan over medium-low heat.
2. Add sugar, cinnamon, and salt and whisk until sugar is dissolved and mixture is smooth and bubbling.
3. Add rum and vanilla. Mix for 1½ minutes over heat to burn off a little of the alcohol and thicken. Remove from heat and stir to finish combining.
4. May be made two days ahead, covered, and refrigerated. Rewarm over low heat before serving over bread pudding.

NUTRITIONAL INFORMATION PER SERVING

SERVING SIZE: 1oz.	SODIUM: 160mg	DIETARY FIBER: 0g
CALORIES: 140cal	TOTAL CARBOHYDRATE: 10g	PROTEIN: 0g
TOTAL FAT: 9g		

Madeleines

Inspired by the delicious soft French cookie, this gluten-free version captures the wonderful texture, lightness, and flavor of the original.

YIELD: 25 COOKIES

¾ cup (6 oz.)	Sugar
2 tablespoons (1 oz.)	Brown sugar
13 tablespoons (6.5 oz.)	Butter
4 ea.	Eggs
¼ teaspoon	Salt
½ teaspoon	Vanilla extract
½ teaspoon	Baking powder
½ teaspoon	Lemon zest
¾ cup (4.5 oz.)	Flour Blend #1
¼ cup + 1 tablespoon (1.75 oz.)	Flour Blend #3
4 tablespoons (2 oz.)	Butter, melted
2 tablespoons (21 g)	Flour Blend #1 for dusting

1. Preheat oven to 350°F.
2. In a large bowl cream the sugar, brown sugar, and butter together using a mixer.
3. While mixing, slowly add the eggs one at a time, along with salt and the vanilla extract.
4. Add the dry ingredients, including the lemon zest, and mix just until incorporated.
5. Cover the mixture and store in the refrigerator to rest for one hour.
6. Prepare the Madeleine mold by brushing it with melted butter and dusting it with Flour Blend #1.
7. Place in the oven for 12 minutes, until lightly golden brown.
8. Transfer mold to wire rack and allow to cool.

NUTRITIONAL INFORMATION PER SERVING
. . . .

SERVING SIZE: 1 cookie   SODIUM: 60mg   DIETARY FIBER: 0g
CALORIES: 120cal   TOTAL CARBOHYDRATE: 14g   PROTEIN: 1g
TOTAL FAT: 7g

Chapter 7

Cakes

*Y*es, you can make a good gluten-free cake, even a fancy one! Now that you have the recipes in this book, the world is your oyster (or opera, since the subject here is fancy cakes). Cakes come in lots of varieties, from very moist ones with lots of sugar to light and dry torte-style cakes that are assembled into layers with moist fillings, compacted together, and sometimes coated with chocolate glaze or icing, as in the above-mentioned opera cake. In the pages that follow, you will find gluten-free versions of everything from the classic and classy Sacher torte to potluck favorites like pineapple upside-down cake.

You'll see that the gluten-free pound cake recipe requires whipping some egg whites to lighten it up. You can use slices of this cake to make a very nice strawberry shortcake dessert.

Sponge cake is a versatile gluten-free recipe that can be made into tortes or jelly rolls: it is still a somewhat complicated affair, requiring the warm foaming method (see page 34). You will need to set aside an hour for all the steps. Once baked, it comes out light and dry, with that unique spongy texture that begs for layering with moist fillings.

Dave's gluten-free pumpkin spice cake is moist and delicious on its own or as cup-cakes—you could top them with streusel and have them for breakfast. When you add the crunchy chocolate nut base and cream cheese frosting to the pumpkin cake, it is sinful. And speaking of sin, there is a rich, delectable devil's food cake that will fulfill the needs of any chocoholic, gluten-free or otherwise.

If you have never baked a cake from scratch before, try using one of the simpler reci-pes the first time, such as velvet cake. Once you gain more experience and confidence, you'll be ready to try something more complicated. The best litmus test for a gluten-free item is to serve it to a group that includes people who are not on the gluten-free diet. At the next birthday party, whip something up from this chapter and pass it out to your guests. You won't have to tell them it's gluten free, and they won't notice the difference, unless they see that you're eating a piece.

Pound Cake

A new take on the recipe known for its classic ratio of a pound of butter to a pound of sugar to a pound of flour. Whether it's paired with coffee in the morning or served after dinner, this pound cake weighs in at the top of the list.

YIELD: TWO STANDARD 8" × 4" × 2¾" LOAVES (20 SERVINGS)

9 tablespoons (4.5 oz.)	Butter, softened
⅝ cups (5 oz.)	Sugar
2 ea.	Eggs
¼ teaspoon (¼ teaspoon)	Vanilla extract
⅓ cup (2 oz.)	Flour Blend #1
⅔ cup (4.5 oz.)	Flour Blend #3
¼ teaspoon	Salt
¼ cup (2 oz.)	Milk
3 ea.	Egg whites
¼ cup (2 oz.)	Sugar

1. Preheat oven to 375°F.
2. Spray loaf pans with cooking spray.
3. Cream together the butter and ⅝ cup sugar on medium speed.
4. Gradually add the eggs and vanilla; scrape down the side of the bowl as needed.
5. Reduce to low speed and add flour blends and salt; scrape bowl again.
6. Gradually pour in milk. Set mixture aside.
7. In a separate bowl, whip egg whites and remaining sugar (¼ cup) to medium peaks. Fold the meringue into the creamed mixture.
8. Pour into prepared pans. Bake for 1 hour or until golden brown on top.
9. Cool on a rack for 10 minutes; unmold to cool completely.

NUTRITIONAL INFORMATION PER SERVING

SERVING SIZE: 1 slice	SODIUM: 60mg	DIETARY FIBER: 0g
CALORIES: 120cal	TOTAL CARBOHYDRATE: 17g	PROTEIN: 2g
TOTAL FAT: 6g		

Sour Cream Coffee Cake

Dawn may look a little brighter with this cake waiting in the kitchen. Created for the morning, this gluten-free coffee cake is moistened with sour cream and sprinkled with a streusel topping to finish. For coffee and non-coffee drinkers alike, this cake will please anyone with a sweet tooth.

YIELD: ONE 9" – 10" BUNDT PAN (12 SERVINGS)

8 tablespoons (4 oz.)	Butter
½ cup (4 oz.)	Sugar
2 ea.	Eggs
⅓ cup +1 tablespoon (2.5 oz.)	Flour Blend #1
1⅓ cups (8 oz.)	Flour Blend #3
1¾ teaspoons	Baking powder
1 teaspoon	Baking soda
½ teaspoon	Salt
1 cup (8 oz.)	Sour cream
3 cups (Double recipe)	Streusel Topping (page 199)

1. Preheat oven to 350°F.
2. Cream together the butter and the sugar.
3. Add the eggs and scrape down the side of the bowl as needed.
4. Add flour blends, baking powder, baking soda, and salt, and blend thoroughly.
5. Add the sour cream and blend until smooth.
6. Fill Bundt pan with batter. Sprinkle streusel topping on top and swirl in with a toothpick.
7. Bake for 40 to 50 minutes, or until a toothpick inserted into the center comes out clean.

NUTRITIONAL INFORMATION PER SERVING

SERVING SIZE: 1 slice	SODIUM: 330mg	DIETARY FIBER: 2g
CALORIES: 360cal	TOTAL CARBOHYDRATE: 46g	PROTEIN: 5g
TOTAL FAT: 19g		

Butter Kuchen

*The German word for cake, Kuchen, is also used to describe a specific baked good—a type of cof-
feecake, often made with the addition of fruit and nuts. This butter kuchen recipe adds bittersweet
chocolate, hazelnuts, and dried cherries; you can serve this cake at breakfast or just as appropriately
as a dessert.*

YIELD: ONE 9" – 10" BUNDT PAN (EIGHT SERVINGS)

7 tablespoons (3.5 oz.)	Butter, softened
½ cup (4 oz.)	Sugar
2 ea.	Eggs
1½ cups (5.25 oz.)	Hazelnuts, ground
⅓ cup + 1 tablespoon	Bittersweet chocolate chips
1¼ teaspoon	Baking powder
½ teaspoon	Cinnamon
2½ teaspoons (6 g)	Cocoa powder, unsweetened
¼ cup + 2 tablespoons (2 oz.)	Flour Blend #3
¾ cup (2.5 oz.)	Cherries, pitted, dried (optional)

1. Preheat oven to 325°F.
2. Whip butter and sugar with whip.
3. Add eggs, one by one. Scrape and whip with each addition.
4. Incorporate ground hazelnuts, bittersweet chocolate, baking powder, cinnamon, cocoa powder, and flour blend, then add cherries if desired.
5. Fill greased Bundt pan.
6. Bake for about 45 minutes.

NUTRITIONAL INFORMATION PER SERVING

SERVING SIZE: 1 slice	SODIUM: 90mg	DIETARY FIBER: 3g
CALORIES: 350cal	TOTAL CARBOHYDRATE: 31g	PROTEIN: 6g
TOTAL FAT: 25g		

Chocolate Banana Bundt Cake

In this recipe, chocolate and banana pair up to add new sweetness to a classic Bundt cake. Swirled together, the banana and chocolate batters add both flavor and visual appeal to the already elegant, molded cake; set on a stand, this cake is sure to impress dinner party guests.

YIELD: ONE CAKE (EIGHT SERVINGS)

1½ cups (9 oz.)	Flour Blend #1
2 teaspoons	Baking powder
¼ teaspoon	Baking soda
¼ teaspoon	Salt
12 tablespoons (6 oz.)	Butter
1¼ cups (10 oz.)	Sugar
3 ea.	Bananas, mashed
1 teaspoon	Vanilla extract
3 ea.	Eggs
6 tablespoons (3 oz.)	Buttermilk
½ cup + 1 tablespoon	Bittersweet chocolate, melted

1. Preheat oven to 350°F.
2. Generously grease a Bundt pan.
3. In a medium bowl, whisk the flour blend, baking powder, baking soda, and salt until well blended. Set aside.
4. With a paddle, beat the butter, sugar, bananas, and vanilla until well blended; scrape down the sides of the bowl as needed.
5. Add the eggs, one at a time, beating until just incorporated.
6. Remove the bowl from the mixer. With a rubber spatula, alternately add half the flour mixture, all the buttermilk, and the rest of the flour mixture, stirring until each addition is just blended.
7. Spoon half the batter into a medium bowl and gently stir in the melted chocolate until just combined.

8. With a large spoon, alternately add a scoopful of each batter (chocolate and non-chocolate) to the prepared pan, working around the pan until all the batter is used.

9. Gently run the tip of a spoon through the batter, once clockwise and once counterclockwise, to slightly swirl the batters.

10. Bake until done, about 60 to 70 minutes.

NUTRITIONAL INFORMATION PER SERVING		
SERVING SIZE: 1 slice	SODIUM: 270mg	DIETARY FIBER: 2g
CALORIES: 390cal	TOTAL CARBOHYDRATE: 47g	PROTEIN: 4g
TOTAL FAT: 24g		

Blueberry Buckle

This buckle is made by incorporating blueberries into a cakelike bottom layer that is topped off with a sugary, gluten-free crumb topping. Simple and deliciously rustic, each juicy bite of this blueberry buckle is likely to call to mind the taste of summer.

YIELD: ONE 9" × 9" PAN (NINE SERVINGS)

½ cup + 1⅓ tablespoons (5.3 oz.)	Sugar
6 tablespoons (3 oz.)	Butter, softened
1 ea.	Egg
1½ teaspoons	Vanilla extract
¼ cup (2 oz.)	Milk
⅝ cup (3.75 oz.)	Flour Blend #1
⅝ cup (3.5 oz.)	Flour Blend #2
1½ teaspoons	Baking powder
⅓ teaspoon	Salt
1¾ cups (9.25 oz.)	Blueberries

Crumb Topping:

¼ cup (2 oz.)	Butter, softened
¼ cup + 1 tablespoon (3 oz.)	Sugar
¼ cup (1.4 oz.)	Flour Blend #2
½ teaspoon	Cinnamon

1. Preheat oven to 350°F.
2. Spray a 9" × 9" pan with pan spray, line with waxed or parchment paper, and spray the paper. Set aside.
3. Cream the sugar and butter together in a mixing bowl with a paddle. Scrape down the sides of the bowl as necessary.
4. In a separate bowl, combine the egg, vanilla, and milk. Add the egg mixture slowly to the creamed butter mixture. Scrape the bowl as necessary.
5. Blend the dry ingredients together in a separate bowl.

6. Add half the dry ingredients to the wet ingredients and blend until combined. Add the other half and continue mixing on medium speed for 2 minutes.
7. Gently fold in the blueberries until incorporated.
8. Spread the batter evenly into the prepared pan. Set aside.
9. To make the crumb topping, mix all the topping ingredients with the mixer until just combined and crumbly. Sprinkle evenly on top of batter.
10. Bake for 50 minutes.

NUTRITIONAL INFORMATION PER SERVING		
SERVING SIZE: 1 slice	SODIUM: 160mg	DIETARY FIBER: less than 1g
CALORIES: 320cal	TOTAL CARBOHYDRATE: 51g	
TOTAL FAT: 14g		PROTEIN: 2g

Devil's Food Cake

An embodiment of the phrase "sinfully delicious," this devil's food cake is a union of rich, dark, elegant flavors that whisper of indulgence. Decorated with whipped cream, dark cherries, and chocolate shavings, this cake is a romantic addition on any occasion.

YIELD: ONE 6" CAKE (SIX SERVINGS)

1 tablespoon (11 g)	Flour Blend #1
2 tablespoons	Bittersweet chocolate chips
1 tablespoon (8.5 g)	Cocoa powder, sifted
⅓ cup (2.7 oz.)	Milk
¼ cup + 1 tablespoon (1.75 oz.)	Flour Blend #3
2 teaspoons	Baking soda
Pinch	Salt
4 tablespoons (2 oz.)	Butter, softened
¼ cup + 1 tablespoon (2.3 oz.)	Dark brown sugar
¼ teaspoon	Vanilla extract
1 ea.	Egg
3 tablespoons (1.5 oz.)	Sour cream
1 cup	Whipped cream
As needed	Shaved dark chocolate
⅓ cup (2 oz.)	Dark cherries

1. Preheat oven to 350°F.
2. Grease a 6" cake pan with cooking spray and dust with Flour Blend #1.
3. Combine chocolate chips and cocoa powder in a small bowl.
4. In a small pot, bring milk to a boil. Pour milk over chocolate and whisk until smooth; set aside.
5. Sift together flour blend, baking soda, and salt. Set aside.
6. Cream butter, sugar, and vanilla until light and fluffy. Gradually add egg.
7. Mix in sour cream on low speed until completely combined.
8. Alternately fold dry and wet ingredients into the creamed mixture, ending with dry ingredients.
9. Fill pan. Wet your hands and smooth the top of the batter after you've put it in the pan, or you could end up with an uneven looking top.

10. Bake for 20 to 30 minutes, or until a toothpick inserted in the center comes out with a few crumbs.

11. Cool upside down on rack before unmolding.

12. Garnish top and sides with whipped cream. Garnish top with dark cherries and chocolate shavings.

NUTRITIONAL INFORMATION PER SERVING		
SERVING SIZE: 1 slice	SODIUM: 660mg	DIETARY FIBER: 1g
CALORIES: 300cal	TOTAL CARBOHYDRATE: 23g	PROTEIN: 4g
TOTAL FAT: 23g		

Vanilla Sponge Cake

Nearly weightless, this blond vanilla sponge cake is a delicate and gentle sweet treat. Serve this cake with a bit of whipped cream and fresh berries for an airy summer dessert, or serve it plain paired with coffee or tea for a nice afternoon or post-meal snack. Note: The secret is in the whipping. This recipe employs the warm foam mixing method (see page 34). You will need to take extra care that it is whipped properly. This can be hard to judge, so make sure you are familiar with the warm foam mixing method before you get started.

YIELD: ONE 10" CAKE OR TWO 6" CAKES (12 SERVINGS)

9 ea.	Eggs
1 cup + 2 tablespoons (9 oz.)	Sugar
1½ cups (9 oz.)	Flour Blend #3
4 tablespoons (2 oz.)	Butter, melted (or oil)
½ teaspoon	Vanilla extract

1. Preheat oven to 325°F.
2. Grease and flour sides of desired pans and place a parchment paper round on the bottom of each pan. Set aside.
3. Combine eggs and sugar in a mixing bowl and heat over a hot water bath until eggs and sugar are warm, about 120°F.
4. Whip the eggs on high speed to maximum volume.
5. Stabilize mixture by whipping on second speed for 10 more minutes.
6. Sift the flour blend. Gradually fold sifted flour into mixture.
7. Stream in melted butter while folding and add the vanilla extract.
8. Fill prepared cake pans two-thirds full.
9. Bake until set, about 45 to 50 minutes. The cake should spring back when you press the center and the sides of the cake should have pulled away from the pan.
10. Let cake cool for 5 minutes in the pan. Then, if you've used a round pan, tilt it sideways and knock the pan, rotating as you go. Flip it over quickly and give it a good knock to get it to unmold. Finish cooling on a rack.

Variation: To make Chocolate Sponge Cake, replace ⅔ cup of the flour with ¾ cup Dutch-process cocoa powder.

NUTRITIONAL INFORMATION PER SERVING		
SERVING SIZE: 1 slice	SODIUM: 85mg	DIETARY FIBER: 1g
CALORIES: 230cal	TOTAL CARBOHYDRATE: 36g	PROTEIN: 7g
TOTAL FAT: 7g		

Trifle

Trifle, a traditional English sweet, is composed of cake layered with custard and fruit and topped with whipped cream. Though simple to make, this moist and fruity dish is seriously delicious.

YIELD: FIVE 8 OZ. SERVINGS

⅓ cake	Vanilla Sponge Cake (page 162)
¼ cup (2 oz.)	Simple Syrup (see page 165)
2 cups (18.7 oz.)	Pastry cream
As needed	Assorted fruit
1 cup	Whipped cream

1. Place a layer of sponge cake on the bottom of each glass and soak with simple syrup.
2. Add a layer of pastry cream.
3. Add a layer of fruit.
4. Top with whipped cream.

NUTRITIONAL INFORMATION PER SERVING

. . . .

SERVING SIZE: 8 oz.	**SODIUM:** 60mg	**DIETARY FIBER:** less
CALORIES: 290cal	**TOTAL CARBOHYDRATE:** 31g	than 1g
TOTAL FAT: 17g		**PROTEIN:** 5g

Simple Syrup

Boiling sugar and water creates a slightly viscous reduction known as simple syrup. Sometimes used to moisten baked cakes, simple syrup is also commonly found in coffee shops as a sweetening agent for drinks as well as being a common ingredient in bar-mixed alcoholic beverages.

YIELD: ONE CUP (8 OUNCES)

½ cup (4 oz.)	Sugar
½ cup (4 oz.)	Water

Bring sugar and water to a boil until sugar is fully dissolved, and remove from heat. Cool and store in refrigerator to room temperature.

NUTRITIONAL INFORMATION PER SERVING

· ·

SERVING SIZE: 1 table-spoon (½ ounce)
CALORIES: 28cal
TOTAL FAT: 0g

SODIUM: less than 1mg
TOTAL CARBOHYDRATE: less than 1g

DIETARY FIBER: 0g
PROTEIN: 0g

Black Bottom Cupcakes

While at first glance these cupcakes may look like standard fare, one bite is all it takes to realize that they are anything but. Filled rather than frosted, these cupcakes hide a creamy, chocolate-chip cream-cheese center inside each rich chocolate cake; it is no secret that these cupcakes are one of a kind.

YIELD: 12 SERVINGS

Cream Cheese Filling:

1 cup (8 oz.)	Cream cheese, softened
⅓ cup (2.7 oz.)	Sugar
Pinch	Salt
1 ea.	Egg
⅔ cup	Chocolate chips

Black Bottom Cupcakes:

2 tablespoons (21 g)	Flour Blend #1
1¼ cups (6.25 oz.)	Flour Blend #4
1 cup (8 oz.)	Sugar
⅓ cup (2.2 oz.)	Cocoa powder
1 teaspoon	Baking soda
½ teaspoon	Salt
1 cup (8 oz.)	Water
⅓ cup	Oil
1 tablespoon	Vinegar
1 teaspoon	Vanilla

1. Preheat oven to 350°F. Grease a muffin pan and flour with Flour Blend #1.
2. Cream the cream cheese, sugar, and salt in mixer bowl with the paddle attachment until completely smooth. Scrape down the bowl as necessary.
3. Add the egg and continue to cream until light in color.
4. Fold in the chocolate chips. Set aside.
5. Mix together the dry ingredients in a bowl. Mix wet ingredients together in a separate bowl. Pour the wet ingredients into the dry and blend until smooth.

6. Put about a tablespoon of cupcake batter into the bottom of each muffin cup.
7. Put a scoop of cream cheese filling on top of the batter, dividing the filling evenly between the 12 muffin cups.
8. Divide the rest of the chocolate batter on top.
9. Bake at 350°F for about 25 to 30 minutes, or until a skewer inserted near the center of a cupcake comes out with a few moist crumbs.

NUTRITIONAL INFORMATION PER SERVING
. . . .

SERVING SIZE: 1 cupcake   SODIUM: 200mg   DIETARY FIBER: 1g
CALORIES: 180cal   TOTAL CARBOHYDRATE: 30g   PROTEIN: 3g
TOTAL FAT: 6g

Carrot Cake

Vegetables have never tasted quite so delicious. Showcasing the natural sweetness of carrots, this cake adds the traditional walnuts and raisins for flavor and texture; finished with cream cheese frosting, this carrot cake is one serving of veggies that will leave you wanting seconds.

YIELD: TWO 6" CAKES (12 SERVINGS)

3 cups (12 oz.)	Carrots, grated
¼ cup (2 oz.)	Sugar
4 tablespoons (2 oz.)	Butter
⅔ cup (4.3 oz.)	Flour Blend #2
1 teaspoon	Baking powder
½ teaspoon	Baking soda
½ teaspoon	Cinnamon
¼ teaspoon	Salt
3 tablespoons (1.5 oz)	Sugar
⅓ cup (2.7 oz.)	Light brown sugar
5 ea.	Eggs, separated
1 teaspoon	Vanilla extract
¼ cup (2 oz.)	Milk
¼ cup (1.25 oz.)	Walnuts, chopped
¼ cup (1.5 oz.)	Raisins
As needed	Cream Cheese Filling (page 192), optional

1. Preheat oven to 350°F.
2. Toss grated carrots with ¼ cup granulated sugar and allow to set for 20 to 30 minutes. Drain off the liquid from the carrots by pressing the solids against the sides of a strainer and set aside.
3. Cook the butter in a small pot until all of the milk solids brown and the butter fat turns amber in color. Allow to cool to room temperature.
4. Sift flour blend, baking powder, baking soda, cinnamon, and salt together and set aside.
5. Whisk together the cooled brown butter, brown sugar, egg yolks, vanilla, and 3 tablespoons granulated sugar.

6. Alternately add the dry ingredients and milk to the butter-sugar-egg mixture and blend until just incorporated.
7. Add the drained carrots, walnuts, and raisins, mixing until just incorporated.
8. In a separate bowl, whisk the egg whites to soft peaks.
9. Stir in ¼ of the whipped egg whites, then gently fold in the rest of the whipped whites.
10. Divide batter evenly between 2 prepared pans.
11. Bake for 40 to 50 minutes or until center is firm when pressed.
12. Cool cakes completely on a wire rack before unmolding and topping with Cream Cheese Frosting (if desired).

NUTRITIONAL INFORMATION PER SERVING		
SERVING SIZE: 1 slice	SODIUM: 240mg	DIETARY FIBER: 1g
CALORIES: 340cal	TOTAL CARBOHYDRATE: 40g	PROTEIN: 6g
TOTAL FAT: 18g		

Assemble the carrot cake by alternating layers of frosting between the layers of cake.

Cream Cheese Frosting

A basic combination of three pure ingredients makes for a frosting that is rich, full, and exceptionally creamy. Use this cream cheese frosting to finish carrot cakes, pumpkin breads, chocolate cupcakes, or other products as you creatively see fit.

YIELD: 10 SERVINGS

4 tablespoons (2 oz.)	Butter, softened
½ cup (4 oz.)	Cream cheese, softened
1 cup (5 oz.)	Powdered sugar, sifted
1 teaspoon	Vanilla extract

1. Cream butter and cream cheese together until smooth.
2. Add in powdered sugar and vanilla. Mix until combined, scraping down occasionally.
3. Mix until completely combined. The longer you mix, the lighter and fluffier it will become.

NUTRITIONAL INFORMATION PER SERVING

SERVING SIZE: 2 tablespoons   SODIUM: 35mg   DIETARY FIBER: 0g

CALORIES: 120cal   TOTAL CARBOHYDRATE: 12g   PROTEIN: 1g

TOTAL FAT: 8g

Molten Chocolate Cakes

These individual cakes are intensely chocolate. Served still hot from the oven, they earn their "molten" title as they ooze rich, creamy chocolate from the core; these cakes may be garnished with powdered sugar, whipped cream, sauces, or ice cream, or simply served as they are for a powerful chocolate experience.

YIELD: SIX INDIVIDUAL CAKES

1 cup + 1 tablespoon	Semisweet chocolate chips
8 tablespoons (4 oz.)	Butter
¼ cup (2 oz.)	Milk
¼ cup	Heavy cream
4 ea.	Eggs
⅓ cup (3 oz.)	Sugar
⅔ cup (4.25 oz.)	Flour Blend #1

1. Preheat oven to 400°F.
2. Prepare six 6 oz. ramekins by spraying generously with cooking spray and sprinkling entire interior with sugar. Set aside.
3. Melt the chocolate and butter together over a hot water bath.
4. Bring milk and cream to a boil.
5. Once the chocolate and butter are melted, pour the hot milk/cream over the chocolate and stir until completely incorporated.
6. In a separate bowl, whisk the eggs and sugar together until smooth. Slowly add the chocolate mixture, stirring to incorporate completely. Add flour blend.
7. Portion 4 ounces of batter into each ramekin and place on a sheet pan.
8. Bake for 8 to 10 minutes or until tops are set but still spring back when touched; internal temperature should be 150° to 160°F. Unmold from ramekins and serve immediately.

NUTRITIONAL INFORMATION PER SERVING

SERVING SIZE: 1 cake	SODIUM: 55mg	DIETARY FIBER: 2g
CALORIES: 490cal	TOTAL CARBOHYDRATE: 48g	PROTEIN: 6g
TOTAL FAT: 33g		

Sacher Cake

This famous chocolate cake gets its name from Franz Sacher, a chef who at the age of sixteen, working as an apprentice in the kitchen of Prince Metternich of Austria, created this recipe on the spot during an evening when the head chef was home ill. Exceptionally rich in chocolate with thin layers of apricot jam spread between the cake, this is a recipe that promises to dazzle guests and delight taste buds.

YIELD: ONE 8" CAKE (SIX SERVINGS)

Cake:

⅔ cup (5.3 oz.)	Butter
⅔ cup (3.3 oz.)	Powdered sugar
3 ea.	Egg yolks
1 ea.	Egg
⅔ cup	Chocolate, melted
5 ea. (5 ea.)	Egg whites
¼ cup (2 oz.)	Sugar
¼ cup + 2 tablespoons (2 oz.)	Flour Blend #3
1½ cups (5.25 oz.)	Almonds, fine ground, toasted
As needed	Apricot jam
1½ cups (12 oz.)	Chocolate Ganache (page 141)

1. Preheat oven to 350°F.
2. Grease and flour sides of an 8" cake pan and place parchment paper round on the bottom. Set aside.
3. Combine butter and powdered sugar; cream together until smooth and light.
4. Gradually add egg yolks and whole egg scraping as necessary.
5. Add warm melted chocolate all at once and incorporate immediately, scraping as necessary.
6. In a separate bowl, whip egg whites and sugar to medium peaks. Gradually fold into creamed mixture by hand.
7. Combine Flour Blend #3 and nuts and gradually fold into creamed mixture by hand.

8. Pour into pan and bake until firm along entire top surface, about 55 to 60 minutes. Allow to cool, then slice cake in half horizontally and spread thin layer of apricot jam on bottom half, and replace top half. Coat top and sides with jam to seal cake.

9. Melting hard ganache over a hot water bath until it is spreadable. Glaze cake with ganache, then refrigerate until ganache is set firm.

NUTRITIONAL INFORMATION PER SERVING		
SERVING SIZE: 1 slice	SODIUM: 95mg	DIETARY FIBER: 4g
CALORIES: 840cal	TOTAL CARBOHYDRATE: 74g	PROTEIN: 14g
TOTAL FAT: 60g		

Opera Cake

Sometimes referred to as "Clichy Cake" honoring French Chef Louis Clichy, the supposed creator of the delicacy, opera cake is six layers of spongy cake and smooth chocolate ganache.

YIELD: ONE 9" × 9" CAKE (NINE SERVINGS)

Cake:

3 ea.	Eggs
⅔ cup (3.3 oz.)	Powdered sugar, sifted
3 ea. (3 ea.)	Egg whites
½ cup (4 oz.)	Sugar
1 cup (3 oz.)	Almond Flour
⅓ cup (2 oz.)	Flour Blend #3
2 tablespoons (1 oz.)	Butter, melted and cooled

Ganache:

1 cup + 1 tablespoon	Bittersweet chocolate chips
1 cup	Heavy cream
¼ teaspoon	Instant coffee powder
¼ cup (4 oz.)	Light corn syrup

Buttercream:

½ cup (4 oz.)	Sugar
2 ea.	Egg whites
1 cup (8 oz.)	Butter, softened
¼ teaspoon	Instant coffee powder

Coffee Syrup:

½ cup (4 oz.)	Brewed coffee
¼ cup (2 oz.)	Sugar

Cake:

1. Preheat oven to 375°F. Allow eggs and egg whites to sit at room temperature for 30 minutes.
2. Whip the whole eggs and powdered sugar together on high speed for 10 to 15 minutes.
3. In a separate bowl, whip together the egg whites and sugar to medium peaks.
4. Fold the two egg mixtures together gently, leaving the result a bit marbled.
5. Combine the dry ingredients and then fold them in until nearly combined, then stream in the cooled butter while folding.

6. Spray and flour three 9" × 9" pans. Divide batter between pans, smoothing tops.

7. Bake for 35 to 40 minutes or until firm.

8. Unmold from pans immediately and cool completely before assembling rest of cake.

Ganache:

1. Place chocolate in a heatproof bowl.

2. In a pan bring cream, coffee powder, and corn syrup to a boil; pour over chocolate.

3. Let mixture sit for 30 seconds, then stir vigorously until completely combined.

4. Set aside to firm up to a frosting-like consistency.

Buttercream:

1. Combine sugar and egg whites in a clean, dry mixer bowl. Heat over a barely simmering water bath, stirring constantly, until mixture reaches 140°F.

2. Place mixer bowl on mixer and whip until medium stiff peaks form and bowl is cool to the touch.

3. While mixer is on medium speed, blend in butter by tossing in small chunks at a time, allowing each addition to be completely blended before adding next chunk.

4. Dissolve coffee powder with 1 tablespoon hot water.

5. Once all the butter has been added, add coffee and mix on high speed until light and fluffy.

Coffee Syrup: Dissolve sugar in coffee.

Assembly:

1. To assemble the opera cake, place one jaconde cake on a plate, brush with the coffee syrup, and spread with half the ganache.

2. Set second cake on top of the ganache, brush with coffee syrup, and spread with all but ½ cup of the butter cream. Set third cake on buttercream and brush with syrup.

3. Spread a very thin layer of buttercream on top, and chill cake until all layers are firm, at least 1 hour.

4. In the meantime, warm the remaining ganache and stir until it is a thick glazing liquid.

5. Remove the cake from the refrigerator and glaze top with warmed ganache.

6. Chill to set ganache. Trim the sides to show the cake's layers.

7. Serve at room temperature.

NUTRITIONAL INFORMATION PER SERVING		
SERVING SIZE: 1 slice	SODIUM: 70mg	DIETARY FIBER: 2g
CALORIES: 630cal	TOTAL CARBOHYDRATE: 66g	PROTEIN: 6g
TOTAL FAT: 41g		

Rum Cake

Soaked in a signature flavor of the Caribbean, this slightly citrus-scented cake is one of the moistest cakes you may ever savor. The final rum-syrup-drizzled dessert is darkly sweet, a vacation from the ordinary.

YIELD: ONE 9" – 10" BUNDT PAN (EIGHT SERVINGS)

½ cup + 3 tablespoons (5.5 oz.)	Butter
1¼ cups (10 oz.)	Sugar
Pinch	Salt
1 teaspoon	Lemon zest
1 teaspoon	Orange zest
2 ea.	Eggs
4 ea.	Egg yolks
1¼ cups (7.5 oz.)	Flour Blend #1
1 teaspoon	Baking powder
½ cup (4 oz.)	Whole milk
½ cup (4 oz.)	Simple Syrup (page 165)
1 teaspoon	Rum

1. Preheat oven to 350°F.
2. Cream together butter, sugar, salt, and zests.
3. Allow eggs and yolks to come to room temperature; add yolks first and then whole eggs in three additions to the butter and sugar mixture.
4. Sift together flour blend and baking powder.
5. Add sifted flour mixture alternately with milk to the creamed mixture.
6. Fill greased Bundt pan.
7. Bake for about 40 to 50 minutes, or until a toothpick inserted in the center comes out clean.
8. Heat simple syrup and rum in a saucepan.
9. Cool cake in the pan for a few minutes, then invert onto a wire rack and soak with warm syrup.

NUTRITIONAL INFORMATION PER SERVING

SERVING SIZE: 1 slice	SODIUM: 230mg	DIETARY FIBER: 0g
CALORIES: 440cal	TOTAL CARBOHYDRATE: 65g	PROTEIN: 4g
TOTAL FAT: 20g		

Blueberry Almond Rum Cake

Add almonds to anything and you're in for a real treat, but when they are coupled with blueberries and a splash of rum, it's even better. This is a good summer dessert when the blueberries are in season and at the peak of their sweetness.

YIELD: ONE 9" × 9" PAN (NINE SERVINGS)

8 tablespoons (4 oz.)	Firmly packed almond paste
7 tablespoons (3.5 oz.)	Unsalted butter, room temperature
⅓ cup (2.7 oz.)	Sugar
3 ea.	Eggs, room temperature
¼ cup + 2 tablespoons (2 oz.)	Flour Blend #3
Pinch	Salt
¾ teaspoon	Vanilla extract
½ tablespoon	Rum
2 cups (11 oz.)	Fresh blueberries
¼ cup (1.25 oz.)	Pine nuts

1. Preheat oven to 325°F.
2. Put almond paste in mixing bowl with paddle and mix on medium-low speed until smooth.
3. Add room temperature butter. Cream together.
4. Add sugar, still mixing on medium-low speed.
5. Add eggs in two additions, allowing the first addition to come together before adding the second.
6. Add in all of the sifted flour and salt and mix on low speed.
7. Add in flavorings and mix until combined.
8. Take off mixer and use spatula to stir in blueberries.
9. Fill oiled pan three-fourths full and sprinkle pine nuts on top.
10. Bake for approximately 40 minutes or until tops are dark golden brown.

NUTRITIONAL INFORMATION PER SERVING

SERVING SIZE: 1 slice	SODIUM: 150mg	DIETARY FIBER: 2g
CALORIES: 270cal	TOTAL CARBOHYDRATE: 27g	PROTEIN: 5g
TOTAL FAT: 17g		

Pineapple Upside-Down Cake

The pineapple finds its way to the top of this gluten-free cake, regarded by many as a symbol of friendship and hospitality. Baked top side down, the final cake, once flipped, displays the recognizable layer of golden pineapple slices that give the upside-down cake its character.

YIELD: ONE 9" CAKE (EIGHT SERVINGS)

½ cup (4 oz.)	Butter
¼ cup + 1 tablespoon (2.3 oz.)	Brown sugar
4 ea.	Pineapple slices, ½" sliced rings
1 teaspoon	Baking powder
½ teaspoon	Salt
½ cup (3 oz.)	Flour Blend #1
½ cup (3 oz.)	Flour Blend #3
¾ cup (6 oz.)	Butter, softened
¾ cup (6 oz.)	Sugar
1 teaspoon	Vanilla extract
1 ea.	Egg
½ cup (4 oz.)	Milk

For the pan smear:

1. Melt the ½ cup butter and brown sugar together in a saucepan.
2. Pour into the bottom of a 9" cake pan.
3. Arrange pineapple slices in desired pattern in the pan smear. Set aside.

Cake:

1. Preheat oven to 375°F.
2. Sift together dry ingredients.
3. In mixer bowl, cream the ¾ cup butter and sugar until light and fluffy. Scrape down the bowl as necessary.
4. Add vanilla and egg and mix until completely combined. Scrape bowl.
5. Alternate adding dry ingredients and milk in three additions to the creamed mixture. Blend completely until no lumps remain.

6. Pour batter on top of pineapple and spread evenly.
7. Place on a sheet pan and bake for 30 minutes, or until a toothpick inserted in the center comes out clean.
8. Cool for 10 minutes. Invert a plate over the cake pan, and invert both cake and plate together. Remove pan carefully to avoid any escaping steam.

NUTRITIONAL INFORMATION PER SERVING		
SERVING SIZE: 1 slice	SODIUM: 220mg	DIETARY FIBER: less than 1g
CALORIES: 470cal	TOTAL CARBOHYDRATE: 49g	
TOTAL FAT: 30g		PROTEIN: 3g

Prepare the pan for the cake by layering pineapples and sugar syrup in the bottom.

Dave's Pumpkin Crunch Cake

Developed by Dave DeCesare, a 2004 Baking and Pastry graduate and current Executive Pastry Chef at Tastebudds Café in Redhook, NY, this pumpkin cake tastes of autumn. The familiar combination of nutmeg, clove, ginger, and cinnamon paired with pumpkin creates an earthy spice that is well balanced with the sharp sweetness of the cream cheese frosting. Set atop a crunchy base of chocolate and pecans, this layered cake is an original embodiment of the flavors of fall.

YIELD: TWO ASSEMBLED 6" CAKES (16 SERVINGS)

Spice Cake:

2 ea.	Eggs
1¼ cups (10 oz.)	Sugar
½ cup	Oil
1 cup (8.5 oz.)	Pumpkin purée
1½ teaspoons	Vanilla extract
1⅓ cups (8 oz.)	Flour Blend #1
¾ teaspoon	Baking soda
½ teaspoon	Baking powder
¼ teaspoon	Salt
¼ teaspoon	Cinnamon
⅛ teaspoon	Nutmeg
⅛ teaspoon	Cloves
⅛ teaspoon	Ginger

Crunchy Base:

¾ cup (¾ cup)	Semisweet chocolate chips, melted
1 cup (5 oz.)	Pecans, chopped

Cream Cheese Frosting: Double the recipe on page 170

Spice Cake:

1. Preheat oven to 350°F.
2. Whip eggs, sugar, and oil for 3 minutes. Scrape down the bowl as necessary.
3. Add pumpkin purée and vanilla; mix to combine.
4. In a separate bowl sift flour, baking soda, baking powder, salt, and spices. Add dry ingredients to pumpkin mixture.

Cheese Straws, page 226
Cheese Puffs, page 229

Opera Cake, page 174

Fruit Tart, page 209

Key Lime Pie, page 206

Velvet Cake, page 182

Pasta Dough, page 234

Beef Pot Pie, page 238

Pizza Crust, page 221

5. Spread evenly into two greased and floured 6" cake pans.
6. Bake for 30 minutes, or until toothpick inserted in the center comes out clean.
7. Allow cakes to cool completely in the pans before unmolding.

Crunchy Base:
1. Add pecans to melted chocolate and mix until completely incorporated.
2. Cut two 6" circles from waxed paper. Place one circle in the bottom of a 6" cake pan.
3. Spread entire mixture in the pan. Top with second waxed paper circle and flatten base into an even layer.
4. Refrigerate until firm. Unmold onto cake plate, removing all waxed paper, and set aside.

Assembly:
1. Lightly coat crunchy base with a very thin layer of frosting and place one cake layer on top.
2. Fill with cream cheese frosting and then put on top layer of cake.
3. Spread remaining cream cheese frosting on top of the cake. Decorate as desired.

NUTRITIONAL INFORMATION PER SERVING		
SERVING SIZE: 1 slice	SODIUM: 220mg	DIETARY FIBER: 2g
CALORIES: 480cal	TOTAL CARBOHYDRATE: 55g	PROTEIN: 4g
TOTAL FAT: 30g		

Velvet Cake

This moist chocolate layer cake, sometimes referred to as Red Velvet cake, is often recognizable by its reddish-brown coloring (often enhanced with red food coloring). The vinegar and the buttermilk in the recipe react to turn the cocoa powder a very slight reddish color. Popular in Southern cooking, this smooth cake is finished with a cream-cheese-based frosting.

YIELD: ONE 6" LAYERED CAKE (SIX SERVINGS)

4 tablespoons (2 oz.)	Butter
¾ cup (6 oz.)	Sugar
1 ea.	Egg
½ teaspoon	Vanilla extract
⅓ cup (2 oz.)	Flour Blend #1
½ cup + 1 tablespoon (3.25 oz.)	Flour Blend #3
4 teaspoons (11 g)	Cocoa powder
½ cup + 2 tablespoons (5 oz.)	Buttermilk
¾ teaspoon	Baking soda
¾ teaspoon	Vinegar
One recipe	Velvet Cake Frosting (page 183)

1. Preheat oven to 350°F.
2. Grease one 6" pan.
3. Beat butter on medium speed until fluffy. Gradually add sugar, beating well.
4. Add egg, beating until blended. Add vanilla and blend well.
5. In a separate medium bowl, combine flour blends and cocoa powder.
6. Add flour mixture to creamed shortening, alternating with buttermilk. After each addition, beat on low speed until blended.
7. Take off mixer and fold in baking soda and vinegar until combined.
8. Pour into prepared pan and bake for 20 to 25 minutes.
9. Cool completely before unmolding, cutting in half, and frosting.

NUTRITIONAL INFORMATION PER SERVING

. . . .

SERVING SIZE: 1 slice	**SODIUM:** 330mg	**DIETARY FIBER:** 3g
CALORIES: 650cal	**TOTAL CARBOHYDRATE:** 75g	**PROTEIN:** 8g
TOTAL FAT: 37g		

Velvet Cake Frosting

This cream-cheese-based white frosting is used to finish a velvet cake. While delicious and striking when spread in between the reddish velvet cake layers, this creamy and thick frosting may also be used to finish cupcakes or other cakes as your taste buds see fit.

YIELD: ENOUGH FOR ONE 6" LAYER CAKE (SIX SERVINGS)

1 cup (8 oz.)	Cream cheese, softened
1 stick (4 oz.)	Butter
1 cup (5 oz.)	Powdered sugar
1 teaspoon	Vanilla extract
3 tablespoons (1 oz.)	Cocoa powder

1. Cream the cream cheese and butter until light and fluffy.
2. Sift the sugar into the cream cheese mixture and blend thoroughly.
3. Add vanilla and cocoa powder and mix until combined.
4. Chill until needed, then whip to desired consistency.
5. Spread over completely cooled cake—one layer in between the two layers of cake and one on top.

NUTRITIONAL INFORMATION PER SERVING

SERVING SIZE: 1 serving
CALORIES: 370cal
TOTAL FAT: 29g

SODIUM: 115mg
TOTAL CARBOHYDRATE: 27g

DIETARY FIBER: 2g
PROTEIN: 4g

Cola Cake

Move aside, milk—in this recipe, cake has a new partner. The addition of cola to this moist chocolate cake lends a truly unique flavor hinting of nuts and caramel. Finished with a cola frosting, the marriage of soda and cake, while perhaps a child's dream come true, is sure to tickle the taste buds at any age.

YIELD: ONE 9" × 9" CAKE (NINE SERVINGS)

1 cup (8 oz.)	Butter, divided
½ cup + 1 tablespoon (5 oz.)	Cola
1 tablespoon	Semisweet chocolate chips
1 ea.	Egg white
1⅓ cups (7.25 oz.)	Flour Blend #4
⅓ cup + 1 tablespoon (2.5 oz.)	Cocoa powder
1 teaspoon	Baking powder
½ teaspoon	Baking soda
¼ teaspoon	Salt
1¼ cups (10 oz.)	Sugar
⅓ cup	Vegetable oil
1¼ teaspoons	Vanilla extract
1 ea.	Whole egg
1 ea.	Egg yolk
½ cup (4 oz.)	Buttermilk
One recipe	Chocolate Cola Frosting (page 186)

1. Preheat oven to 350°F.
2. In a small pot, bring 10 tablespoons butter, cola, and semisweet chocolate to a boil. Remove from heat and fold in egg whites; set aside.
3. Sift together the flour blend, cocoa powder, baking powder, baking soda, and salt; set aside.
4. Cream the sugar, ⅓ cup butter, oil, and vanilla until smooth.
5. Gradually add the whole egg, egg yolk, and buttermilk and beat until smooth.
6. Add half of the dry ingredients to the creamed mixture and beat until smooth. Scrape the sides of the bowl as needed.
7. Add the cooled cola mixture and beat until incorporated.
8. Add the remaining dry ingredient mixture and beat for 4 minutes. The batter will be thick.

9. Pour the batter into a prepared 9" square pan and place the pan onto a cookie sheet.

10. Bake for 35 to 40 minutes, or until a toothpick inserted in the center comes out clean.

11. Cool for 10 minutes on a wire rack. Frost with Chocolate Cola Frosting while still warm.

NUTRITIONAL INFORMATION PER SERVING		
SERVING SIZE: 1 slice	SODIUM: 260mg	DIETARY FIBER: 5g
CALORIES: 660cal	TOTAL CARBOHYDRATE: 81g	PROTEIN: 8g
TOTAL FAT: 38g		

Chocolate Cola Frosting

Here, chocolate and cola together create a sweet and playful flavor unlike that of any chocolate frosting to come before. Used to top the Cola Cake, this fun frosting may also be delicious creatively spread on cake or cupcakes of other flavors.

YIELD: ICING FOR ONE 9" × 9" CAKE (NINE SERVINGS)

¼ cup (2 oz.)	Butter, softened
¼ cup (2 oz.)	Cocoa powder
¼ cup (2 oz.)	Cola
3 tablespoons (2 oz.)	Chocolate Ganache (page 141)
1 teaspoon	Vanilla extract
1½ cups (7.5 oz.)	Powdered sugar, sifted

1. To make the frosting, cream the butter and add the cocoa powder, cola, ganache, and vanilla extract and beat until smooth, scraping down the side of the bowl as necessary.
2. Add sifted powdered sugar slowly and mix to thoroughly combine, scraping the side of the bowl as necessary. If needed, add more cola until the desired spreading consistency is achieved.
3. Frost the Cola Cake while warm.

NUTRITIONAL INFORMATION PER SERVING

SERVING SIZE: 1 serving   SODIUM: 0mg   DIETARY FIBER: 1g
CALORIES: 138cal   TOTAL CARBOHYDRATE: 23g   PROTEIN: 1g
TOTAL FAT: 5.5g

Boston Cream Pie

Don't let the name fool you; though cut in wedges like a pie, this "pie" is actually a cake. Layered with pastry cream and coated with chocolate ganache, this sponge cake creation may have been called a pie because of the availability of pie tins over cake pans during the nineteenth century. Whatever you call it, this favorite dessert is sure to please pie and cake lovers alike.

YIELD: ONE PIE (EIGHT SERVINGS)

1 10" cake	Sponge Cake, vanilla or chocolate (page 162)
1½ cups (14 oz.)	Pastry Cream (page 140)
2 cups (14 oz.)	Chocolate Ganache (page 141)
½ cup + 1 tablespoon	White chocolate, melted

1. Slice cooled cake in half.
2. Spread pastry cream in between the two halves.
3. Warm the ganache and spread on top of the cake. To finish, create a spider web effect with the white chocolate on top of the cake.

NUTRITIONAL INFORMATION PER SERVING

SERVING SIZE: 1 slice	SODIUM: 55mg	DIETARY FIBER: 2g
CALORIES: 400cal	TOTAL CARBOHYDRATE: 43mg	PROTEIN: 5g
TOTAL FAT: 25g		

Fruitcake

This gluten-free version of the famed holiday cake is a tribute to tradition—packed with dried and candied fruit and soaked in brandy, colorfully fruity and scattered with toasted pecans. This fruitcake will entertain as a festive addition to your winter meal table.

YIELD: ONE STANDARD 8" × 4" × 2¾" LOAF (10 SERVINGS)

Soaker:

½ cup (3 oz.)	Raisins, golden seedless
½ cup (3 oz.)	Currants, dried
½ cup (3 oz.)	Apricots, dried
½ cup (3 oz.)	Cherries, dried
¼ cup	Lemon peel, candied
¼ cup	Orange peel, candied
¼ cup	Brandy
1 cup (5 oz.)	Pecans, toasted, chopped

Cake:

½ cup + 2 tablespoon (5 oz.)	Butter
⅔ cup (5.3 oz.)	Sugar
3 ea.	Eggs
2 teaspoons (17 g)	Corn syrup, light
1 tablespoon + ¼ cup	Brandy, divided
1 teaspoon	Lemon zest
1 teaspoon	Orange zest
1 cup (6 oz.)	Flour Blend #1
4 cups (22 oz.)	Fruit soaker
¼ cup (2 oz.)	Orange juice

Soaker:

Combine all ingredients and let sit covered overnight, in refrigerator.

Cake:

1. Preheat oven to 300°F.
2. Cream together the butter and the sugar.
3. Add eggs one at a time, scraping bowl when necessary.
4. Combine corn syrup, 1 tablespoon brandy, lemon zest, and orange zest and add to the creamed mixture.
5. Sift the flour blend. Take a handful and toss with the fruit soaker; add remaining flour to the batter.
6. Fold the fruit soaker into the batter.
7. Pour into a greased, lined loaf pan.
8. Bake at 300°F for 1 hour, then lower to 275°F and bake for an additional 30 minutes.
9. Unmold and let cool.
10. Brush with ¼ cup brandy and orange juice.

NUTRITIONAL INFORMATION PER SERVING		
SERVING SIZE: 1 slice	SODIUM: 25mg	DIETARY FIBER: 4g
CALORIES: 480cal	TOTAL CARBOHYDRATE: 66g	PROTEIN: 5g
TOTAL FAT: 21g		

Jelly Roll

✳

Sometimes referred to as Swiss rolls, jelly rolls are an old-fashioned simple dessert made from rolling up a sponge-like cake with jam spiraled throughout. Choose whatever flavor of jam you prefer.

YIELD: ONE-HALF SHEET PAN (12 SERVINGS)

9 ea.	Eggs
1¼ cups (10 oz.)	Sugar
1½ cups (9 oz.)	Flour Blend #3
¼ cup (2 oz.)	Butter, melted (or oil)
½ teaspoon	Vanilla extract
3 tablespoon (1 oz.)	Flour Blend #1
3 tablespoons (11 g)	Powdered sugar
½ cup	Jam

1. Preheat oven to 400°F.
2. Grease and flour sides of pan and place a parchment paper on the bottom of the pan. Set aside.
3. Combine eggs and sugar in a mixing bowl and heat over a hot water bath or direct flame until eggs and sugar are warm, about 120°F.
4. Whip the egg mixture on high speed to maximum volume.
5. Stabilize mixture by whipping on second speed for 10 to 15 more minutes.
6. Sift Flour Blend #3. Gradually fold sifted blend into mixture. Stream in melted butter and vanilla while folding.
7. Fill prepared cake pans two-thirds full. Bake until set, about 10 minutes.
8. Unmold immediately onto a sheet that has been dusted with Flour Blend #1 and powdered sugar.
9. When cool, spread with jam and roll up. Slice to serve.

Variation: For a Chocolate Jelly Roll, replace ⅔ cup (4 oz.) of Flour Blend #3 with ½ cup (4 oz.) of Dutch-process cocoa powder.

NUTRITIONAL INFORMATION PER SERVING

SERVING SIZE: 1 slice	SODIUM: 85mg	DIETARY FIBER: 1g
CALORIES: 280cal	TOTAL CARBOHYDRATE: 49g	PROTEIN: 7g
TOTAL FAT: 7g		

Pumpkin Roll

A pumpkin roll is essentially very thin pumpkin bread rolled around a sweet cream cheese filling.

YIELD: ONE-HALF SHEET PAN (14 SERVINGS)

¾ cup (4.5 oz.)	Flour Blend #1
1 teaspoon	Baking powder
2 teaspoons	Cinnamon
1 teaspoon	Nutmeg
1 teaspoon	Ginger
¼ teaspoon	Salt
3 ea.	Eggs
1 cup (8 oz.)	Sugar
⅔ cup (6.6 oz.)	Canned pumpkin
1 teaspoon (6 g)	Lemon juice
1½ cups (14.5 oz.)	Cream Cheese Filling (recipe follows)

1. Preheat oven to 350°F.
2. Sift the flour blend and baking powder. Add the spices and salt and set aside.
3. Combine the eggs and sugar and mix on medium speed with the paddle attachment for 3 to 5 minutes, scraping down the bowl as necessary.
4. Add the pumpkin and lemon juice to the egg mixture and mix until incorporated, about 3 to 5 minutes on medium speed.
5. Add the flour mixture to the pumpkin mixture until it is fully incorporated. Be sure to scrape down the bowl.
6. Lightly grease a half sheet pan and line with a piece of lightly greased parchment paper.
7. Spread the batter evenly in the sheet pan.
8. Bake for about 7 to 10 minutes, or until it is dry to the touch.
9. When the cake is done, remove from pan and transfer onto a cool surface; let it cool, then sprinkle with powdered sugar. Turn onto a piece of parchment paper and remove the bottom parchment paper.
10. When cool, spread with Cream Cheese Filling and roll up. Slice to serve.

NUTRITIONAL INFORMATION PER SERVING

SERVING SIZE: 1 slice	**SODIUM:** 170mg	**DIETARY FIBER:**
CALORIES: 300cal	**TOTAL CARBOHYDRATE:** 31g	less than 1g
TOTAL FAT: 18g		**PROTEIN:** 4g

Cream Cheese Filling

YIELD: 1½ CUPS (14.5 OZ.)

1 cup (5 oz.)	Powdered sugar
1 cup (8 oz.)	Cream cheese
4 tablespoons (2 oz.)	Butter
½ teaspoon	Vanilla extract

1. Sift the powdered sugar; set aside.
2. Soften the cream cheese and butter in the microwave to remove the chill (1 minute), or let it sit at room temperature until tempered (20 minutes).
3. Mix the cream cheese and butter together with the paddle or whisk attachment of the electric mixer on high speed for 5 to 7 minutes, scraping down the bowl as necessary.
4. Add the vanilla and mix at low speed until incorporated. Gradually add in the sifted powdered sugar.
5. Mix until smooth, about 5 minutes.

NUTRITIONAL INFORMATION PER SERVING

SERVING SIZE: 1oz.	SODIUM: 50mg	DIETARY FIBER: 1g
CALORIES: 130cal	TOTAL CARBOHYDRATE: 11g	PROTEIN: 1g
TOTAL FAT: 9g		

Chapter 8

Pies and Tarts

*S*ome people would go to the ends of the earth to find a recipe for the perfect pie crust—and even farther for one that is also gluten free. Fortunately, all you have to do is turn to page 195; gluten-free 3-2-1 Pie Dough has everything you need. Once you've blended the flours together, you can proceed just as you would with regular wheat-based pie crust. It rolls out easily, flutes beautifully, and bakes up perfectly. The taste and texture is hard to distinguish from regular pie crust. Now you just need to choose your favorite filling. All the classics are here: pumpkin, apple, pecan, lemon meringue. You can even make a rustic apple crostata. Recipes for gluten-free quiche, the brunch classic with custard, cheese, vegetables, and meat fillings, can be found in the "Savories" chapter on page 219.

Sometimes a pie demands a sweeter crust. Cream pies work well with a crust made from gluten-free 1-2-3 Cookie Dough. Roll it out as you would any pie dough and prebake the crust. Then proceed with banana cream, coconut cream, chocolate cream, or banana chocolate cream fillings. You can take the same cookie dough recipe, bake it, crumble it, and press it into a pan for the perfect counterpoint to tangy Key lime filling.

Tarts also lend themselves to a crust made from gluten-free 1-2-3 Cookie Dough. Roll it out, press it into a pan, and you've got a beautiful, high-quality tart crust that can handle a wide variety of fillings. Pipe some pastry cream into the baked crust, top with fruit, and brush on some glaze (an easy way to do this is to just heat some apricot jam). You will be amazed at how beautiful it turns out. And try these other tasty varieties: lemon curd, streusel apple, chocolate and caramel, or maple and pecan.

There is also a tart recipe that requires no crust at all: almond pear apple tart is made with a mixture of almond meal, gluten-free flours, eggs, ricotta cheese, and yogurt. Pour the batter into a greased pan, top with a spiral of pear slices, and bake. Then you can sit down with a warm slice of tart and a cup of tea or coffee. A perfectly normal thing to do—which, for those on the gluten-free diet, is hard-won.

3-2-1 Pie Dough

No baker's repertoire is complete without a recipe for the perfect pie crust; this recipe is the end to the gluten-free baker's quest for such. A simple combination of gluten-free flour blends, butter, and water, the resulting crust is a staple base for all pie fillings.

YIELD: TWO 12 OZ. CRUSTS (8 SERVINGS PER CRUST)

12 tablespoons (6 oz.)	Butter, cold
⅔ cup (4.3 oz.)	Flour Blend #2
¾ cup (4 oz.)	Flour Blend #4
⅔ cup (4 oz.)	Flour Blend #5
⅔ cup (5.3 oz.)	Water, cold

1. Cut butter in ¼" chunks.
2. Combine the flour blends with the butter, using your fingertips to rub the butter into the flour in pea-size pieces.
3. Add the cold water and combine just until smooth with your hands or a paddle attachment (hands are best).
4. Refrigerate, unwrapped, for 60 minutes. At this point, the pie dough can be wrapped and frozen for up to one month.
5. When ready to bake, preheat oven to 350°F.
6. Roll out dough and line pie pan. Dock dough with fork and bake for 15 minutes or until pale golden for a parbaked crust; bake for 20 minutes, or to the desired golden brown, for a fully baked crust.

Note: When prebaking shells (some recipes call for the shell to be baked before the filling is placed in the shell), line the crust with parchment paper and dried beans or pie weights.

NUTRITIONAL INFORMATION PER SERVING

SERVING SIZE: 1.5 oz.	**SODIUM:** 10mg	**DIETARY FIBER:** 21g
CALORIES: 150cal	**TOTAL CARBOHYDRATE:** 16g	**PROTEIN:** 3g
TOTAL FAT: 9g		

Apple Pie

This gluten-free version of the American classic is delicious any time of the year—flaky pie crust filled with warm, buttery sweet apples and topped with freshly whipped cream or vanilla ice cream makes for a wonderful dessert.

YIELD: ONE 9" PIE; 8 SERVINGS

One recipe (24 oz.)	3-2-1 Pie Dough, uncooked (page 195)
½ cup (3.75 oz.)	Light brown sugar, packed
½ cup (3 oz.)	Flour Blend #1
1 teaspoon	Cinnamon
4 cups (1 lb. 3 oz.)	Apples, tart, sliced
6 tablespoons (3 oz.)	Butter, cut into small chunks
One recipe	Egg Wash (page 197)

1. Preheat the oven to 375°F.
2. Divide the pie dough in half. Wrap one half and place in the refrigerator. Roll out the other half into a circle large enough to line the bottom of a 10" pie pan on a work surface lightly dusted with Flour Blend #1. Place in the pie pan.
3. Whisk together the sugar, flour blend, and cinnamon. Toss together with the sliced apples.
4. Roll out the remaining pie dough into a circle large enough to cover the pie on a work surface lightly dusted with flour.
5. Place the pie filling into the dough-lined pie pan. Sprinkle the butter over the filling.
6. Lightly brush the edges of the pie dough with egg wash and drape the rolled-out pie dough over the top of the pie.
7. Trim the edges of the crust and crimp the top and bottom together. Lightly brush the top of the pie with egg wash and cut vents in the top with a sharp paring knife.
8. Place the pie on a baking sheet and bake for 50 to 60 minutes, or until the crust is golden brown and the filling is bubbling.

NUTRITIONAL INFORMATION PER SERVING

SERVING SIZE: 1 slice	SODIUM: 30mg	DIETARY FIBER: 3g
CALORIES: 500cal	TOTAL CARBOHYDRATE: 64g	PROTEIN: 6g
TOTAL FAT: 27g		

To create the bottom crust for a pie, roll the flattened dough onto a rolling pin and gently drape it over the pie plate.

Once the pie is filled and topped with another layer of crust, crimp the edges to help seal the dough and create a decorative finishing touch.

Egg Wash

Incorporating eggs with water creates what is referred to as an egg wash. Able to be brushed over breads and pastries, egg wash is typically used in order to give finished baked goods a golden brown, glossy finish.

YIELD: EIGHT SERVINGS, 4 OUNCES

2 ea.	Eggs
1 tablespoon (14 g)	Water
Small pinch	Salt

Whisk together until completely combined.

Blueberry Streusel Pie

Fresh or frozen, blueberries bring a pleasant balance of sweetness and tartness to any dessert. The streusel topping adds an extra burst of sugar and texture to this summertime favorite.

YIELD: ONE 9" PIE, 8 SERVINGS

One recipe (12 oz.)	Streusel Topping (page 199)
¾ cup (6 oz.)	Sugar
¼ cup (1.5 oz.)	Flour Blend #1
¼ teaspoon	Salt
3 cups (1 lb. 3 oz.)	Blueberries, fresh or frozen
One-half recipe (one crust) (12 oz.)	3-2-1 Pie Dough, parbaked (page 195)
2 tablespoons (1 oz.)	Butter

1. Prepare the streusel topping. Preheat the oven to 400°F.
2. Whisk together sugar, Flour Blend #1, and salt. Toss together with the blueberries and immediately place in the parbaked pie shell. Top with the butter and then the streusel topping.
3. Place the pie on a baking sheet and bake for 45 to 55 minutes, or until the crust and streusel are golden brown and the filling is bubbling.

NUTRITIONAL INFORMATION PER SERVING

SERVING SIZE: 1 slice	SODIUM: 135mg	DIETARY FIBER: 3g
CALORIES: 520cal	TOTAL CARBOHYDRATE: 79g	PROTEIN: 5g
TOTAL FAT: 23g		

Streusel Topping

This topping is characteristically crumbly and sweet; most often found atop pies, cakes, and muffins, streusel adds both flavor and texture when used to finish a baked product.

YIELD: 2 CUPS (12 OZ.), ENOUGH FOR ONE 9" PIE

⅔ cup (4.25 oz.)	Flour Blend #1
¼ teaspoon	Baking soda
¼ cup (2 oz.)	Butter, cold
½ cup (2.5 oz.)	Walnuts or pecans, chopped
½ cup (3.75 oz.)	Brown sugar

1. Rub together flour blend, baking soda, butter, and brown sugar until crumbly.
2. Mix in nuts.

NUTRITIONAL INFORMATION PER SERVING

SERVING SIZE: ¼ cup (1.5 oz.)
CALORIES: 200cal
TOTAL FAT: 11g

SODIUM: 45mg
TOTAL CARBOHYDRATE: 27g

DIETARY FIBER: Less than 1g
PROTEIN: 1g

Apple Crostata

This Italian dessert is a variation on a fruit tart. Crostatas get their characteristic appearance from having the edges of the dough folded in around the filling rather than left pressed into the edges of a pan. Once baked, the crostata embraces the homespun look and embodies the flavors of sweet Italy.

YIELD: SIX CROSTATAS

One-half recipe (one crust) (12 oz.)	3-2-1 Pie Dough, uncooked (page 195)
1 cup (4.75 oz.)	Apples, peeled, cored, and sliced
¼ cup (2 oz.)	Brown sugar, packed
⅓ cup (2 oz.)	Flour Blend #1
1 teaspoon	Cinnamon
One recipe (12 oz.)	Streusel Topping
As needed	Egg Wash (page 197)
½ cup (4 oz.)	Cinnamon sugar

1. Divide the pie dough into 6 equal pieces (2 oz. each) and shape into balls. Roll out each piece of the pie dough in a circular shape with a 4" diameter.
2. Mix together apples, brown sugar, flour blend, and cinnamon.
3. For each crostata, place one-sixth of the prepared filling off-center of a dough circle and top with streusel. Carefully fold the dough in the form of overlapping pleats outside to inside, making sure the filling and crumb stay in the center at all times.
4. Chill crostatas until firm.
5. When ready to bake, preheat oven to 375°F.
6. Just before baking, gently brush with egg wash and lightly sprinkle with cinnamon sugar.
7. Bake until browned, 20 to 25 minutes—check that base is cooked and not raw.

NUTRITIONAL INFORMATION PER SERVING

SERVING SIZE: 1 crostata	SODIUM: 80mg	DIETARY FIBER: 3g
CALORIES: 570cal	TOTAL CARBOHYDRATE: 84g	PROTEIN: 6g
TOTAL FAT: 27g		

Banana Cream Pie

Pleasingly simple, this pie is a nearly effortless combination of soft, sweet flavors. Pastry cream layered over sliced bananas is topped with whipped cream; this light, smooth pie is the perfect dessert to relax with on a warm spring or summer's night.

YIELD: ONE PIE (EIGHT SERVINGS)

One-half recipe (one crust) (12 oz.)	3-2-1 Pie Dough, uncooked (page 195)
One recipe (28 oz.)	Pastry Cream (page 140)
2 ea.	Bananas, medium
One recipe	Whipped Cream (page 203)

1. Preheat oven to 350°F.
2. Roll out pie dough to ⅛" thick, line the pie tin, and dock. Place a piece of parchment paper over the pie crust, so that it overhangs the sides, and fill it with dry beans or pie weights.
3. Bake the shell for 20 to 25 minutes or until golden brown.
4. Set aside to cool.
5. Slice bananas lengthwise and lay along the bottom of the pie shell.
6. Fill shell with pastry cream. Place in refrigerator to cool for 45 minutes.
7. Spread whipped cream on top and serve.

NUTRITIONAL INFORMATION PER SERVING

SERVING SIZE: 1 slice	SODIUM: 19mg	DIETARY FIBER: 2g
CALORIES: 260cal	TOTAL CARBOHYDRATE: 30g	PROTEIN: 4g
TOTAL FAT: 15g		

Chocolate Cream Pie

Satisfy your chocolate hunger with this flavored version of a simple cream pie. Chocolate melted into pastry cream creates a milky sweet filling for a gluten-free pie crust; topped with whipped cream, this pie is smooth through the last bite.

YIELD: ONE PIE (EIGHT SERVINGS)

One-half recipe (one crust) (12 oz.)	3-2-1 Pie Dough, uncooked (page 195)
One recipe (28 oz.)	Pastry Cream (page 140)
½ cup + 2 tablespoons	Chocolate chips
One recipe	Whipped Cream (page 203)

1. Preheat oven to 350°F.
2. Roll out pie dough to ⅛" thick, line the pie tin, and dock. Place a piece of parchment paper over the pie crust, so that it overhangs the sides, and fill it with dry beans or pie weights.
3. Bake the shell for 20 to 25 minutes or until golden brown.
4. Set aside to cool.
5. Once pastry cream is made and still warm, fold in chocolate until melted.
6. Fill pie shell with chocolate pastry cream. Place in refrigerator to cool for 45 minutes.
7. Spread whipped cream on top and serve.

NUTRITIONAL INFORMATION PER SERVING

SERVING SIZE: 1 slice	SODIUM: 21mg	DIETARY FIBER: 2g
CALORIES: 300cal	TOTAL CARBOHYDRATE: 32g	PROTEIN: 5g
TOTAL FAT: 19g		

Whipped Cream

Whipping heavy cream with the gradual addition of sugar creates the famous simple and sweet topping that we all know and love so well. From pies to cakes, ice cream to drinks, the list of possibilities in which to use whipped cream is nearly endless.

1 cup	Heavy cream
4 tablespoons (2 oz.)	Sugar

1. Beat cream until frothy, then gradually add sugar.
2. Continue whipping until desired peaks are achieved.

NUTRITIONAL INFORMATION PER SERVING

SERVING SIZE: 1.5 oz. or ¼ cup	**TOTAL FAT:** 10g	**DIETARY FIBER:** 0g
CALORIES: 130cal	**SODIUM:** 10mg	**PROTEIN:** 1g
	TOTAL CARBOHYDRATE: 8g	

Lemon Meringue Pie

This meringue pie is a showcase for lemon. Bright with golden yellow hues and ethereal and light in consistency, from top to bottom this lemon meringue is uncomplicatedly sweet and tart, a perfectly refreshing end to a meal.

YIELD: ONE 9" PIE (EIGHT SERVINGS)

One-half recipe (one crust) (12 oz.)	3-2-1 Pie Dough, uncooked (page 195)
1 cup (8 oz.)	Sugar, divided
½ cup + 2 tablespoons (5 oz.)	Lemon juice
1¼ cups (10 oz.)	Water
1 teaspoon	Lemon zest
¼ cup + 2 tablespoons (2.2 oz.)	Cornstarch
3 ea.	Egg yolks
1 tablespoon (14 g)	Butter
One recipe	Meringue (page 205)

1. Preheat oven to 350°F.
2. Roll out dough and line a 9" pie tin; dock bottom.
3. Prebake for 20 minutes or until fully baked.
4. Cool to room temperature and set aside.
5. Bring ¾ cup sugar, half of the water, lemon juice, and zest to a boil.
6. Combine the cornstarch with the remaining water and add to the egg yolks combined with ¼ cup sugar.
7. Slowly pour the boiling liquid into a bowl with the above mixture, whisking constantly.
8. Return to heat and bring to a boil while whisking constantly.
9. Pour into the pie tin.
10. Chill completely.
11. Top the pie with meringue and brown the meringue in a 500°F oven.

NUTRITIONAL INFORMATION PER SERVING		
SERVING SIZE: 1 slice	SODIUM: 45mg	DIETARY FIBER: less than 1g
CALORIES: 450cal	TOTAL CARBOHYDRATE: 82g	
TOTAL FAT: 12g		PROTEIN: 6g

Meringue

When heated and whipped, egg whites and sugar combine to make meringue, a light and fluffy mixture that is used as an element in countless baking and pastry recipes. Whether it's baked as a topping on pies or folded into batters for aeration, the basic meringue should be used immediately so as not to lose the volume created from whipping.

YIELD: 8 SERVINGS

4 ea.	Egg whites
1 cup (8 oz.)	Sugar

1. Combine whites and sugar in top of double boiler over nearly simmering water.
2. Stir to dissolve sugar; and heat mixture to 145°F.
3. Pour mixture into a mixing bowl, and whip to medium-firm peaks. Use immediately.

NUTRITIONAL INFORMATION PER SERVING

SERVING SIZE: 1.5 oz.	SODIUM: 25mg	DIETARY FIBER: 0g
CALORIES: 120cal	TOTAL CARBOHYDRATE: 29g	PROTEIN: 2g
TOTAL FAT: 0g		

Key Lime Pie

Headline ingredient of the pie, the Key lime is a variety of lime with a strong aroma and bold acidity that grows readily in the Florida Keys. Key lime pie has a pale yellow filling; topped with a baked meringue, this pie is a guaranteed sweet-and-sour success.

YIELD: ONE 9" PIE (EIGHT SERVINGS)

One-half recipe (one crust) (12 oz.)	3-2-1 Pie Dough, uncooked (page 195)
⅝ cup (5 oz.)	Key lime juice
1 teaspoon	Lime zest
1 cup (8 oz.)	Sugar, divided
1 can (12 oz.)	Evaporated milk
¼ cup + 2 tablespoons (2.2 oz.)	Cornstarch
3 ea.	Egg yolks
One recipe	Meringue (page 205)

1. Preheat oven to 350°F.
2. Roll out pie dough to ⅛" thick, line pan, and dock.
3. Bake for about 20 to 25 minutes or until golden brown. Set aside.
4. Boil juice, zest, ¾ cup sugar, and 8 oz. of the evaporated milk.
5. Whisk the cornstarch, egg yolks, and remaining sugar and remaining evaporated milk and set aside.
6. Temper boiling ingredients into the rest and return all to heat immediately.
7. Whisk vigorously until mixture thickens and boils.
8. Remove mixture from heat.
9. Fill pie shell with filling. Cool in the refrigerator.
10. Top with meringue and brown in a 500°F oven.

NUTRITIONAL INFORMATION PER SERVING

SERVING SIZE: 1 slice (with meringue)	**TOTAL FAT:** 14g	**DIETARY FIBER:** less than 1g
CALORIES: 490cal	**SODIUM:** 85mg	
	TOTAL CARBOHYDRATE: 43g	**PROTEIN:** 8g

Chocolate Tart Dough

The addition of cocoa powder to this tart dough creates a recipe whose result is deliciously elegant. Use this deep-brown tart dough year-round to add a new and chocolaty element to your favorite tart recipe.

YIELD: 12 SERVINGS

6 tablespoons (3 oz.)	Butter, cold
¼ cup + 2 tablespoons (3 oz.)	Sugar
½ cup (3 oz.)	Flour Blend #2
⅔ cup (3.3 oz.)	Cocoa powder
1 ea.	Egg, room temperature
¼ cup + 3 tablespoons (3.5 oz.)	Milk

1. Cut the butter into 1" cubes.
2. Combine all ingredients into a bowl.
3. Mix (by hand or with a paddle) until combined.
4. Wrap the dough in plastic or waxed paper. Refrigerate for 1 to 2 hours before use.

NUTRITIONAL INFORMATION PER SERVING

SERVING SIZE: Approximately 1.5 oz.	TOTAL FAT: 8g	DIETARY FIBER: 3g
	SODIUM: 10mg	PROTEIN: 3g
CALORIES: 129cal	TOTAL CARBOHYDRATE: 17g	

Cookie Crumb Crust

Yielding the freshest possible crust, this recipe calls for the baking of a simple gluten-free cookie that, when cooled, is crushed to crumbs appropriate for pressing into a pie crust. This sweet and crunchy pie crust is ideal for holding cream pie fillings.

YIELD: EIGHT SERVINGS

½ cup (4 oz.)	Butter, cold
¼ cup (2 oz.)	Sugar
1 cup + 1 tablespoon (6 oz.)	Flour Blend #2
1 ea.	Egg, room temperature

1. Cut the butter into 1" cubes.
2. Combine all ingredients in a bowl.
3. Mix (by hand or with a paddle) until combined.
4. Wrap the dough in plastic or waxed paper. Refrigerate for 1 hour.
5. When ready to bake, preheat oven to 400°F.
6. Roll chilled dough into a flat piece and place on a sheet pan.
7. Bake for about 30 minutes or until golden brown. Cool.
8. Crush crust into crumbs. Press crumbs into pie pan and fill as desired.

NUTRITIONAL INFORMATION PER SERVING

SERVING SIZE: 1.75 oz.	SODIUM: 10mg	DIETARY FIBER: 0g
CALORIES: 210cal	TOTAL CARBOHYDRATE: 25g	PROTEIN: 2g
TOTAL FAT: 12g		

A quick cookie crust can be made by sandwiching cooking crumbs between two pie plates.

Fruit Tart

Unfold your checkered tablecloth and color your picnic table with fruit tarts made from this recipe, baked as individual-sized tarts or made as one larger portionable dessert. Choose whatever fruit is freshest to top the tart; with berries or kiwis or plums, this glazed and almond-sprinkled fruit tart is a bright and festive finale to a summer dinner.

YIELD: SIX 4½" TARTS

One-half recipe (7 oz.)	1-2-3 Cookie Dough, uncooked (page 103)
1¼ cups (11.7 oz.)	Pastry cream (page 140)
16 oz. (1 lb.) (as needed)	Fresh fruit, sliced
¼ cup (2 oz.)	Water
¼ cup (2 oz.)	Sugar
¼ cup	Apricot jam
¼ cup (1.25 oz.)	Almonds, sliced, toasted

1. Preheat oven to 350°F.
2. Roll out dough to ⅛" thick, place in greased tart pan, and dock.
3. Bake for about 15 to 20 minutes or until golden brown. Let cool.
4. Fill shell with pastry cream.
5. Top with sliced fruit.
6. Heat water, sugar, and jam together in a saucepan on the stove over medium heat until sugar is dissolved and jam is liquid. Bring to a boil, then simmer before brushing over fruit.
7. Top edges with crushed toasted almonds.

NUTRITIONAL INFORMATION PER SERVING

SERVING SIZE: 1 tart	SODIUM: 42mg	DIETARY FIBER: 3g
CALORIES: 500cal	TOTAL CARBOHYDRATE: 74g	PROTEIN: 6g
TOTAL FAT: 22g		

Pecan Pie

Nut lovers will be thrilled to indulge in this version of a Southern pie staple. In this pecan pie, the nuts are cloaked in an appropriately dark and gooey filling, held together in a gluten-free pie crust. This comforting home-style pie is sure to evoke sweet-tooth cravings in all.

YIELD: ONE 9" PIE (EIGHT SERVINGS)

1 cup (5 oz.)	Pecan halves
One-half recipe (one crust) (12 oz.)	3-2-1 Pie Dough, parbaked (page 195)
¼ cup + 2 tablespoons (3 oz.)	Sugar
¼ cup + 2 tablespoons (2.75 oz.)	Brown sugar
½ teaspoon	Salt
¾ cup (9 oz.)	Light corn syrup
3 ea.	Eggs

1. Preheat oven to 375°F.
2. Spread pecans evenly into the bottom of the pie crust and set aside.
3. By hand, whisk together the granulated sugar, brown sugar, salt, corn syrup, and eggs until the mixture is well blended.
4. Pour over the pecans until filling reaches the top of the pie crust.
5. Bake until the filling no longer jiggles and is completely firm, about 45 minutes.

Note: If necessary, to prevent burning the top edge of the pie crust, wrap an aluminum foil collar around the top edge while baking.

NUTRITIONAL INFORMATION PER SERVING

SERVING SIZE: 1 slice	**SODIUM:** 210mg	**DIETARY FIBER:** 3g
CALORIES: 440cal	**TOTAL CARBOHYDRATE:** 56g	**PROTEIN:** 7g
TOTAL FAT: 24g		

Pumpkin Pie

❋

A North American tradition from Halloween through Christmas, this pie is a holiday tabletop essential. The standard pumpkin filling is seasoned with the spices of the colder months; combined and baked to its finished form, this pie tastes like home.

YIELD: ONE 9" PIE (EIGHT SERVINGS)

One-half recipe (one crust) (12 oz.)	3-2-1 Pie Dough, uncooked (page 195)
2 cups (15 oz.)	Pumpkin, canned (sweet potatoes may be used instead in equal portions)
½ cup (4 oz.)	Sugar
¼ cup (2 oz.)	Brown sugar
Pinch	Salt
½ teaspoon	Cinnamon
¼ teaspoon	Ginger
¼ teaspoon	Nutmeg
¼ teaspoon	Cloves
½ cup (4 oz.)	Whole milk
½ cup	Evaporated milk
2 ea.	Eggs

1. Preheat oven to 350°F.
2. Roll out dough to ⅛" thick, line pan, and dock.
3. Parbake for about 15 minutes or until dough no longer looks wet. Let cool.
4. Mix all other ingredients together.
5. Fill pie shell with filling.
6. Bake about 50 minutes or until filling is set.

NUTRITIONAL INFORMATION PER SERVING

SERVING SIZE: 1 slice	SODIUM: 150mg	DIETARY FIBER: 2g
CALORIES: 293cal	TOTAL CARBOHYDRATE: 44g	PROTEIN: 7g
TOTAL FAT: 11g		

Almond Pear/Apple Tart

Embrace the fall orchard harvest with this pear and apple tart. Sliced apples and pears are displayed atop an exceptionally flavorful mixture of ricotta cheese, yogurt, milk, and eggs, all enhanced by ground almonds. The resulting tart is a peaceful, rustic dessert, ideal as a centerpiece to your autumn table.

YIELD: ONE 10" TART (12 SERVINGS)

1 ea.	Apple
1 ea.	Pear, firm
1¼ cups (6.25 oz.)	Almonds, sliced
¾ cup (6 oz.)	Sugar
½ cup + 1 tablespoon (3.15 oz.)	Flour Blend #2
¼ teaspoon	Mace
¼ teaspoon	Cinnamon
¼ teaspoon	Nutmeg
¼ teaspoon	Salt
2 ea.	Eggs
¼ cup (2 oz.)	Skim milk
½ teaspoon	Vanilla extract
3 tablespoons (2 oz.)	Ricotta cheese
2 tablespoons (1.25 oz.)	Nonfat yogurt
¼ cup	Cinnamon
¼ cup (2 oz.)	Sugar

1. Preheat oven to 350°F.
2. Grease a 10" tart pan.
3. Peel, seed, quarter, and slice pears and apples.
4. Grind almonds and sugar in a food processor until finely ground.
5. In a bowl, mix almond/sugar mixture, flour blend, spices, and salt.
6. In a separate bowl, combine eggs, milk, vanilla, ricotta, and yogurt.
7. Add wet ingredients to dry ingredients and mix thoroughly.
8. Pour batter into the tart pan and smooth surface.

9. Place the sliced pears/apples on top of batter; dust lightly with cinnamon and sugar.

10. Bake for 45 to 60 minutes until the top is lightly golden brown and firm to the touch.

11. Allow to cool, then remove from pan.

NUTRITIONAL INFORMATION PER SERVING		
SERVING SIZE: 1 slice	SODIUM: 67mg	DIETARY FIBER: less than 1g
CALORIES: 95cal	TOTAL CARBOHYDRATE: 19g	
TOTAL FAT: 1.5g		PROTEIN: 2g

Hawaiian Chocolate Tart

A caramel chocolate tart goes Hawaiian in this recipe that is layered with toasted macadamia nuts. Complementing the smoothness of the tart with their creamy nut flavor, the taste and texture of the island native macadamias take this chocolate tart to new places.

YIELD: ONE 10" TART (12 SERVINGS)

One recipe (14 oz.)	1-2-3 Cookie Dough (page 103) or Chocolate Tart Dough (page 207), uncooked
2¼ cup	Heavy cream
¾ cup (6 oz.)	Sugar
3 tablespoons (1.5 oz.)	Butter
1 cup (5 oz.)	Macadamia nuts, toasted, rough chopped or quartered
2 cups	Semisweet chocolate chips
⅛ cup	Coffee liquor, optional

1. Preheat oven to 350°F.
2. Roll out dough to ⅛" thick, place in tart pan, and dock bottom.
3. Bake shell for 25 minutes or until fully baked. Cool to room temperature.
4. Bring ¾ cup heavy cream to a boil and set aside.
5. Caramelize the sugar by coating the bottom of a saucepan with ⅓ of remaining sugar. Place over heat and stir in small circles. Once sugar starts melting, slowly add sugar in increments, waiting until the previous has been melted. Once all sugar is melted, let sugar caramelize to a medium amber color.
6. Slowly add the hot cream while stirring.
7. Remove from heat and add the butter.
8. Spread half the caramel evenly into the bottom of the baked tart shell. Set other half aside.
9. Sprinkle with half the chopped nuts. Place shell in the refrigerator to cool and firm the product.

10. Boil 1⅓ cups of heavy cream.
11. Pour over chopped chocolate in a bowl and stir well. Add the coffee liquor if desired.
12. Fill the chilled shell just up to the rim with the ganache and then cool in the freezer.
13. Top with the rest of the caramel (warm slightly before pouring) and garnish with remaining nuts.

NUTRITIONAL INFORMATION PER SERVING		
SERVING SIZE: 1 slice	SODIUM: 26mg	DIETARY FIBER: 3g
CALORIES: 563cal	TOTAL CARBOHYDRATE: 50g	PROTEIN: 4g
TOTAL FAT: 42g		

Apple Tart

✳

Elegance intersects with classic comfort food in this apple tart. Cradled in a golden tart shell, juicy spiced apples layered underneath a crumbly streusel topping make this recipe both attractive and delicious.

YIELD: ONE 10" TART (12 SERVINGS)

One recipe (14 oz.)	1-2-3 Cookie Dough, uncooked (page 103)
4 cups (1 lb. 3 oz.)	Apples
½ cup (4 oz.)	Sour cream
½ cup (3.75 oz.)	Brown sugar
1 teaspoon	Cinnamon
1 teaspoon	Nutmeg
⅛ teaspoon	Salt
One-half recipe (6 oz.)	Streusel Topping (page 199)

1. Preheat oven to 350°F.
2. Roll out the cookie dough to approximately ⅛" thickness. Carefully lift the dough, place it over the tart pan, and gently press it to the bottom and sides. Trim any excess dough from the edges using a sharp paring knife.
3. Line the unbaked tart shell with parchment paper and fill with dry beans or pie weights. Bake the crust at 350°F for 8 to 10 minutes, or just until the crust is set. After removing the crust, raise the oven temperature to 375°F.
4. Peel the apples and thinly slice ⅛" thick.
5. Mix together the sour cream, brown sugar, cinnamon, nutmeg, and salt.
6. Toss the apples together with the sour cream mixture and pour into the tart shell, arranging the apples so that they lie flat.
7. Sprinkle the streusel topping in an even layer over the filled tart. Place tart shell on cookie tray to prevent overspill from burning during baking.
8. Bake at 375°F for 60 minutes or until streusel topping is golden.

NUTRITIONAL INFORMATION PER SERVING

SERVING SIZE: 1 slice	SODIUM: 150mg	DIETARY FIBER: 2g
CALORIES: 290cal	TOTAL CARBOHYDRATE: 42g	PROTEIN: 2g
TOTAL FAT: 14g		

Maple Pecan Tart

Maple replaces molasses in this elegant variation of a pecan pie. Prepared in a buttery tart shell, pecans are mixed into a maple syrup mixture to create a finished tart that is a woodsy sweet end to any winter meal.

YIELD: ONE 10" TART (12 SERVINGS)

One recipe (14 oz.)	1-2-3 Cookie Dough, uncooked (page 103)
3 ea.	Eggs
½ cup + 2 tablespoons (8 oz.)	Pure maple syrup
¼ cup (2 oz.)	Butter, melted
1¼ teaspoons	Vanilla extract
1¼ cups (6.25 oz.)	Pecans, chopped

1. Preheat oven to 375°F.
2. Roll out dough or press into pan to ⅛" thick, dock the dough with a fork, and parbake for 20 minutes. After removing the pan, raise the oven temperature to 400°F.
3. Whisk eggs until combined.
4. Add maple syrup, melted butter, and vanilla.
5. Stir in pecans.
6. Pour into parbaked crust.
7. Bake at 400°F on a sheet pan for 30 minutes, then reduce heat to 375°F and continue baking 45 minutes.

NUTRITIONAL INFORMATION PER SERVING

SERVING SIZE: 1 slice	**SODIUM:** 25mg	**DIETARY FIBER:** 2g
CALORIES: 350cal	**TOTAL CARBOHYDRATE:** 32g	**PROTEIN:** 4g
TOTAL FAT: 24g		

Linzer Torte

This classic Austrian dessert is thought by some to be the oldest known cake in the world. Golden strips of crust latticed on top of a classic jewel-toned jam filling make this gluten-free Linzer Torte strikingly delicious.

YIELD: ONE 10" FLUTED TART PAN (12 SERVINGS)

Double recipe	Linzer Cookies dough (page 120)
¾ cup	Raspberry or apricot jam

1. Preheat oven to 350°F.
2. Roll out the Linzer cookie dough into a circle 1½" larger than the diameter of the tart tin onto a piece of parchment. Place in refrigerator to cool slightly.
3. Place the rolled-out dough into the tart tin and work into the sides and up the side.
4. Fill with jam, leaving a ¼" rim around the edge.
5. Roll out the remaining cookie dough into a square 1" larger than the diameter of the tart tin. Cut the square into strips ¾" wide and place in the freezer until firm. Lay the strips across the tart in one direction, leaving a ½" gap between each strip. Lay the remaining strips over the first, at a 45° angle, leaving a ½" gap between each strip. Trim the edges of the strips around the edge of the tart pan.
6. Bake for 20 to 25 minutes or until golden brown.

NUTRITIONAL INFORMATION PER SERVING

SERVING SIZE: 1 slice	SODIUM: 40mg	DIETARY FIBER: 1g
CALORIES: 300cal	TOTAL CARBOHYDRATE: 39g	PROTEIN: 3g
TOTAL FAT: 16g		

Chapter 9

Savories

*P*izza! Pot pies! Roux! Stew! This may sound like a litany of foods you have to avoid on the gluten-free diet, but it's really just a small sample of the terrific savory gluten-free recipes in this chapter. When you ask a person on a gluten-free diet what he or she misses most, the answer is often "Take-out pizza." Most people don't live near a gluten-free pizzeria, so ordering a pie for delivery is out of the question. But you can enjoy making your own custom pizza: think of smelling the yeast as the crust bakes, simmering your own sauce, sprinkling on just the right amount of cheese, and hand-picking your toppings. Gluten-free pizza crust is easy to make with a piping bag, thick or thin.

You want a soft pretzel? You got it! Just put the dough in your piping bag and make them whatever shape you want. A quick dip in a baking soda solution before baking and you get that wonderful brown crust. There is also stick-to-your-ribs quiche, a great brunch classic. Use 3-2-1 Pie Dough, parbake your crust, then fill with sautéed vegetables and your favorite cheeses and pour on the eggs and cream. Creamy custard, savory fillings, and a flaky crust—a winning combination.

That same gluten-free pie crust can be used to top meat and vegetables for a delicious pot pie. And how about stew, another enduring comfort food? You can have that, too, because thickeners and sauces are fairly easy to make gluten free, if you have the right flour blend for the job. In this chapter you will learn what works—opening the door to roux, béchamel, and brown sauce, traditionally flour-based sauces that are banned from the gluten-free diet. You can also look forward to gluten-free versions of dumplings (bring on the soup!), cheese straws, and the cheese puffs known as gougères. Enjoy!

Pizza Crust

If you like your pizza with more toppings and less crust, this recipe is for you. Gluten-free crust dough is piped onto parchment paper to create a final cooked dough that is light and crisp. After topping, put the crusts on the grill for an extra flavor and crunch.

YIELD: TWO APPROX. 6" DIAMETER CRUSTS (8 SERVINGS)

3⅔ cups (1 lb. 3 oz.)	Flour Blend #4
1 teaspoon	Instant yeast
2¼ cups (18 oz.)	Water
1 teaspoon	Salt
1¼ teaspoons (3.5 g)	Guar gum
¼ cup	Vegetable oil

1. Combine 1 cup of the flour blend, the yeast, and 1 cup of water and mix until smooth. Cover the top with plastic wrap and let it rise for 45 minutes.
2. Thoroughly mix the remaining flour blend with the salt and guar gum.
3. Combine the two flour mixtures and add the remaining 1¼ cups of water and the oil.
4. Mix for 2 minutes using paddle attachment on low speed.
5. After mixing, pipe the mixture onto parchment paper into a 8" disk shape (or shape of your choice, such as triangles for instant slices or animal shapes) or directly into greased pie tin. Rest the crust for 30 minutes in a warm, humid environment.
6. When ready to bake, preheat oven to 375°F. Parbake crust for 15 minutes.
7. Allow crusts to cool. Turn over so the bottom of the crust is now facing upward and top with your favorite toppings. Complete the baking in the oven for 8 to 10 minutes.

NUTRITIONAL INFORMATION PER SERVING

SERVING SIZE: 1 slice	SODIUM: 300mg	DIETARY FIBER: 5g
CALORIES: 290cal	TOTAL CARBOHYDRATE: 46g	PROTEIN: 12g
TOTAL FAT: 8g		

Pizza Corn Crust

Friday nights may never be the same again. This recipe for thick, gluten-free cornmeal pizza dough allows you to create a soft base for a pie that invites customization according to personal taste. Whether it's topped with veggies or meat, this substantial crust complements all.

YIELD: ONE PIZZA (FOUR SERVINGS)

½ cup (3 oz.)	Flour Blend #4
½ cup (3 oz.)	Flour Blend #5
¾ teaspoon	Instant yeast
¼ cup (1.5 oz.)	Yellow cornmeal
¾ cup (6 oz.)	Water
1¼ teaspoons	Extra virgin olive oil
1 teaspoon	Salt

1. Mix all ingredients on low speed for 4 minutes, scraping bowl as needed.
2. Mix on medium speed for 6 minutes.
3. Cover with plastic wrap and allow to rise for 50 minutes.
4. Shape into a ball and rest for 15 minutes.
5. Refrigerate overnight, covered.
6. When ready to bake, preheat oven to 350°F. Flatten the ball of dough in a greased pie tin.
7. Parbake in a pie tin until a skin is formed and center is partially baked.
8. Cover with sauce, cheese, and choice of toppings and continue baking until crust is golden brown and cheese is melted, about 15 minutes.

NUTRITIONAL INFORMATION PER SERVING

SERVING SIZE: 1 slice	SODIUM: 720mg	DIETARY FIBER: 3g
CALORIES: 200cal	TOTAL CARBOHYDRATE: 39g	PROTEIN: 8g
TOTAL FAT: 2.5g		

Crackers

Flavored with cheddar and hints of cayenne pepper and garlic, these crunchy crackers have bite.
Serve them beside a sandwich or alongside a bowl of soup—this snack is perfect for munching.

YIELD: 20 2" × 2" CRACKERS

¼ cup (1.4 oz.)	Flour Blend #2
¼ cup (1 oz.)	Flour Blend #4
¼ cup (1.5 oz.)	Flour Blend #5
¼ teaspoon	Cayenne pepper
½ teaspoon	Garlic powder (or 2 cloves fresh)
¼ teaspoon	Salt
¼ cup + 1 tablespoon (2.5 oz.)	Butter, cold
¼ cup (1.2 oz.)	Cheddar cheese, shredded
¼ cup (2 oz.)	Water, cold
¼ cup (2 oz.)	Egg Wash (page 197)
Garnish	Salt

1. Combine flour blends, cayenne, garlic, and salt in mixer bowl. Cut cold butter into ½" cubes. Add to bowl with dry ingredients, then add cheese.
2. Mixing on low speed, gradually add cold water. Mix until dough just comes together; there should be chunks of butter visible.
3. Remove from bowl and shape into a rectangle about 1½" thick. Cover and chill about 2 hours or until firm and pliable.
4. Using additional flour, roll to a rectangle ¼" thick and longer than wide. Dust off excess flour and give rectangle a four-fold (fold in half twice). Cover and chill 30 minutes. Repeat rolling and folding two more times, allowing a 30-minute chill between each fold.
5. When ready to bake, preheat oven to 300°F.
6. Roll dough out to approximately ⅛" and cut into desired shapes. Move to a sheet pan, brush with egg wash, dock, and sprinkle with garnish salt.
7. Bake for about 20 minutes or until dry and crispy.

NUTRITIONAL INFORMATION PER SERVING

SERVING SIZE: 1 cracker	SODIUM: 80mg	DIETARY FIBER: 0g
CALORIES: 60cal	TOTAL CARBOHYDRATE: 5g	PROTEIN: 2g
TOTAL FAT: 4g		

Puff Dough

This dough, used to create flaky puff pastry products, gets its "puff" from being folded many times, thus creating layers before the dough is molded into its final shape. Stabilized with a small addition of guar gum in place of gluten structure, the finished puff dough has an endless list of applications. From cream puffs to wrappings for savory items such as spinach, this recipe delivers an airy product sure to satisfy your pastry needs.

YIELD: 24 SERVINGS

½ cup (4 oz.)	Butter
1 cup (8 oz.)	Water
2 cups (8 oz.)	Flour Blend #1
½ cup (3 oz.)	Flour Blend #3
⅓ cup (2 oz.)	Flour Blend #4
4 ea.	Eggs
½ cup (4 oz.)	Butter, softened, shaped into 3" x 5" rectangle
2 cups (8 oz.)	Flour Blend #1

1. In a saucepan, bring ½ cup of butter and the water to a boil.
2. Add Flour Blend #1. Stir and cook for 1 minute over medium heat.
3. Remove from the heat and pour the mixture into the bowl of an electric mixer. Mix with the paddle attachment for 1 minute to cool. Add one egg at a time and mix until incorporated. Scrape down the bowl as needed.
4. Add Blends #3 and #4 and mix for 1 minute until the mixture comes together.
5. Put the dough in the refrigerator uncovered for 1 hour.
6. Shape the remaining ½ cup butter into a rectangle 3" x 5". Place it in refrigerator to firm up, 20 minutes.
7. Using the 2 cups of Flour Blend #1 to dust the surface of your workspace, roll dough into the shape of a rectangle, about 12" × 5". Place the 3" x 5" butter on one side of the rectangle.
8. Immediately give a three-fold: with a long edge of the rectangle facing you, fold one of the short ends two-thirds of the way to the end of the other side and fold the remaining one-third of dough over it, as if you are folding a business letter. Press down the three sides to lock in the dough. Rest the dough uncovered in the freezer for 20 minutes.

9. Roll the dough into a 12" × 7" rectangle and administer another three-fold. Repeat four more times with a 15-minute rest in the freezer between each folding.

10. Rest the dough, wrapped, overnight in the refrigerator before shaping.

11. When ready to bake, preheat oven to 400°F. Shape and bake as indicated in recipes used.

NUTRITIONAL INFORMATION PER SERVING

SERVING SIZE: 1.75 oz.   SODIUM: 20mg   DIETARY FIBER: 0g
CALORIES: 160cal   TOTAL CARBOHYDRATE: 21g   PROTEIN: 2g
TOTAL FAT: 8g

Folding puff dough creates its signature layered texture. Begin a book fold with the dough by folding each edge of the dough in to meet at the center.

Using a piece of parchment paper for leverage, finish the book fold by folding one half of the dough on top of the other.

Cheese Straws

These are a variation on the puff dough recipe, which would be a great addition to a soup or salad or as a snack just on their own.

YIELD: 15 SERVINGS

One-half recipe	Puff Dough (page 224)
As needed	Egg Wash (page 197)
½ cup (2.3 oz.)	Cheese, grated

1. Preheat oven to 400°F.
2. Roll the puff dough into a 12" × 7" x ¼" thick rectangle, brush the top of the dough with egg wash, and evenly sprinkle over the top ½ cup of grated cheddar cheese.
3. To shape, cut into ¾" wide strips. Lay the strips on a parchment-lined baking sheet.
4. Bake in a preheated 400°F oven for 15 minutes or until golden brown.

Note: For cheese straws half a cup of any hard cheese may be used, such as Asiago, Parmesan, or Manchego. Finely chopped herbs may be folded in as well.

For a variation in shape, twist the cheese straws as you lay them on the parchment just before baking.

NUTRITIONAL INFORMATION PER SERVING

SERVING SIZE: 1 cheese straw	TOTAL FAT: 8g	DIETARY FIBER: 0g
	SODIUM: 80mg	PROTEIN: 4g
CALORIES: 150cal	TOTAL CARBOHYDRATE: 17g	

Butterflies

For a sweet variation of puff dough, sprinkle some coarse sugar and bake these butterfly-shaped treats. Both the taste and the shape will bring a smile to your face.

YIELD: 15 SERVINGS

One-half recipe	Puff Dough (page 224)
1 cup (8 oz.)	Coarse sugar
As needed	Egg Wash (page 197)

1. Preheat oven to 400°F.
2. Sprinkle ½ cup of the sugar onto the table and roll the puff dough on top of it into a 12" × 7" x ¼ " thick rectangle. Brush the top of the dough with egg wash and evenly sprinkle the remaining sugar over the top.
3. To shape, roll the two sides of the pastry toward the center until they meet. Wrap the roll with plastic wrap and refrigerate until firm, at least 15 minutes.
4. Unwrap the puff pastry roll and slice it into ¼" thick slices.
5. Lay the slices on a parchment lined baking sheet about 1-inch apart.
6. Bake until light golden brown, 6 to 7 minutes and then flip the butterflies over and bake for an additional 6 to 7 minutes, until golden brown.

NUTRITIONAL INFORMATION PER SERVING

SERVING SIZE: 1 butterfly	SODIUM: 15mg	DIETARY FIBER: 0g
CALORIES: 190cal	TOTAL CARBOHYDRATE: 32g	PROTEIN: 2g
TOTAL FAT: 7g		

Pâte à Choux

Pâte à choux is a versatile dough that can be used for either sweet or savory applications. Try adding your favorite cheese to the dough to make a tasty snack.

YIELD: SIX ÉCLAIRS OR 10 TO 12 PUFFS

4 tablespoons (2 oz.)	Butter
¼ cup (2 oz.)	Water
½ teaspoon	Salt
3 tablespoons (1 oz.)	Flour Blend #2
¼ cup (1.5 oz.)	Flour Blend #3
1 tablespoon (8 g)	Guar gum
4 ea.	Eggs

1. Preheat oven to 375°F.
2. In a medium saucepan bring the butter, water, and salt to a full boil.
3. Add the flour blends all at once and stir vigorously to combine. Cook while stirring constantly for 1 minute over a high heat.
4. Transfer the mixture to the bowl of a mixer and beat with a whisk for 1 minute or until the batter begins to cool. While mixing constantly, mix in the guar gum.
5. Add the four eggs one at a time while continuing to mix. The mixture may appear broken, but will come together with continued mixing.
6. Pipe the batter into the desired shape onto a parchment-lined baking sheet.
7. Bake for 10 to 15 minutes or until golden brown and crisp.

NUTRITIONAL INFORMATION PER SERVING

SERVING SIZE: 1 éclair shell

CALORIES: 150cal

TOTAL FAT: 11g

SODIUM: 240mg

TOTAL CARBOHYDRATE: 10g

DIETARY FIBER: 1g

PROTEIN: 4g

Cheese Puffs

These puffs are the perfect cheesy gluten-free snack at any time of day or night.

YIELD: 24 CHEESE PUFFS

| 1 recipe | Pâte à Choux (page 228) |
| ½ cup (1.6 oz.) | Parmesan cheese, grated |

1. Preheat oven to 400°F.
2. Mix ½ cup (1.6 oz.) grated Parmesan cheese into the finished batter and pipe into puffs onto a parchment-lined baking sheet.
3. Bake for 12 minutes until golden brown and crisp.

NUTRITIONAL INFORMATION PER SERVING		
SERVING SIZE: 1 cheese puff	**TOTAL FAT:** 3.5g	**DIETARY FIBER:** 0g
CALORIES: 50cal	**SODIUM:** 90mg	**PROTEIN:** 2g
	TOTAL CARBOHYDRATE: 3g	

Southwestern Quiche

Go west while staying right where you are with this colorful quiche. Chiles, peppers, corn, and sun-dried tomatoes load this recipe with the distinctive flavor of the southwest—heartily spicy and sun soaked. You can almost feel the desert heat with each bite of this satisfying quiche.

YIELD: ONE 9" SHELL (EIGHT SERVINGS)

One-half recipe (one crust) (12 oz.)	3-2-1 Pie Dough, uncooked (page 195)
¼ cup (2 oz.)	Sun-dried tomatoes, small diced
5 tablespoons (2 oz.)	Green chiles, small diced
½ cup (1 oz.)	Scallion onions, small diced
½ cup (3 oz.)	Corn
3 tablespoons (20 g)	Jalapeño peppers, fresh, small diced
1 cup (4 oz.)	Monterey jack cheese, grated
4 ea.	Eggs
½ cup (4 oz.)	Milk
½ cup	Heavy cream
½ teaspoon	Black pepper
½ teaspoon	Nutmeg

1. Preheat oven to 350°F.
2. Roll out pie dough to ⅛" thick, line the pie tin, and dock. Place a piece of parchment paper over the pie crust, so that it overhangs the sides, and fill it with dry beans or pie weights.
3. Bake at 350°F for 20 minutes or until golden brown. After removing the tin, raise the oven temperature to 375°F.
4. Place sun-dried tomatoes in a bowl and cover them with water. Let them sit and rehydrate for about 15 minutes, then strain.
5. Combine all vegetables.
6. Toss grated cheese with all of the vegetables.
7. In a separate bowl, combine the eggs, milk, heavy cream, and spices. Whisk together.

8. Place the vegetable mixture in the parbaked pie shell and make sure it is level.
9. Pour the egg mixture into the shell over the vegetable mixture to just under the edge. Don't let it spill over.
10. Bake in 375°F oven for 45 to 60 minutes.

NUTRITIONAL INFORMATION PER SERVING		
SERVING SIZE: 1 slice	SODIUM: 290mg	DIETARY FIBER: 3g
CALORIES: 330cal	TOTAL CARBOHYDRATE: 29g	PROTEIN: 11g
TOTAL FAT: 20g		

Quiche Lorraine

Indulge your palate with this definitively rich, classic French quiche. Salty, full-flavored bacon and the distinctive yet not overpowering flavor of the Gruyère combine to create a savory quiche as wonderful for breakfast as it is pleasing for dinner.

YIELD: ONE 9" SHELL (EIGHT SERVINGS)

One-half recipe (one crust) (12 oz.)	3-2-1 Pie Dough, uncooked (page 195)
¾ cup (6 oz.)	Bacon, cooked, chopped
⅔ cup (2.5 oz.)	Gruyère cheese
⅔ cup (2.5 oz.)	Onions, large yellow
4 ea.	Eggs
½ cup (4 oz.)	Milk
½ cup	Heavy cream

1. Preheat oven to 350°F.
2. Roll out dough to ⅛" thick, place in a pie tin, and dock the bottom.
3. Bake crust fully for 20 to 25 minutes; let cool.
4. Mix together all remaining ingredients with a whisk.
5. Fill pie shell and place back in oven. Bake for 30 to 35 minutes or until set.

NUTRITIONAL INFORMATION PER SERVING

SERVING SIZE: 1 slice	**SODIUM:** 580mg	**DIETARY FIBER:**
CALORIES: 400cal	**TOTAL CARBOHYDRATE:** 19g	less than 1g
TOTAL FAT: 28g		**PROTEIN:** 17g

Potato Leek Quiche

Potatoes and leeks combine in subtle flavors to create a complementary duo of ingredients. Cheddar cheese and accents of onion and a splash of hot sauce add finishing touches to this hearty quiche.

YIELD: ONE 9" PIE TIN (EIGHT SERVINGS)

One-half recipe (one crust) (12 oz.)	3-2-1 Pie Dough, uncooked (page 195)
½ cup	Heavy cream
½ cup (4 oz.)	Whole milk
4 ea.	Eggs
1¼ teaspoons	Salt
¼ teaspoon	Black pepper
¼ teaspoon	Hot sauce
1¾ cups (9 oz.)	Potatoes, peeled, cubed, cooked
1 cup (3 oz.)	Leeks, chopped
⅓ cup (1.25 oz.)	Onions, diced
1 cup (4.7 oz.)	Cheddar cheese, shredded

1. Preheat oven to 350°F.
2. Roll out dough to ⅛", place into pie tin, and dock. Place a piece of parchment paper over the pie crust, so that it overhangs the sides, and fill it with dry beans or pie weights.
3. Bake at 350°F for 20 minutes or until golden brown. After removing the tin, raise the oven temperature to 375°F.
4. Mix together cream, milk, eggs, salt, pepper, and hot sauce.
5. Place potatoes, leeks, onions, and cheese inside the shell.
6. Fill shell with egg mixture until everything is coated.
7. Bake for 30 to 35 minutes or until set.

NUTRITIONAL INFORMATION PER SERVING		
SERVING SIZE: 1 slice	SODIUM: 200mg	DIETARY FIBER: 2g
CALORIES: 350cal	TOTAL CARBOHYDRATE: 26g	PROTEIN: 11g
TOTAL FAT: 22g		

Pasta Dough

This was a difficult item to develop. It makes simple pasta shapes and it cooks very quickly; do not overcook the pasta for it will become very rubbery. The garnishing sauce that you choose is what helps to give it character.

YIELD: 18 OUNCES (EIGHT SERVINGS)

¾ cup (5 oz.)	Flour Blend #3
2½ cups (14 oz.)	Flour Blend #4
1 teaspoon	Salt
2 ea.	Eggs
⅛ cup	Vegetable oil
1 cup + 2 tablespoons (9 oz.)	Water

1. Combine flour and salt in a mixing bowl. In a separate bowl combine eggs, vegetable oil, and water.
2. Blend wet ingredients into the dry using a paddle. Mix thoroughly.
3. Place the dough on a parchment-lined sheet tray and cover with wax paper.
4. Rest overnight in the refrigerator before forming into desired shapes such as gnocchi or ravioli.

To cook pasta:
1. In a large pot, bring heavily salted water to a boil.
2. Add pasta and cook 1 minute, until pasta is floating and completely cooked through.
3. Drain.

NUTRITIONAL INFORMATION PER SERVING

SERVING SIZE: 2.25 oz.	SODIUM: 340mg	DIETARY FIBER: 4g
CALORIES: 260cal	TOTAL CARBOHYDRATE: 46g	PROTEIN: 12g
TOTAL FAT: 5g		

Ham and Cheese Scones

This recipe transforms a classic sandwich into a new breakfast treat. Gluten-free scones are enhanced with deli-style ham, cheese, and a touch of fresh green onions to create a savory baked good perfect for a hearty breakfast or satisfying lunch.

YIELD: SIX 2" × 3" SCONES

⅔ cup (4.25 oz.)	Flour Blend #1
½ cup (3 oz.)	Flour Blend #2
¼ teaspoon	Salt
4 teaspoons (19 g)	Sugar
1½ teaspoons	Baking powder
1 ea.	Egg
⅛ cup (1 oz.)	Buttermilk
¼ cup	Heavy cream
⅓ cup (2 oz.)	Deli honey ham lunchmeat, diced
⅓ cup (1.5 oz.)	Cheddar cheese, shredded
½ bunch	Fresh green onion, chopped
As needed	Egg Wash (page 197)

1. Blend flour blends, salt, sugar, and baking powder together.
2. In a separate bowl combine egg, buttermilk, and cream.
3. Combine dry and wet ingredients and mix until smooth.
4. Add ham, cheese, and onions.
5. Refrigerate mixture, uncovered, for 1 hour.
6. When ready to bake, preheat oven to 400°F.
7. Using a large ice cream scoop, scoop out batter. If not using an ice cream scoop, make sure to scoop or cut dough into portions with a 3" diameter.
8. Brush dough with egg wash.
9. Bake for 12 to 15 minutes.

NUTRITIONAL INFORMATION PER SERVING

SERVING SIZE: 1 scone
CALORIES: 210cal
TOTAL FAT: 8g

SODIUM: 380mg
TOTAL CARBOHYDRATE: 32g

DIETARY FIBER: less than 1g
PROTEIN: 6g

Brazilian Cheese Rolls

Known as Pão de Queijo in Brazil, these cheese rolls are a very popular gluten-free bread. Made with tapioca starch, which is made from the yuca plant indigenous to Brazil, these rolls turn out light and fluffy yet dense at the same time.

YIELD: 30 ROLLS

¾ cup (6 oz.)	Water
1 cup (8 oz.)	Whole milk
½ cup (½ cup)	Vegetable oil
1 tablespoon	Salt
3½ cups (18 oz)	Tapioca starch
4 ea.	Eggs
2½ cups (8 oz.)	Parmesan cheese, grated

1. Bring water, milk, oil, and salt to a boil. Add tapioca starch to boiled mixture and stir. Lower heat and continue to cook for 2 minutes.
2. Transfer to mixing bowl. Mix using a paddle until smooth and somewhat cool.
3. Add eggs, one at a time, until incorporated.
4. Incorporate the Parmesan.
5. Allow mixture to cool for 2 hours in refrigerator.
6. When ready to bake, preheat oven to 400°F.
7. Shape by hand or with an ice cream scoop. Shape into balls using oiled hands. Bake for approximately 20 minutes until risen and golden brown.

NUTRITIONAL INFORMATION PER SERVING

SERVING SIZE: 1 roll   SODIUM: 370mg   DIETARY FIBER: 0g

CALORIES: 123cal   TOTAL CARBOHYDRATE: 16g   PROTEIN: 3g

TOTAL FAT: 6g

Jalapeño Cheddar Scones

In this recipe the bold pair of jalapeños and cheddar cheese turn a typical scone into anything but. Made with buttermilk and cream, these moist and flavorful scones are a satisfying accompaniment to breakfast or lunch.

YIELD: SIX 2" × 3" SCONES

⅔ cup (4.25 oz.)	Flour Blend #1
½ cup (3 oz.)	Flour Blend #2
¼ teaspoon	Salt
4 teaspoons (19 g)	Sugar
1½ teaspoons	Baking powder
1 ea.	Egg
⅛ cup (1 oz.)	Buttermilk
¼ cup	Heavy cream
⅓ cup (2 oz.)	Fresh jalapeño peppers, diced
⅓ cup (1.5 oz.)	Cheddar cheese, shredded
As needed	Egg Wash (page 197)

1. Blend flour blends, salt, sugar, and baking powder.
2. In a separate bowl combine egg, buttermilk, and cream.
3. Pour the dry into the wet ingredients and mix until smooth.
4. Add jalapeños and cheese.
5. Refrigerate mixture, uncovered, for 1 hour.
6. When ready to bake, preheat oven to 400°F.
7. Using a large ice cream scoop, scoop out batter. If not using an ice cream scoop make sure to scoop or cut dough into portions with a 3" diameter.
8. Brush dough with egg wash.
9. Bake for 12 to 15 minutes.

NUTRITIONAL INFORMATION PER SERVING

SERVING SIZE: 1 scone	SODIUM: 360mg	DIETARY FIBER: less than 1g
CALORIES: 210cal	TOTAL CARBOHYDRATE: 32g	
TOTAL FAT: 8g		PROTEIN: 5g

Beef Pot Pie

On cold winter nights, there's nothing like the warmth and heartiness of beef pot pie. This favorite is the ultimate comfort food that makes you forget about how harsh some winters can be.

YIELD: SIX 4" PIES (6 SERVINGS)

4½ cups (3 lb.)	Boneless beef shank, chuck, or round
1 tablespoon	Salt
½ tablespoons	Black pepper
4 tablespoons	Vegetable oil, divided
1 small (7 oz.)	Yellow onion, diced
2 tablespoons (1 oz.)	Tomato paste
3 tablespoons (1.1 oz.)	Flour Blend #3
2 cups (16 oz.)	Beef broth
1 large (6 oz.)	Yellow or white waxy potato, peeled and cut into large dice
12 ea. (11 oz.)	Pearl onions, peeled
1 stalk (3 oz.)	Celery, coarsely diced
1 ea. (4 oz.)	Carrot, coarsely diced
½ cup (3 oz.)	Fresh or thawed frozen peas
One recipe (24 oz.)	3-2-1 Pie Dough, uncooked (page 195)

1. Trim the beef of excess fat and gristle. Cut into 2" cubes and season with salt and pepper.

2. Heat 2 tablespoons of the oil in a Dutch oven over high heat. Working in batches without crowding, sear the beef to a deep brown on all sides, about 8 minutes. Transfer the beef to a pan and set aside.

3. Add the remaining 2 tablespoons oil to the Dutch oven and heat over medium-high heat. Add the onion and cook, stirring occasionally, until golden, about 5 minutes. Add the tomato paste and cook until it darkens, about 1 minute. Add the flour blend and cook, stirring frequently, to make a white roux, about 5 minutes.

4. Add the beef broth to the pot, whisking well to work out any lumps.

5. Return the beef cubes to the pot along with any juices released by the beef.

6. Bring to a gentle simmer over low to medium heat. Cover the pot and continue to stew over very low heat, or transfer to a 350°F oven. Stew the beef for 45 minutes, stirring occasionally. Add the potato, pearl onions, celery, and carrot and stew until the beef is tender to the bite and the vegetables are fully cooked, 30 to 35 minutes more.

7. Add the peas and simmer 2 to 3 minutes more, or until all of the ingredients are very hot. Taste and season with salt and pepper.

8. When cooking is complete, divide the stew evenly among six ovenproof bowls or ramekins.

9. For the top crust: Divide the pie dough into 6 even portions and roll each into a circle large enough to cover one of the bowls. Drape a circle of the dough over each of the bowls, lightly brush with egg wash, and cut vents with a sharp paring knife.

10. Bake in a preheated 375°F oven until golden brown, about 25 minutes. Serve while piping hot.

NUTRITIONAL INFORMATION PER SERVING

SERVING SIZE: 1 pot pie	SODIUM: 770mg	DIETARY FIBER: 6g
CALORIES: 1080cal	TOTAL CARBOHYDRATE: 73g	PROTEIN: 60g
TOTAL FAT: 63g		

Roux

This classic thickening agent created by cooking fat with flour is reinvented in this recipe by using a gluten-free flour blend. Use your finished roux to aid in creating thickened sauces such as béchamel, velouté, and brown sauce.

YIELD: 1⅛ CUPS (12 OUNCES)

1⅓ cups (8 oz.)	Flour Blend #3
½ cup (4 oz.)	Clarified butter* or vegetable oil

1. Preheat oven to 300°F.
2. Place flour blend in a mixing bowl.
3. Stir in oil, or melted (not too hot) clarified butter.
4. Place into a 9" × 9" baking dish. Place baking dish on a cookie sheet.
5. Bake for 30 minutes.
6. Allow to cool to room temperature before use.
7. Keep covered and store in refrigerator. Allow to warm up to room temperature before using to thicken a soup or sauce.

*Clarified butter: Bring butter to a boil, then turn the heat down and let it simmer for 5 minutes. Let the butter cool for 2 hours; the milk solids will stay on the bottom of the pot; the clarified butter will be on the top of the sauce pot. Scoop out the clarified top part of the butter and use for any recipe that calls for clarified butter.

NUTRITIONAL INFORMATION PER SERVING

SERVING SIZE: 1 oz.	SODIUM: 35mg	DIETARY FIBER: less than 1g
CALORIES: 140cal	TOTAL CARBOHYDRATE: 13g	
TOTAL FAT: 10g		PROTEIN: 2g

Cream Sauce

This recipe uses a gluten-free roux that when cooked together with milk creates a version of the classic French béchamel sauce. Considered in the culinary world to be one of the five "grand" or "mother" sauces, this simple sauce is used as the base for countless others by simply adding additional flavors as needed.

YIELD: 11 SERVINGS

1¼ cups (10 oz.)	Milk
1½ tablespoons (1 oz.)	Roux (page 240)

1. Stir together in a saucepan over medium heat. Bring to a boil, then simmer for 10 minutes. Strain.

> ### NUTRITIONAL INFORMATION PER SERVING
> . . . .
>
> SERVING SIZE: 1 oz.   SODIUM: 15mg   DIETARY FIBER: 0g
> CALORIES: 30cal   TOTAL CARBOHYDRATE: 2g   PROTEIN: 1g
> TOTAL FAT: 1.5g

Brown Sauce

Sometimes referred to as sauce Espagnol, this combination of brown veal or beef stock and gluten-free roux creates a version of a rich culinary mother sauce. Able to stand alone, brown sauce also works as a base for additional flavorings as appropriate for a given dish.

YIELD: SEVEN SERVINGS

¾ cup (6 oz.)	Beef broth
1½ tablespoons (1 oz.)	Roux (page 240)

1. Stir together in a saucepan over medium heat. Bring to a boil, then simmer for 10 minutes. Strain.

> ### NUTRITIONAL INFORMATION PER SERVING
> . . . .
>
> SERVING SIZE: 1 oz.   SODIUM: 55mg   DIETARY FIBER: 0g
> CALORIES: 25cal   TOTAL CARBOHYDRATE: 2g   PROTEIN: 1g
> TOTAL FAT: 1.5g

Chicken Velouté

Another of the famous culinary mother sauces, this velouté is created by cooking chicken stock in combination with a gluten-free white roux. Use velouté as a base for other sauces by adding ingredients such as mushrooms, herbs, wine, or cream.

YIELD: NINE SERVINGS

1 cup (8 oz.)	Chicken stock
1½ tablespoons (1 oz.)	Roux (page 240)

1. Stir together in a saucepan over medium heat. Bring to a boil, then simmer for 10 minutes. Strain.

NUTRITIONAL INFORMATION PER SERVING

SERVING SIZE: 1 oz.   SODIUM: 70mg   DIETARY FIBER: 0g
CALORIES: 15cal   TOTAL CARBOHYDRATE: 2g   PROTEIN: 0g
TOTAL FAT: 1g

Recipe Credits

Orange Cranberry Muffins
Developed by Rilwan Danmola and Emily Kinner

Lemon Poppy Seed Muffins
Developed by Rachel Oliver from Wauwatosa, Wisconsin

Scones
Developed by Stacey Drewisis from Middle Island, New York

Buttermilk Biscuits
Developed by Ian Taylor from Egg Harbor City, New Jersey

Funnel Cake
Developed by Rachel Reuter from New Jersey

Coconut Macaroons
Developed by Chef Marc Haymon, CMB

Pizzelles
Developed by Rosemarie Marotti from Kalamazoo, Michigan

Chocolate Crinkles
Developed by Jeremy Sawicki from Tewksbury, Massachusetts

Sand Cookies
Developed by Ryan Ruda from Dallas, Pennsylvania

Whoopie Pie
Developed by Ashley O'Neil from Londonderry, New Hampshire

Blondies
Developed by Lauren Elliott from Delaware

Hip Hugger Bars
Developed by Tara Smith from Duluth, Minnesota

Cannoli Shells
Developed by Elizabeth Shaw from Philadelphia, Pennsylvania

Éclairs
Developed by Alesha Rice from Madison, Wisconsin

Apple Strudel
Developed by Sam Major from Milwaukee, Wisconsin

Madeleines
Developed by Hayoung Kim from Seoul, South Korea

Blueberry Buckle
Developed by Jenna Leuchak

Devil's Food Cake
Developed by Erin McDowell from Lawrence, Kansas

Carrot Cake
Developed by Deborah Wise
and
Samara Yigitsoy from Holbrook, New York

Sacher Cake
Developed by Brielle Hutchinson from Overland Park, Kansas

Pineapple Upside-Down Cake
Developed by Nicole Bonfante from Jackson, New Jersey

Cola Cake
Developed by Janette Collins from Valley Falls, New York
and
Julia Nadler from Acton, Massachusetts

Fruitcake
Developed by Sungrok Kang from Seoul, South Korea

Pumpkin Roll
Developed by Nada Harris from Lincoln, Delaware

Blueberry Streusel Pie
Developed by Caitlin Crowley from Lake Geneva, Wisconsin

Apple Crostata
Developed by Gitanjali Siddharth-Shah from Mumbai, India

Key Lime Pie
Developed by Jared Lowry from Stoystown, Pennsylvania
and
Steven Cak from Minneapolis, Minnesota

Fruit Tart
Developed by Kaitlyn Norton from New Jersey

Pumpkin Pie
Developed by Marisa High from Maryland

Pizza Crust, Cornmeal
Developed by Selina LaVista from New Jersey

Brazilian Cheese Rolls
Developed by Marcello Amaral from Brazil

Readings and Resources

BOOKS

Bowland, Susan. *The Living Gluten-Free Answer Book*. Naperville, IL: Sourcebooks, Inc., 2008.

Case, Shelley, BSc, RD. *Gluten-Free Diet: A Comprehensive Resource Guide, Expanded Edition*. Regina, Saskatchewan, Canada: Case Nutrition Consulting, 2006.

Donovan, Mary, ed. *Baking at Home with the Culinary Institute of America*. Hoboken, NJ: John Wiley & Sons, Inc., 2004.

Fenster, Carol. *Cooking Free: 200 Flavorful Recipes for People with Food Allergies and Multiple Food Sensitivities*. New York: Avery, 2005.

Green, Peter H.R., M.D. and Rory Jones. *Celiac Disease: A Hidden Epidemic*. New York: HarperCollins, 2006.

Hagman, Bette. *The Gluten-Free Gourmet Bakes Bread*. New York: Henry Holt, 2000.

Hamelman, Jeffrey. *Bread: A Baker's Book of Techniques and Recipes*. Hoboken, NJ: John Wiley & Sons, Inc., 2004.

Korn, Danna. *Living Gluten-Free for Dummies*. Hoboken, NJ: Wiley Publishing, Inc., 2006.

Thompson, Tricia. *Celiac Disease Nutrition Guide, 2nd ed*. Chicago: American Dietetic Association, 2006.

MAGAZINES AND NEWSLETTERS

Gluten-Free Living
19A Broadway
Hawthorne, NY 10532
✆ 914-741-5420
✍ *www.glutenfreeliving.com*

Scott-Free Newsletter
✍ *www.celiac.com*

Sully's Living Without
P.O. Box 2126
Northbrook, IL 60065
✆ 847-480-8810
✍ *www.livingwithout.com*
Gluten-free/allergy awareness magazine;
dining cards.

OTHER PUBLICATIONS

The CSA Gluten-Free Product Listing
Celiac Sprue Association
P.O. Box 31700
Omaha, NE 68131-0700
✍ *www.csaceliacs.org*
Product listing published annually; 11th
edition was published in 2006.

ARTICLE

Dowd, B. and J. Walker-Smith. "Samuel
Gee, Aretaeus, and the coeliac affection."
Abstract, *British Medical Journal*, April
6, 1974; 2(5909): 45–47.

Green, Peter, M.D. and Christophe
Cellier, M.D. "Celiac Disease." *The New
England Journal of Medicine,* October
25, 2007; 1731-43.

WEB SITES

Advocacy
American Celiac Disease Alliance
✍ *www.americanceliac.org*

Celiac Disease Foundation
✍ *www.celiac.org*

Celiac Sprue Association
✍ *www.csaceliacs.org*

Gluten Intolerance Group
✍ *www.gluten.net*

Medical Publications
MedicineNet.com
✍ *www.medicinenet.com*

MedlinePlus, a service of the U.S.
National Library of Medicine and the
National Institutes of Health
✍ *www.nlm.nih.gov/medlineplus*

National Center for Biotechnology
Information
✍ *www.ncbi.nlm.nih.gov*

National Digestive Diseases Information
Clearinghouse (NDDC)
✍ *http://digestive.niddk.nih.gov/ddiseases/
pubs/celiac/index.htm#1*

PubMed, a service of the National
Library of Medicine and the National
Institutes of Health
✍ *www.pubmed.gov*

Government Food Labeling
U.S. Food and Drug Administration
Center for Food Safety and Applied
Nutrition
✍ *www.cfsan.fda.gov/*

Patient Care and Research Centers
Celiac Disease Center at Columbia
University
✍ *www.celiacdiseasecenter.org*

University of Chicago Celiac Disease
Program
✍ *www.celiacdisease.net*

University of Maryland Center for
Celiac Research
✍ *www.celiaccenter.org*
William K. Warren Medical Research
Center for Celiac Disease at University of
California, San Diego
✍ *http://celiaccenter.ucsd.edu*

*Autism and the Gluten-
Free/Casein Free Diet*
ANDI Autism Network for Dietary
Intervention
✍ *www.autismndi.com*

Gluten-Free Casein Free Diet
✍ *www.gfcfdiet.com*

Other Helpful Web Sites
Wikipedia, the free encyclopedia
✍ *www.wikipedia.org*

For converting weights and measures
✍ *www.onlineconversion.com/weight*

GLUTEN-FREE FLOURS AND INGREDIENTS

Arrowhead Mills
The Hain Celestial Group
4600 Sleepytime Drive
Boulder, CO 80301
✆ 800-434-4246
✍ *www.arrowheadmills.com*
✍

Bob's Red Mill Natural Foods
5209 SE International Way
Milwaukie, OR 97222
✆ 800-349-2173
✍ *www.bobsredmill.com*

Cream Hill Estates
9633 rue Clément
LaSalle, Québec
Canada H8R 4B4
✆ 866-727-3628
✍ *www.creamhillestates.com*
Manufactures and distributes gluten-free
oats.

Enr-G Foods, Inc.
5960 First Avenue South
P.O. Box 84487
Seattle, WA 98124-5787
✆ 800-331-5222
✍ *www.ener-g.com*
Carries gluten-free starches and egg
replacer.

Gulf Pacific Rice Company, Inc.
✆ 800-999-RICE
✍ *www.gulfpac.com*
Has rice flours.

Heartland's Finest
24291 Veterans Memorial Highway
Hillman, MI 49746
✆ 888-658-8909
✍ *www.heartlandsfinest.com*
Has precooked navy bean flour.

Manitoba Starch Products
P.O. Box 749
10 Fredrick Street
Carberry, Manitoba, Canada R0K 0H0
✆ 204-834-2702
✑ *www.manitobastarch.com*
Source for potato starch.

TIC Gums
4609 Richlynn Drive
Belcamp, MD 21017
✆ 800-899-3953
✑ *www.ticgums.com*
Has gums for baking, including guar
gum and xanthan gum.

GLUTEN-FREE YEAST

Red Star Yeast
✆ 877-677-7000
✑ *http://redstaryeast.com*
Red Star is a division of SAF Yeast
Company, P.O. Box 737, Milwaukee, WI
53201-0737, 800-445-4746,
✑ *www.safyeast.com.*

GLUTEN-FREE BAKING POWDER

Davis Baking Powder
Clabber Girl Corporation
P.O. Box 150
Terre Haute, IN 47808-0150
✆ 812-232-9446
✑ *www.davisbakingpowder.com*

PURE VANILLA EXTRACT

Kestrel Growth Brands Inc.
DBA Singing Dog Vanilla, Inc.
P.O. Box 50042
Eugene, OR 97405
✆ 888-343-0002
✑ *www.singingdogvanilla.com*

GLUTEN-FREE BEER

Bard's Tale Beer Co., LLC
25 Van Zant Street, Suite 8E
Norwalk, CT 06855-1713
✆ 816-524-3270
✑ *www.bardsbeer.com*
Makes Dragon's Gold, gluten-free sorghum lager.

Lakefront Brewery
1872 North Commerce Street
Milwaukee, WI 53212
✆ 414-372-8800
✑ *www.lakefrontbrewery.com*
Makes New Grist gluten-free beer from
sorghum and rice.

Anheuser-Busch, Inc.
St. Louis, MO
✑ *www.redbridgebeer.com*
Makes Redbridge Beer from sorghum.

KITCHEN AND BAKING EQUIPMENT

Demarle, Inc.
www.demarleusa.com
Carries flexible bakeware that can be ordered online.

J.B. Prince Company
36 East 31st Street
New York, NY 10016-6821
☎ 800-473-0577
www.jbprince.com
Has piping bags, digital scales, and flexible baking mats and pans.

NordicWare
Hwy 7 and 100
Minneapolis, MN 55416-2274
☎ 877-466-7342
www.nordicware.com
Carries Bundt-style baking pans.

Ohaus Corporation
19A Chapin Road
P.O. Box 2033
Pine Brook, NJ 07058
☎ 973-377-9000
www.ohaus.com
Has digital scales.

Warren Kitchen & Cutlery
6934 Route 9
Rhinebeck, NY 12572
☎ 845-876-6208
www.warrenkitchentools.com
Has baking pans, molds, and tools.

HOME OVENS WITH STEAM

KitchenAid
☎ 800-886-8318
www.kitchenaid.com
Gaggenau
☎ 877-4GAGGENAU
www.gaggenau.com

Miele, Inc.
☎ 800-843-7231
www.miele.com

Sharp
☎ 800-237-4277
www.sharpusa.com

GLUTEN-FREE FOODS ONLINE SHOPPING

Allergy Grocer.com, formerly Miss Robens
☎ 800-891-0083
www.allergygrocer.com

Foods By George
3 King Street
Mahwah, NJ 07430
☎ 201-612-9700
www.foodsbygeorge.com

Gluten-Free Mall
4927 Sonoma Highway, Suite C1
Santa Rosa, CA 95409
☎ 800-986-2705
www.glutenfreemall.com

GlutenFree.com
☎ 800-291-8386
🖱 www.glutenfree.com

Gluten Solutions, Inc.
8750 Concourse Court
San Diego, CA 92123
☎ 888-845-8836
🖱 www.glutensolutions.com

Vance's Foods
☎ 800-497-4834
🖱 www.vancesfoods.com
Manufactures DariFree casein-free dried
milk substitute.

OTHER GLUTEN-FREE/ ALLERGY AWARENESS RESOURCES

Bob and Ruth's Travel Club
205 Donerail Court
Havre de Grace, MD 21078
☎ 410-939-3218
🖱 www.bobandruths.com
Source for gluten-free catered trips and
tours.

R.O.C.K. (Raising Our Celiac Kids)
🖱 http://celiackids.com
Support group for parents of children
with celiac disease, founded by Danna
Korn.

The Gluten-Free Lifestyle
🖱 www.theglutenfreelifestyle.com
Holds annual gluten-free foods seminar
in Colorado; source for newsletter.

The Gluten-Free Guide to New York
Mari Productions, LLC
P.O. Box 8477
Sleepy Hollow, NY 10591
🖱 www.gfguideny.com
Source for comprehensive guide to gluten-
free dining in the metro New York, tri-
state area.

Gluten-Free Passport
27 N. Wacker Drive, Suite 258
Chicago, IL 60606-2800
☎ 312-952-4900
🖱 www.glutenfreepassport.com
Offers gluten-free, allergy-free dining
awareness guides.

Triumph Dining
1200 N. Herndon St., Suite 605
Arlington, VA 22201
☎ 609-564-0445
🖱 www.triumphdining.com
Offers gluten-free restaurant guides and
dining cards.

Index